A SMALL NATION'S CONTRIBUTION TO THE WORLD
ESSAYS ON ANGLO-IRISH LITERATURE AND LANGUAGE

A SMALL NATION'S CONTRIBUTION TO THE WORLD ESSAYS ON ANGLO-IRISH LITERATURE AND LANGUAGE

EDITED BY
DONALD E. MORSE, CSILLA BERTHA
AND ISTVÁN PÁLFFY

Irish Literary Studies: 45

COLIN SMYTHE
Gerrards Cross

LAJOS KOSSUTH UNIVERSITY
Debrecen, 1993

First published in 1993 by Lajos Kossuth University
Debrecen, Hungary 4010

ISBN 9 634 71907 4

This book is published with the financial assistance
of the Hungarian National Scholarly and Scientific Research
Fund (OTKA)

Published in 1993 in Great Britain by Colin Smythe Limited,
Gerrards Cross, Buckinghamshire SL9 8XA

British Library Cataloguing in Publication Data

A catalogue record for this book is available from
the British Library

ISBN 0—861340—375—4 ○

ACKNOWLEDGEMENTS

The editors and publishers have made every effort
to obtain permission to reprint copyrighted materials
and gratefully acknowledge permission to reprint the following:
From *More Real than Reality: the Fantastic in Irish Literature
and the Arts* edited by Donald E. Morse and Csilla Bertha.
Used by permission of Greenwood Press an imprint
of Greenwood Publishing Group, Inc., Westport, CT, USA.
From *Journal of the Fantastic in the Arts,* 4.3 edited
by Carl B. Yoke. Used by permission of the editor.
Other copyright holders are urged to contact the publishers.

Produced in Hungary
Typeset, printed and bound by Alföldi Nyomda Rt.,
Debrecen

CONTENTS

Contents   vii

For Colin Smythe
for his generous encouragement and support
of Irish Studies at Lajos Kossuth University

PREFACE

The 1989 Debrecen conference of the International Association for the Study of Anglo-Irish Literature was the first to be held behind the iron curtain — a curtain which we now realize with the advantage of hindsight was that summer becoming increasingly porous where it was not rusting to pieces. The conference brought together over one hundred and fifty Irish scholars from around the world and from every continent to Hungary for a lively, festive few days.

A milestone in itself, the Debrecen conference was the direct descendent of another IASAIL conference held in 1984 in Graz, Austria which set the equally important precedent of inviting Eastern European scholars of Anglo-Irish literature, culture and language to participate in discussions with their Western colleagues. The convener of the Graz conference, Professor Wolfgang Zach, University of Graz, arranged for the first time for Eastern European scholars to attend — arrangements which then included the difficult task of helping them with exit visas, transportation and accommodation.

At Graz Professor István Pálffy of Lajos Kossuth University in Debrecen courageously invited IASAIL to hold its 1989 conference in Hungary. Given the novelty of his and his colleagues' participation this invitation was greeted with profound gratitude and encouragement. What sounded uniquely daring from Professor Pálffy and rather impossible in 1984, became reality in 1989. The fact that it took so long — almost another five years — to publish a volume of the selected essays of the conference shows, on the one hand, the — mostly financial — difficulties these past tumultuous years presented to such projects, and gives us, on the other, a vantage point from which to see the last decade as a continuous process of change, in the middle of which this conference stands as both the result of, and a participant in, the thawing of the political atmosphere in Hungary.

Most conferees were deeply aware of the special nature of the Debrecen conference: scholars from this part of the world had entered into the international discussion of Anglo-Irish literature, culture, and language through the historic Graz conference. Now Irish studies helped another small nation, Hungary, to contribute more directly to scholarship by bringing together scholars from around the world. In addition, the conference enjoyed the enlivening presence of two Irish writers, Jennifer Johnston and Michael Cook. Students and faculty of Kossuth University presented a staged reading of Cook's radio play, *Ireland's Eye,* about a deserted island off Newfoundland, Canada, originally settled by the Irish. Cook himself introduced the play and afterward commented graciously upon the performance. Jennifer Johnston gave an electrifying reading at the closing banquet of a prose piece which could easily fit within the Hungarian genre of the monodrama.

This volume, a small selection of the many papers and lectures presented, demonstrates how international the study of Anglo-Irish literature and language became in Debrecen from the host Hungarians, to the Irish, Canadian, American, English, German and Greek contributors represented here. Its publication has been unavoidably delayed by sometimes chaotic, often confusing, but ultimately hopeful events which followed the conference as within a year's time Hungary welcomed its first freely elected Parliament and within months after that saw the departure of the last occupying foreign soldier. Significant change also came to Lajos Kossuth University as the new university president, deans and department heads were freely elected by the faculty and the arduous work of overhauling completely an obsolete curriculum began. So looking back from the vantage point of late summer 1993 we see that the 1989 IASAIL conference was yet another visible sign of the change taking place in Hungary — a change that moved with increasing rapidity in late 1989 and early 1990 — as the country moved ever closer to democracy and independence.

Without the concern and generosity of Professor Zach, the courage of Professor Pálffy, the hard work of the local organizing committee, especially Péter Szaffkó, and the enthusiastic response of Irish scholars from every part of the world, the IASAIL conference in 1989 would not have happened. The presence and active participation of the Irish Ambassador to Hungary, Joseph Small and the late President of the Hungarian Academy of Scholars, László Kéry attests to its importance as does the substantial grant from the Hungarian National Scholarly and Scientific Research Fund (OTKA) which has made the publication of this volume possible. Finally, we would like to thank all the contributors for their patience and especially Tamás Kabdebó who at the expense of his summer holiday in Italy prepared his lecture for publication on terribly short notice.

Donald E. Morse and *Csilla Bertha*
Debrecen, July 1993

INTRODUCTION.
A SMALL NATION'S
CONTRIBUTION TO THE WORLD

CSILLA BERTHA and DONALD E. MORSE

A nation's contribution to the world does not depend on the nation's or the country's size. Yet it often is more noticeable when a small nation enriches the world's culture with an unproportionately great contribution. It has a certain appeal to the great nations, who often express their admiration, sometimes in a somewhat patronizing way, sometimes with honest respect and encouragement. For another small nation, however, the example can be encouraging, bringing about a feeling of familiarity, sympathy, even deeper self understanding and identification. So it is with Irish culture which has won the admiration of the whole world, but which offers, in addition, a special brotherly-sisterly feeling to the Hungarians.

Ireland's contribution to world literature, arts, architecture, scholarship and other fields of culture is highly respected in and outside the country. His Excellency, Joseph Small, the then Irish Ambassador to Hungary, in his opening speech to the conference quoted Herbert Kenny's summary of some of the most significant Irish contributions to world literature, leaving it to the audience's judgement whether Kenny's 'modest' claims are justified or not:

> Dublin has produced the greatest novelist of the twentieth century (James Joyce), the greatest poet of the twentieth century (William Butler Yeats), the greatest playwrights of the English stage in this century (Bernard Shaw and Sean O'Casey), the greatest modern national theatre (the Abbey with John Millington Synge, William Butler Yeats, T. C. Murray, Lady Gregory, Padraic Colum, Sean O'Casey, Brendan Behan), the greatest English playwrights since Shakespeare (William Congreve, Richard Brinsley Sheridan, Thomas Southerne, Oliver Goldsmith, Oscar Wilde), ... the greatest satirist the language has known (Jonathan Swift) ...[1]

Ambassador Small continued by describing Ireland's contribution to the world, more particularly to Europe in earlier centuries, not only in terms of literature but also in the broader sense of 'learning and civilization':

> The fact that [this] Congress is being held ... in continental Europe, and given the theme of the Congress ['a small nation's contribution to the world'], reminds one of an earlier age when Irish monks brought back to the continent in its darkest days not only Christianity but also learning and civilization. The Irish imprint was deep and lasting, as Cardinal Tomás O Fiaich's recent book, *Gaelscrinte San Eoraip* indicates. The contributions of St. Columbanus, St. Gall, St. Feargal (or Virgilius) and St. Kilian whose 1300th anniversary is being celebrated this year — to mention but a few — were very substantial indeed. Even in Prague ... [there is] a street name based on Hibernia ... [with] a disused Irish Franciscan Church situated on it. Another Irish monk, St. Fiacre, has given his name to a horse-drawn vehicle which is called the Fiaker in certain parts of Europe. St. Feargal, 1400 years ago, preached that the earth was round and that there were people living on the other side of it ...

Ireland's fame reached Hungary already in the Middle Ages, through the spiritual radiance of the Irish monasteries in Europe, through Irish pilgrims and martyrs[2] and through the Hungarian knights visiting St. Patrick's 'Purgatory' in the fourteenth and fifteenth centuries. Political interest grew and 'the idea of a parallel fate of Hungary and Ireland was first hinted at by Prince Ferenc Rákóczi II ... in trying to liberate Hungary from Habsburg rule ... [When] in 1707, Rákóczi dethroned the house of Habsburg ... [it] was seen by him to be an act similar to the Jacobean restoration that had been attempted in Ireland.'[3]

The historical parallel between the two countries was more consciously explored in the nineteenth century, first by those who prepared the way for another War of Independence against the Habsburgs in 1848–49. As the late László Kéry, President of the Hungarian Academy of Scholars in his introductory speech at the opening of the conference emphasized:

> Those politicians, statesmen and men of letters ... turned with genuine interest and great sympathy towards Ireland. From the 1830s onwards an increasing quantity of information found its way to this

country about the heroic struggles of the Irish past, as well as about their hardships and endurance at the time ... If, for example, Joseph Eötvös [a leading nineteenth century writer and statesman] spoke highly of Daniel O'Connel, the Hungarian reader could not help thinking of Louis Kossuth ... [at that] phase of upswing in the history of the national movement in our country.[4]

Irish politicians returned this kind of interest in the middle and the second half of the nineteenth century, first the Young Irelanders, who, as Thomas Kabdebo describes, in

> the Irish aftermath of 1848, Michael Doheny, John Mitchel and William Smith O'Brien each, in his own way, 'discovered' for himself — and through their journals, correspondence and agitation discovered it for others too — that there was a similarity between the 'Hungarian cause' and the Irish struggle.[5]

Later Arthur Griffith's famous pamphlet *The Resurrection of Hungary* (1904) called attention to Hungary, regarding this country as a model for Ireland, especially praising the Reconciliation (or rather: Compromise) with Austria in 1867 which, after the defeated War of Independence and much retaliation succeeded in assuring at least partial independence for Hungary.

This kind of interest in each other's history and historical figures also colours the appreciation of literature. 'Interest in any foreign national literature in a certain country at a certain time depends', István Pálffy contends — we may add: at least partly —:

> on whether the actual political and social conditions in the given country are ripe enough to induce the would-be-recipients to acquaint themselves with, and accept, that particular foreign literature. These social-political conditions are more important than linguistic contacts or relationships, more significant than the question of how widely the given language is known in the recipient country ...[6]

Seeing Ireland not only as another small nation but as one which exhibits so many parallels to Hungary in its history, culture, national heritage and in the attitudes to history and culture, Hungarian writers, thinkers, men of letters have often turned to Irish literature and culture for inspiration and example. This helps explain for example, in Professor Kéry's words, the exceptional popularity of the Irish national poet, Thomas Moore in Hungary during the 19th century. Translations of his poems started appearing from the 1830s on, and we find among his translators the three leading Hungarian poets of the century, Vörösmarty, Petőfi and Arany, who practically entered into a competition with each other in producing the Hungarian version of a poem in the *Irish Melodies* series, beginning with the words: 'Forget not the field where they perished, / The truest, the last of the brave . . .' This poem, together with many others, provided a suitable inspiration for Hungarian patriots in the period before the War of Independence and assuaged their despair after the defeat in 1849.

Similarly, in the 1920s and 1930s, after the shock of historic Hungary's being cut into pieces, with two thirds of its land and one third of its population suddenly belonging to neighbouring countries, Hungarians in Transylvania (now Rumania) wrote extensively about Irish literature to show how a small nation under oppression can preserve its identity through culture.[7] In the efforts of the Irish Literary Renaissance and the Irish Dramatic Movement they found inspiration and a model of resisting forced assimilation in an alien nation by the means of preserving and reviving the national heritage, past values, cultural treasures and through them forming anew the nation's — now reduced to a national minority — own spiritual features. Even as late as the 1980s Irish literature in Hungary could serve not only as a rich body of aesthetic values to study but also as a metaphor. So, for example, in discussing Brian Friel's *Translations* (1981) it was possible to draw parallels with contemporary Hungarian drama (such as that of András Sütő, the Transylvanian-Hungarian writer and playwright).[8] Questions of colonization, preservation or loss of the native tongue, religion, culture, individual and collective human rights and through them the nature and the importance of national identity could be examined at a time when it was not permitted in Hungary to discuss openly such problems.

These few examples of Hungarian interest in and attention to Irish literature, culture, history and politics do not attempt to cover the cultural contacts and influences between the two countries, but only serve to emphasize that the relationship between them is not new and not quite ordinary, and thus it was an all the more welcome occasion that IASAIL was able to convene in Hungary in 1989. Like so many aspects and phenomena of life in Hungary and in Ireland — small countries with long histories of fighting against colonialism and post-colonial confusion, and struggling for national self-realization — this occasion also pointed beyond itself by being freighted with symbolical and metaphorical significance. Professor Kéry even found an explanation of why it was appropriate to hold the conference in Debrecen:

> I consider it an excellent idea that your choice fell on the City of Debrecen and on Kossuth Lajos University as the venue of your deliberations. You probably know that there is a good reason why this University took Lajos Kossuth's name, that of the great nineteenth century national leader, one of the most highly celebrated figures in the history of this country. It was in Debrecen, on the 14th of April 1849, that after more than three centuries of subjection to Austria he [Kossuth] declared the dethronement of the House of Habsburg and the independence of Hungary. True, within a few months the noble struggle ended in failure, but the courageous decision of Kossuth and the revolutionary Parliament in Debrecen has kept its historical and political significance to this day.

Events like the IASAIL 1989 conference keep adding to the historical, political and cultural significance of Debrecen, of Hungary, and strengthen the brotherly feelings and the appreciation of each other's culture and literature between the two small nations of the Hungarians and the Irish. The essays in this volume will, we hope, testify to the exceptional richness of Irish literature and culture and broaden both small nations' contribution to the world.

STARTING FROM THE EARTH, STARTING FROM THE STARS: THE FANTASTIC IN SAMUEL BECKETT'S PLAYS AND JAMES JOYCE'S *ULYSSES*

DONALD E. MORSE

Our definition of the fantastic depends upon our view of reality, since the two terms are symbiotically linked. What we call 'reality' reflects our notions of what we believe is possible, while the fantastic is what we believe is impossible. Given the limits of bovine possibility, for example, all farmers and even most city people would agree with the statement: *'Bulls do not fly'*, as an accurate description of reality. At the end of Tom Mac Intyre's novel, *The Charollais* (1969), when the huge heroic bull takes off into the empyrean propelled by his vigorously twisting gonads, we know we are in the fantastic wind-up of a fantastic novel and not in the more mundane reality of a Farm and Food column in the *Irish Times*. A flying bull is clearly an impossible event in our everyday world and may, therefore, be properly labelled 'fantastic'.

Yet what we agree is 'impossible' today, hence fantastic, may become possible tomorrow or perhaps was actually possible at some time in the past. George P. Landow makes this point about changing conceptions of the fantastic in painting and literature:

> ... what we find improbable and unexpected follows from what we find probable and likely, and the fantastic will therefore necessarily vary with the individual and the age. Many of the basic assumptions which the Middle Ages or the eighteenth century made about society, human nature, the external world and the laws that govern it appear bizarre today, while many of our century's attitudes towards body and spirit, like its technological, artistic, and political creations, would appear as pure fantasy to earlier times.[1]

There is a real sense, for instance, in which the situation in Northern Ireland in the late 1980s 'would appear as pure fantasy to earlier times'. In the 1960s most people for very good reasons were optimistic about a peaceful solution to the Northern Ireland question. Looking back on the 1960s from the vantage point of twenty years later, F. X. Martin, co-author of the best-selling survey of Irish history, *The Course of Irish History* (1967 and 1982), reflects that optimism: 'All was then changing, and mostly for the better'.[2] Most predictions made at that time were for more and better contacts between the Republic and Northern Ireland (See, for example, F. X. Martin, pp. 2–3), yet in the early 1960s Seamus Heaney warned us: 'that kind of thing could start again'.[3] Heaney's poem, 'Docker', goes so much against the commonly held assumptions of the day about what was possible or impossible that it has about it the ring of prophecy which in this limited sense makes it also part of the fantastic.

What we choose to call 'fantastic' depends as well upon our personal beliefs. To cite a well-known example from Irish letters: in the last years of the nineteenth century Yeats and Æ (George Russell) came to believe that the 'external world' was undergoing a major change in that the ancient gods were returning to Ireland.[4] These gods, which they saw as having been a living reality in the past, would, both men believed, manifest themselves in the present, thereby compelling belief in what was now considered purely fantastic. Their millennial beliefs proved too optimistic, however, and the history of most of Ireland from the beginning of the twentieth century until today is that of the destruction of the habitat of these gods as well as that of the Little People. Both today remain remote in time and place, and both today are considered fantastic in Ireland except in those few older rural, agrarian, and usually isolated places where such belief persists — places where the natural and the supernatural keep close and frequent company. Dermot Mac Manus describes the relationship between these worlds while lamenting the 'lost knowledge' of the faerie kingdoms:

In Ireland the world of the Shee *[Sidhe]*, that is, of the faeries and of all those spirits which are elemental and have never been human, was called the Middle Kingdom, a satisfactory and expressive term. In ancient times, and almost up to this very age, this world of 'faerie' has been as much an accepted reality to the country people as has the normal material world around them. But today [1959], though belief still remains widespread, the old knowledge of the organization, of the ordered hierarchy of the classes and castes that compose the spirit world has almost disappeared.[5]

With its disappearance has gone as well a rich literary tradition[6] for, as Augustine Martin observes: '... this concern with the unseen world gave rise to a great body of writing — poetry, drama and fiction — which employed the methods of fable and fantasy to express its peculiar idea of life and reality'.[7] This ancient, rich tradition has now all but disappeared under modern highways and suburban housing estates.[8] What remains is a literary convention, rather than a living body of belief.[9] At its worst there are the caricatures to be found in virtually every Irish souvenir shop where the once-powerful Little People are reduced to cute pins to decorate blouses, or to plaster statues to adorn the lawn. Typical are remarks attributed to the Chair of Bord Failte (the Irish Tourist Board) in a 1989 interview in *Newsweek:* 'Visitors are looking for a land of shamrocks and leprechauns, and we should give it to them'.[10]

This process of domesticating the strange, unknown, and inexpressible, of taming the fantastic, is admirably caught in Tom Stoppard's example of the sighting of 'a unicorn': a fantastic mythical beast of no time or place which becomes reduced through familiarity and repetition to the known and easily described 'horse with an arrow in its forehead [which must have]... been mistaken for a deer'.[11] Nor is literary criticism immune to the temptation to transform the unicorns of the fantastic into 'the horses of instruction', as is apparent in the interpretation of much of Irish literature, including Samuel Beckett's plays or James Joyce's 'Circe' chapter in *Ulysses* (1922). Geoffrey Hartman might have been speaking about the reading or misreading of such texts, as well as 'Leda and the Swan', when he warned:

> That writing is a calculus that jealously broods on strange figures, on imaginative otherness, has been made clear by poets and artists rather than by the critics. The latter are scared to do anything except convert as quickly as possible the imaginative into a mode of the ordinary — where the ordinary can be the historically unfamiliar familiarized.[12]

Yet despite such efforts, Beckett's work remains outside the pale of 'the ordinary' as a meditation on impotence and failure. What many spectators find unacceptable in his early plays, for example, is the 'imaginative otherness' encountered in his view of reality as reflected in that startling, unremitting picture of life lived in time as 'moments for nothing'.[13]

This vision, found throughout his work, clearly focuses on what decades ago he termed 'impotence': 'I am working with impotence, ignorance', he declared then.[14] Beckett's work remains remarkable for the intensity and integrity with which he confronted, pursued, and presented his vision of impotence. Only in his earliest play, *Waiting for Godot* (1952), do we find any suggestion that there might be something to do and something with which to do it. Yet even in *Godot* the underlying reality of time for Beckett continues as a constant, as 'moments for nothing'. It is this vacuity which drives the characters into immobility, with the possible exception of the tramps in *Waiting for Godot,* and leads readers and audiences to substitute other values, any other values, for Beckett's. Michael Levenson describes precisely this kind of shift in his review of the beautiful book of photographs, *The Beckett Country:*

> ... the book includes scores of landscapes (rocky beaches, mountain vistas, banks of clouds), included on the strength of any passing mention in Beckett's writing. David Davison, a gifted photographer, renders these landscapes beautifully, apparently without stopping to consider whether his canons of the beautiful have anything to do with Beckett's own. Where, one wonders, are the severed heads and the bloody torsos? What would blind Hamm make of the sunset? In which heap of sand would Winnie be buried up to her neck? Where are the ash bins, the tape machines, the harsh lights, the urns?[15]

Here in these lovely photographs is 'the ordinary... the historically infamiliar familiarized' with the resulting loss of what is strange and disturbing in Beckett's plays — the unicorn is reduced to a 'horse with an arrow in its forehead'. But all of Beckett's settings with the possible exception of the two radio plays, 'Embers' and 'All That Fall', many of his characters, much of the action, and most often the time in his plays violate our sense of reality, and are truly fantastic: none can be photographed. For example, here are the settings for *Happy Days* and 'Play' which, Levenson points out, are missing from *The Beckett Country:*

> *Expanse of scorched grass rising centre to low mound. Gentle slopes down to front and either side of stage. Back an abrupter fall to stage level. Maximum of simplicity and symmetry.*
> *Blazing Light.*
> *Very pompier trompe–l'oeil backcloth to represent unbroken plain and sky receding to meet in far distance.*
> *Embedded up to above her waist in exact centre of mound, WINNIE.*[16]

> *Front centre, touching one another, three identical grey urns ... about one yard high. From each a head protrudes, the neck held fast in the urn's mouth. The heads are those, from left to right as seen from auditorium, of w2 [Second Woman], m [Man], and w1 [First Woman]. They face undeviatingly front throughout the play. Faces so lost to age and aspect as to seem almost part of urns. But no masks.*[17]

In such plays we enter a world obviously very different from our own, one which does not reflect 'consensus reality'[18] but Beckett's own, and which is not captured in a beautiful photograph of a sunset, beach, or bank of clouds. Rosemary Jackson accurately describes the estranging effect achieved by these several fantastic settings, characters and actions, when she asserts:

> To introduce the fantastic is to replace familiarity, comfort ... with estrangement, unease, the uncanny. It is to introduce dark areas, of something completely other and unseen, the spaces outside the limiting frame of the 'human' and 'real', outside the control of the 'word' and of the 'look'.[19]

Clearly Beckett's goal in his plays and prose is 'to replace familiarity ... with estrangement, unease' — as is Joyce's in the 'Circe' chapter of *Ulysses* where he does 'introduce dark areas, of something completely other and "unseen"'. Since this chapter is probably the most famous use of the fantastic in all of modern Irish literature, I will discuss Joyce's specific uses of the fantastic in some detail, showing how the fantastic may yield new insights into human beings, their behaviour, feelings, and thoughts, as well as how it leads to innovations in art. Many have tried to 'read' the unconscious through analyzing dreams or working with symbols, but no one has actually been inside anyone's unconscious — no one that is except readers of Joyce's *Ulysses*.

In 'Circe' Joyce paints Bloom's unconscious using various techniques borrowed from fantastic literature; an ideal choice, since, as Bellemin-Noel observes: 'One could define fantastic literature as that in which the question of the unconscious emerges'.[20] Kathryn Hume might well have been referring directly to 'Circe' when she states: 'Fantasy . . . aims for richness, and often achieves a plethora of meanings. This polysemousness of fantasy is its crucial difference from realism as a way of projecting meaning'.[21] Although Richard Kearney was speaking of *Finnegans Wake* (1939), his observation fits exactly Joyce's use of the fantastic in this chapter of *Ulysses:*

> Joyce subverted the established modes of linear or sequential thinking in order to recreate a mode of expression which would foster rather than annul heterogeneous meanings, which would, in his own words, permit us to have 'two thinks at a time'.[22]

Drawing upon the conventions of the fantastic, Joyce presented not simply the strange, unfamiliar setting of what Richard Ellmann has called 'the worst slum in Europe' — a reality unfamiliar to most readers of *Ulysses* then and now — but also the hallucinations of Stephen Dedalus and Leopold Bloom, a running commentary on events and characters in the chapter, and then the tour de force at the center of the chapter and the book itself: the kaleidoscopic presentation of the images from Bloom's unconscious.

'Hovering between the marvellous and the mimetic modes . . . floats fantasy, a mode that confounds and confuses the marvellous and the mimetic. It plays one mode off the other, creating a dialectic which refuses synthesis', writes Lance Olsen.[23] Nowhere is this description of the fantastic more clearly illustrated than in 'Circe' where we encounter the mimetic in Bloom's and Stephen's peregrinations through Nighttown complete with the Watch, dogs, whores, dialogue, music, and so forth; the marvellous in the appearance of the dead changeling child, Rudy, and the ghost of Stephen's mother — truly incredible events, but ones which are carefully grounded by Joyce in each character's actions, emotions and physical states; and the fantastic in the brief comments on the action — mostly on Stephen's in figures such as Lynch's Cap and 'Gummy Granny' — and in the deeply disturbing nighttime world of Bloom's unconscious which 'confounds and confuses the marvellous and the mimetic' in the fantastic.

The chapter opens with the unfamiliar but 'real' setting of the Mabbot Street entrance to 'Nighttown'. In the mimetic mode grotesque figures shuttle in and out of shadows:

> *A pigmy woman swings on a rope slung between the railings, counting. A form sprawled against a dustbin and muffled by its arm and hat moves, groans, grinding growling teeth, and snores again. On a step a gnome totting among a rubbishtip crouches to shoulder a sack of rags and bones. A crone standing by with a smoky oil lamp rams the last bottle in the maw of his sack.*[24]

Strange cries echo down the street:

> I gave it to Molly
> Because she was jolly.
> The leg of the duck
> The leg of the duck.
> (p. 430)

Insidious invitations are whispered from doorways: 'Sst! Come here till I tell you. Maidenhead inside. Sst!' (p. 431).

Into this already strange cityscape of the night comes the fog, not with 'little cat feet' but as 'snakes... creep[ing] slowly' (p. 433). And with the fog comes Bloom out of breath, *'flushed, panting'*, to encounter mysterious *'cyclists, with lighted paper lanterns aswing, [who] swim by him, grazing him, their bells rattling'* (p. 435), and the sandstrewer, dragonlike, enormous, *'its huge red headlight winking, its trolley hissing on the wire. The motorman bangs his footgong,'* and narrowly misses running Bloom down (p. 435). All very strange, but nothing — as yet — truly fantastic. This is what Aladár Sarbu calls this 'thin... narrative plane' of events, but which he also notes 'is firm enough to support the elaborate fantasies enacted on it'.[25]

Contrast Joyce's use of mimesis in Bloom's frightening, but substantial encounter with the sandstrewer with his use of the marvellous in Bloom's encounter at the end of the chapter with Rudy, his long dead son *'a fairy boy of eleven, a changeling, kidnapped, dressed in an Eton suit with glass shoes and a little bronze helmet'* (p. 609). Bloom is *'Wonderstruck'*, and his reaction is as immediate as it is deeply felt: '([he] ...*calls inaudibly.*) Rudy!' (p. 609). Clearly· in the marvellous rather than the mimetic mode, this vision is a projection of Bloom's own deepest feelings. It is he who recalls his son as a changeling — at once his own and a fairy child taken away cruelly and abruptly — the mauve face indicating the cause of death. Similarly we are in the mode of the marvellous when Stephen raises the ghost of his mother through drink and physical exertion, when: *'(He lifts his ashplant high with both hands and smashes the chandelier)'* (p. 583), as he attempts to destroy his projection of her with all its horrifying details contributed by his guilt. Hence his violent and immediate reaction: *'(Strangled with rage.)* Shite! *(His features grow drawn and grey and old)'* (p. 582). There is no doubt about what Stephen sees or that he sees it. Nor is there any doubt that he alone of all the people present encounters this apparition, since no one else in the room witnesses his horrifying confrontation with the ghost of his mother. Joyce thus takes great pains to make clear to the reader that at two separate moments in the chapter for well-established physical and emotional reasons, first Stephen, then Bloom hallucinate.

During the remainder of the chapter, however, we are plunged into the mode of the fantastic: '... a mode that confounds and confuses the marvellous and the mimetic ... creating a dialectic which refuses synthesis'.[26] There is, for example, no evidence that either man hallucinates the strange phantasmagoric scenes, characters, and events which occur beginning with the appearance of Bloom's father. Rudolph Virag is not an apparition born out of excessive drink, physical exhaustion, or emotional imbalance — to say so is to 'convert... the imaginative into a mode of the ordinary'[27] and thus to do away with the strangeness of this chapter and its attendant insight into the character of Bloom. Given such a setting, in time and place and given Bloom's physical condition it might not surprise us if he did hallucinate, seeing his father *'Yellow poison streaks'* and all (pp. 437ff). But there is no evidence that Bloom notices or is aware of him. He gives him no greeting (something impossible to imagine for the son of an Hungarian father); evinces no surprise at his strange appearance, but behaves as if such encounters were perfectly normal; and returns readily to his role as the guilty son in attempting unsuccessfully to hide the forbidden pig's trotter. At the end of their meeting, Bloom continues where he left off before their meeting — indicating that nothing has happened, no time has elapsed, no event has occurred of which he is aware. Similarly with the fantastic set pieces in the chapter: Bloom as Lord Mayor or as Blazes Boylan's flunky, Bloom and the new Bloomu-

salem, or Bloom and Bella-Bello are each an image drawn from the
unconscious without Bloom's awareness.[28]

As readers, we must accept the dialectic created by this use of the
fantastic which 'refuses synthesis' rather than attempting to make
sense out of events as Bloom's hallucinations[29] or, worse, reducing
the incredible to the 'ordinary', as Wolfgang Iser does when he
contends that such events are 'potential revelations of character'.
Iser attempts to account for the sequence of events as if they took
place in 'real time' by suggesting that 'everything becomes real for
Bloom that is omitted, concealed, or repressed in his daily life',[30]
but surely the point of 'Circe' is that none of the events which takes
place in his unconscious is 'real' for Bloom, because he remains
unaware of them. Iser's comments are reminiscent of many early
readers attempting to puzzle through the novel as if it were wholly
mimetic. For example, Paul Jordan Smith wrote in 1927: 'Bloom in
the redlight district imagines himself met by respectable folk. He
imagines defenses, imagines the overthrow of the defenses, imagines himself persecuted for his conduct; has illusions of grandeur,
followed immediately by a debased wallowing in the very pits of
humility'. Yet Smith, one of the best of Joyce's early public readers,
sensed what lay at the center of 'Circe' when he remarked: 'This
entire chapter ["Circe"] is made up of noble nonsense, a tissue of
remarkable daydreams — of what Mr. D. H. Lawrence would call
fantasia of the unconscious'.[31] 'Nonsense ... daydreams ... fantasia ...' or what we today term the mode of the fantastic.

Thanks in large measure to Joyce's use of the fantastic, at the end
of *Ulysses* we know Bloom far better than he knows himself or we
can ever know ourselves! While a similar statement might be made
of, say, Oedipus, the difference between Sophocles and Joyce's
hero lies in the nature of the reader's or audience's knowledge of
him. *Oedipus Rex* remains rooted in dramatic irony. As audience
we have knowledge of the past and we know the outcome of events
of which the king remains ignorant. But there is no such dramatic
irony in 'Circe'. Although we encounter images which reside in
Bloom's unconscious, that does not enable us to predict future
events; nor is any action described or new knowledge given of
Bloom in future or past space/time. (For such possibilities, see
'Ithaca'.) Instead, our knowledge is of the dark mirror of the unconscious wherein we see refracted events, people, and emotions
experienced during the daylight hours in the real space/time of
turn-of-the-century Dublin on 16 June 1904. Compare, for example,

the daytime Bloom we meet in the prosaic images of the nurturing man feeding and comforting people, animals, and birds with the nighttime androgynous Bloom we encounter in the fantastic images of the 'new womanly man' fathering children and giving birth. Of the people we meet during the day in Dublin, Bloom alone feeds the gulls, the dog, the cat; he alone at the lying-in hospital identifies with poor Mrs. Purefoy during her long labour and goes and visits her; only he truly sympathizes with Mrs. Breen having to cope with her slightly mad, addled husband Denis who 'is off his chump'. When challenged he stands up for his rights, but also defends love in the face of prejudice and hate. If the male cast of characters in *Ulysses* consists of alcoholic layabouts (Bob Doran), failures (Simon Dedalus), sentimentalists (Father Cowley), and myopic chauvinists (The Citizen), with a huge gathering of hangers-on, freeloaders, and generally ineffective men, Bloom stands out clearly as the exception: he is 'the competent keyless citizen' who negotiates his way through a difficult day, earns a modest living, while performing acts of charity, and generally behaves as 'the most Christian man' in Dublin.[32] Much of his effectiveness arises from his acceptance of his anima, the feminine side of his character and personality which most of the other male characters reject.[33]

He is, in other words, a model of emotional health in the daytime, male-dominated world of Dublin. But in the images of his unconscious, the images of 'Nighttown', his feminine traits and his passive behaviour become transformed into the fantastic images of the 'new womanly man' who gives birth to *'eight male yellow and white children ... with valuable metallic faces'* (p. 494), and who must undergo Bello's examination and humiliating treatment (pp. 530–544). Joyce thus uses the fantastic to establish the relationship of Bloom's conscious acts to his unconscious self. In doing so he illustrates Hume's contention that: 'There is an elegant efficiency to fantasies' which enables a writer to express ideas, emotions, and insights not available through mimesis. Her argument continues:

> Mimesis still demonstrates its power when an author's [such as Joyce's] chief concerns are social interaction and human behavior. Mimesis excels at establishing the relationships between people and the likenesses between the fictive world and our own.... Fantasy serves many other functions.... It provides the novelty that circumvents automatic responses and cracks the crust of habitude. Fantasy also encourages intensity of engagement, whether through novelty or

psychological manipulation... provides meaning-systems to which
we can try relating our selves, our feelings, and our data... encourages
the condensation of images which allows it to affect its readers at
many levels and in so many different ways... [a]nd it helps us en-
vision possibilities that transcend the purely material world which
we accept as quotidian reality.[34]

Where daytime logic and mimesis see two opposing forces or
statements as a contradiction and demand that such contradictions
be resolved, nighttime unreason and the fantastic allow Joyce — or
any author — to hold two opposing forces together as an oxymoron
without moving toward resolution.[35] For example, during the day
Bloom experiences deeply conflicting emotions which will return
in 'Circe': he dreads and abhors the approaching assignation of
Boylan with Molly, but neither resists nor resents it, and even
cooperates in it by not going home. (One of his greatest conscious
worries is that Boylan might be diseased and so infect Molly!) Such
conflict demands resolution: Is he a man or is he not? Why does he
not go home and confront them? How can he do nothing? Why does
he not divorce her? These are questions provoked in readers by this
unresolved situation. Within 'Circe', however, we encounter not
Bloom's calm acceptance of the inevitability of events (that will
happen in 'Ithaca'), but the vivid turmoil produced in his unconscious by both his dread of the event and his failing to resist or
effectively prevent it. Joyce offers a series of fantastic, unresolved
images: first those which name Bloom as a well-known cuckold (p.
469; and see pp. 468—470); then those where he conspires in his
own cuckolding by aiding Boylan. After Boylan *'hangs his hat
smartly on a peg of Bloom's antlered head'*, Bloom *'in a flunkey's
plush coat and kneebreeches'* watches through a keyhole and
cheers on Molly and Blazes as they copulate: 'Show! Hide! Show!
Plough her! More! Shoot!' (p. 565, p. 567). There is no possibility
of bringing such images into the daylight world of space/time or
into Bloom's consciousness — that is, domesticate them — without
destroying the humanity and heroism of Bloom. During the day it is
enough that he experience the humiliation caused by Molly's
adultery and his conspiring in it. Although it involves deep
suffering, he 'turns the other cheek', accepts what happens with
'equanimity' (pp. 732—33), forgives, and goes on loving. 'Circe'
reveals, in the searing images of Bloom as Boylan's flunky and
Bloom as exposed cuckold, what 'the pain of love' actually entails

for him, and it is that pain which lies at the very heart of *Ulysses* (p. 5).

Besides employing 'the dialectic which refuses synthesis', Joyce also makes good use of another characteristic of the fantastic in literature: its insistence on literalness; that is, the fantastic does not say one thing in terms of another.[36] Gregor Samsa is not *like* a cockroach, he *is* a cockroach. Leopold Bloom is not *like* the Lord Mayor of Dublin, in 'Circe' he *becomes* the Lord Mayor of Dublin; it is not *as if* Leopold Bloom gives birth, he *does* give birth. Moreover, Bloom undergoes metamorphosis literally as he changes from male to female to male. Yet, as in many traditional fantasies (for example, in the Alice books), no meaning resides in these changes. The sequence of Bloom's images 'does not lend itself to assimilation into pleasurable or consoling schemes. It has', as Massey maintains of all post-romantic metamorphosis, 'something typically ugly, monstrous, unabsorbable about it'.[37] Like in most modern fantasy, there is 'little purposive transformation. Changes are without meaning. There is no overall teleological scheme to give the transformation a meaning'.[38] This lack of an overall scheme emphasizes the radical instability of the images themselves in the unconscious as they meld into one another. Such metamorphosis is congenial not to conscious, rational, articulate thought, but to the dark, inarticulate, and unarticulable side of humans.

Joyce's use of the fantastic also emphasizes his insistence on a secular as opposed to a sacred interpretation of character in *Ulysses*. At the time Joyce wrote, the fantastic, according to Rosemary Jackson had:

> move[d] away from orthodox demonology towards psychology, to account for difference and strangeness. Literary fantasies from *The Castle of Otranto* to *Jekyll and Hyde* are determined by these transitions: from conventional diabolism in Beckford's *Vathek*, through the equivocations of *Frankenstein*, *Melmoth* and *The Confessions of a Justified Sinner*, to the internalized figures of Dorian Grey or...[39]

might we add: to the internalized images in Leopold Bloom's unconscious.

In 1901 Æ remarked to William Byrne: 'I started from the stars and never succeeded in getting my feet firmly on the earth, but if you start from the earth you can go as far as you like'.[40] Beckett and

Joyce started 'from the earth', that is, from reality as they understood it. Then using the fantastic they were able to 'go as far as
[they]... like[d]'. For Beckett that meant using the fantastic to
explore the reality of human impotence and ignorance which led
him almost inevitably to such works as the 'aesthetically terminal
remnant' 'Breath',[41] while for Joyce that meant using the fantastic
to explore the unconscious, which in turn led him to the richly
human portrait of Dublin's most famous citizen, Leopold Bloom.

If readers do not domesticate their vision, but allow the unicorn
to remain its fantastic self and not reduce it to 'a horse with an arrow
in its forehead', if readers allow the imaginative to remain the
imaginative and not 'convert [it] as quickly as possible... into a
mode of the ordinary', then they may discover that the fantastic
allows each writer and artist, though in very different ways, to do
what fantasy has always been best at; that is, to 'assert the importance of things which cannot be measured, seen, or numbered',[42] which for most of us are those things most worthwhile in
human experience. But it is necessary to acknowledge both reality
and the fantastic: as the unicorn said to Alice: 'Well, now that we
have seen each other... if you'll believe in me, I'll believe in
you'.[43]

ROMANTIC AND MODERN: VISION AND FORM IN YEATS, SHAW AND JOYCE

ALADÁR SARBU

This essay is a by-product of two, mutually complementary, interests of mine: Modernism and Romanticism. The former is a rather old, the latter a relatively recent affair. What is more, my interest in Modernism is focused on British and Anglo-Irish literature, while my more recent study of Romanticism encompasses mainly American fiction and philosophy. Yet what at first seemed no more than an accidental juxtaposition of two disparate phases of the history of literature, has in the course of years turned out to be a stimulating connection. Owing to the peculiar position, to the belatedness of American literature, and also to the fast accelerating pace of social and economic change in the United States in the second and longer half of the nineteenth century, many of the latent Modernist elements within Romanticism became manifest in what is now called the American Renaissance. Which in turn directed attention to similar, although less marked, characteristics of English Romanticism. What I am going to present here is a more or less systematic, although far from full, review of some of the more important problems posed by the relationship between Romanticism and Modernism, where most of my material, as far as the latter is concerned, is supplied by the three outstanding Anglo-Irish writers named in the title.

Movements in art and literature are never easy of define. Those two that I have to deal with are no exception. Instead of going by definitions, it is more fruitful, therefore, to think in terms of paradigms, which are more elastic, less categorical, and always modifiable, when the need arises, with no significant loss to what has previously been established. Luckily, we have some very good paradigmatic studies both of Romanticism and Modernism, which save us much of the labour involved in finding points of departure for a study of the theme. F. C. MacGrath in *The Sensible Spirit: Walter Pater and the Modernist Paradigm* (1986) constructs his conceptual scheme of Modernism from Pater's texts 'around eleven cardinal principles and constellations of corollaries', of which 'the subjectivity and relativity of knowledge', 'epistemological skepticism', 'the primacy of sensory experience', 'aesthetic and historical idealism' and 'an ascetic devotion to aesthetic craftsmanship' appear to be the most relevant.[1] I do not claim that these are to be found in equal measure in Shaw, Yeats and Joyce; by a strict application of the above principles we can even deny Shaw admission into the modernist circle. Let me, in anticipation, stress, however, that 'the primacy of sensory experience', 'the subjectivity and relativity of knowledge' and 'historical', if not 'aesthetic idealism', are important aspects of his work as well. I do not mean, however, that the work of any of these writers fully corresponds to the paradigm.

There is in this paradigm an obvious contradiction between two philosophical orientations. The emphasis on sensory experience, on the subjectivity and relativity of knowledge — both expressed succinctly and effectively in the memorable 'Conclusion' to *The Renaissance* — is eloquent testimonial to Pater's debt to British empiricism. Historical idealism, on the other hand, with its absolutist implications, indicates a strong dose of German idealist philosophy, mainly of the Hegelian variety. The work of Pater as the synthesizer and mediator of these philosophical positions was seminal. As a generation or two before him the great Romantics had also conceptualized their vision 'by sucking at the dugs' of Germany, he was eminently qualified to serve as a bridge between Romanticism and Modernism.

Central though the above components of the paradigm are, they do not include one of the most important — probably because Pater did not see much significance in it, and thus it fell beyond the ken of McGrath as well. This missing component is what Ihab Hassan calls *elitism* (aristocratic or crypto-fascist), which is inseparable from what in another place he describes as 'the pride of art, of the self, defining the conditions of its own grace'.[2] I do not contend that with the inclusion of *elitism* we shall have a satisfactory description on Modernism; but then my objective is only the staking-out of the turf on which I will now move.

One of the numerous temptations is to try and demonstrate that each of the principles posited applies to each of the writers under review. This is clearly not the case here. For Shaw, for instance, the primacy of sensory experience is never in question; as an advocate and practitioner of social realism in his early plays, the creative principle that guides him is mimetic in the strictest sense of the word. When he departs from it, he usually leans towards the grotesque, the absurd or the fantastic. He takes it for granted that sensory perception, combined with intellection, is the source of all knowledge. Apparently, this position is abandoned when, around the turn of the century, he adopts the Bergsonian concept of *élan vital* or *Life Force,* but the fact of the matter is that for all their intuition of the will of the *Life Force,* John Tanner and Saint Joan perceive the physical world in much the same way as everybody else. The relativity of knowledge is an important notion in Shaw, but its connotations are eminently social; Mendoza is a brigand or a practical man of business, depending on one's attitude to society. Cauchon and Warwick and Joan's judges are either wicked men, 'full of corruption, cozenage, fraud and malice', or 'an honest lot of poor fools', where our choice is determined by our view of history. But as Shaw is not a relativist himself, and draws a very clear line between the correct and the incorrect view, perception, in the final analysis, is also correct or incorrect. Reality is objective, regardless of what the mind porjects into it.

Not so for Yeats and the Symbolists, for whom as Arthur Symons put it, 'the visible world is no longer a reality, and the unseen world no longer a dream'.[3] To continue where Symons leaves off: for Yeats the true reality is the unseen, superior, transcendent world. This, however, is not a matter of perception, either; shadow and substance, the two worlds are there, and the poet obtains experience of the latter by following 'the crooked road of intuition', symbolized by the butterfly. What changes is not the reality, but only our knowledge of it. In poetry this means that by the appropriate choice of ancient symbols the poet penetrates 'into the depths of nature', and that by discovering the meanings inherent in the symbol, the reader also descends into those depths.[4] In this respect Pater, who was the fountainhead of Yeats's philosophy, clearly left him unaffected. Knowledge is relative, even subjective, but both the visible and the invisible world exist independently of how we see them.

With Joyce the whole picture changes. The artistic use of language as envisaged by Stephen Dedalus is one half of an important statement. He draws 'less pleasure from the reflection of the glowing sensible world through the prism of a language many-coloured and richly storied than from *the contemplation of an inner world of individual emotions mirrored perfectly in a lucid, supple periodic prose'.*[5] The other half of the statement is the book itself: the world is as Stephen sees it, and how he sees it is suggested by the language conveying the vision. The same world appears in ever changing terms, through an ever changing prism of language, as more and more of it is embraced by Stephen's mind. (A brief reference to the broadening scope and increasingly complex language of *Dubliners* is also apposite here.) But that world is, in part, made by language, and by that 'inner world of individual emotions' which it reflects. In *Ulysses* this method is maintained wherever the point of view is that of the hero of the particular episode (as, for instance, in 'Telemachus', 'Nestor', 'Proteus', 'Calypso' and 'Penelope'). Where it is not, or not quite (as, for instance, in 'The Oxen of the Sun' or 'Circe'), language indicates a marked authorial presence, and thus the abandoning of the illusion that the work is an objective transcript of the mind of the hero. Joyce's fiction is certainly the perfect embodiment of the primacy of sensory experience and thus of perception; it also exemplifies the subjectivity and relativity of knowledge.

Historical idealism is something that all three of the writers share. This perhaps sounds surprising with regard to Shaw, but the *Life Force* as the prime mover of history and evolution places his work on an idealist footing from *Man and Superman* and *Major Barbara* to *Heartbreak House* and *Saint Joan.* It has long been established that the *Life Force* has at least as much to do with Hegel's formula for the progress of the *Spirit* or *Idea* as with Bergson's *élan vital.*[6] Likewise, the predominance of the cyclical pattern of history in Yeats and Joyce is only indirectly Viconian in origin, because much of it represents the Hegelianized variety of Vico.[7] The agent of historical change, the 'world historical man' of Hegel, is also there: Saint Joan is undoubtedly of this class.[8] Whether the Irish airman Robert Gregory, the fisherman, or Stephen Dedalus belong to her company is another matter, and can best be answered by looking at the Romantic legacy as well. Which brings me to the major problem of my paper: to what extent do these artists meet the criteria of the Romantic rather than the Modernist paradigm?

Hopefully, it is clear from what has been said so far that I have concentrated on the above constituents of Modernism because I accord them special place also in Romantic literature, of which the best paradigmatic study is still M. H. Abrams's *The Mirror and the Lamp. Romantic Theory and the Critical Tradition* (1953). What I imply is not only that certain Romantic qualities survived into Modernism. Of course they did, and to this extent we can indeed talk of the Romantic legacy of Joyce or Yeats and even of that most formidable enemy of Romanticism, Shaw. But there is another way of looking at this relationship: that certain Modernist principles, ideas, sensibilites — and techniques for realizing them — had, in embryonic form, been available a hundred years before these writers made their impact. Thus, on the one hand, we have to acknowledge that the old survives into the new, on the other, that the new is anticipated by the old.[9] If in the forthcoming analysis my focus occasionally shifts, that shift only reflects the relative importance of old and new in the particular situation.

So the principles I have just discussed under the heading 'Modernism' are not confined to that one movement. If I now go over the familiar ground I do so in order to accentuate aspects and implications which are particularly pertinent to my theme: the Romantic and the Modern; for the same reason, I shall also call attention to aspects and implications accentuated by the writers themselves. The first two of these, the primacy of sensory perception, the subjectivity and relativity of knowledge — closely related, by the way — inhere in what is conventionally called the 'expressive theory'. This ultimately Plotinian view of art and creation found its way, through Locke, Hume and Young, into the aesthetics of Coleridge and Wordsworth.[10] True, there is a good deal of difference between Young's 'Our senses, as our reason, are divine / And half create the wondrous world they see' and Wordsworth's 'The excellence, pure function and best power / Both of the object seen and the eye that sees',[11] the essential thing, however, is unchanged: the senses contribute to the creation of the reality, as we know that reality, in the very act of perception. Let me stress, however, that this is not yet the primacy of perception, but merely a recognition of the subjective element in knowledge. But then there is an even greater distance between Young, Wordsworth *and* Pater, who reduces the world to impressions. 'Our physical life is a perpetual motion' of natural elements, Pater writes, and '[t]hat clear, perpetual outline of face and limb is but an image of ours, . . . a design in a web'.[12] Yet, despite his much heavier emphasis on the proposition that the forms of the world are what we perceive them to be, Pater does not lapse into total subjectivism, either.

The expressive theory is only one of several which inform the Romantic movement; an equally distinguished place is held in it by neo-Platonism and the Transcendentalist variety of German idealism (Kant and Schelling). This is a fairly long story, let me therefore raise only a few of the more important points we should bear in mind. First, that there is a strong neo-Platonic element in German idealism, and the dual terms (idea and reality, spirit and nature) in which romantic philosophy interpreted the world can be traced back to both. As Coleridge put it in 'The Destiny of Nations':

> *For all that meets the bodily sense I deem*
> *Symbolical, one mighty alphabet*
> *For infant minds; and we in this low world*
> *Placed with our backs to bright reality*
> *That we may learn with young unwounded ken*
> *The substance from its shadow.*

This interpretation is extended to cover history, lending it the kind of idealism that Pater will learn from Hegel;[13] it also produces a particular brand of aesthetic idealism, the gist of which is that art, regarded as essentially mimetic, should concern itself with discovering the ideal behind the phenomenal world. Appearances in this, or such, systems are contiguous with reality; they do not conceal but manifest that reality. This, however, is far from being the only or the dominant view; there is another one, equally important, which posits the possibility that appearances are not necessarily contiguous with reality. When this occurs, they function as disguises and not as manifestations. Which necessitates a brief look at the philosophy of Transcendentalism.

The most influential native Transcendentalist in England was, of course, Carlyle. In view of the roundabout way in which ideas travel, we should not omit to mention Emerson, who was strongly influenced by Carlyle, and Nietzsche, who in turn was influenced by Emerson. Some Modernist notions traced to the German philosopher are in fact traceable as far back as Carlyle. The Nietzschean superman, for instance, is clearly an adaptation of Carlyle's concept. The hero, whom Carlyle calls the 'realized ideal of everybody',[14] is of a piece with his overall philosophy; we only have to place the emphasis on the word *ideal,* and consider that the assigned task of the hero is to penetrate into 'the Divine Idea of the world',[15] and we have the essential Carlyle in a nutshell. But there is something that distinguishes the Scotch philosopher from the run-of-the-mill Transcendentalists: that in addition to the duality of *spirit* and *nature* (vesture of spirit), he sets up another duality: *nature,* defined as reality or fact, and *appearance,* defined as unreality, sham, shape, formula.[16] Thus penetrating into 'the Divine Idea of the world' involves striking through appearances and reaching the realities of life. It is worth remembering that the Carlylean incarnations of the hero, capable of performing this task, include fewer men of action than men of thought; they also include the man-of-letters.[17]

Now, if we return to Shaw, Yeats, and Joyce and reexamine those features of their work which I have just cited as particularly relevant in the context of Modernism, we shall have compelling reasons for regarding them as survivals of the ethos of the Romantic period. Language in *A Portrait* demonstrates not only how perception, operating on behalf of the sensitive *self* (the *soul,* as they called it in the early nineteenth century), imposes form on chaotic reality. It also demonstrates how perception as an instrument of the soul lends qualities of excellence to objects. The epiphanies integrated into the text, but not only the epiphanies, assert the operancy of the creative impulse in perception. Compare only Stephen's image of the brothel on his first and on subsequent visits. If Joyce is in the debt of Pater here, he owes at least as much to the much older tradition associated with the name of Hume, Locke, Young and Wordsworth. This might also be interpreted as Joyce's assertion of the subjective — therefore relative — nature of knowledge, but here I need a more complex approach to make my case convincing. All the more so as the evolution of Modernism did not stop at acknowledging that man's access to the truth was partial and personal; the scepticism that such a position betrays changed into full-scale agnosticism in the work of novelists like James, Conrad and Virginia Woolf, for whom the world consisted only of *appearances,* that is, *illusions,* or — to use Coleridge's concepts — the world was only shadow, but no substance. It would have been impossible to formulate disillusionment in such terms, had it not been for the long tradition of interpreting the world as a duality (substance and shadow, appearance and reality), of which Romanticism was a glorious phase. But some of the more daring representatives of this movement already had what the Modernists would believe to be their own brand of hopelessness and despair — and it is here that certain American writers assume special significance. Melville, in *Pierre,*

likens the search for truth to the work of the archaeologist bur-
rowing into an Egyptian pyramid and discovering, when he finds
the sarcophagus, that 'no body is there'.[18] Even that reputedly un-
shakeable optimist, Emerson, does at times consider the elusiveness of truth, as for instance in a journal entry for 1845: '[t]he universe is like an infinite series of planes, each of which is a false bottom'.[19]

Now, in the light of this we may safely say that in so far as the
world is seen as a duality of material appearance and spiritual
reality, both parts of this duality are assumed to exist by Shaw and
Yeats. The force that in *Saint Joan* drives history does so for the
sake of man — its objective being not merely self-realization but
also the perfection of man and his world. For Yeats 'art / Is but a
vision of reality' in 'Ego Dominus Tuus', which is echoed by 'Seek
out reality, leave things that seem' even in a much later poem,
'Vacillation'. Shaw and Yeats uphold the more conservative Romantic attitude, although the latter in his mature poetry often
wavers between pure spirituality (consider 'Sailing to Byzantium') and the 'quotidian' world[20] (as in the Crazy Jane poems or
'The Wild Old Wicked Man'), and asserts only occasionally, but
then all the more powerfully, that the spiritual and the material
should coexist (this is conveyed beautifully by the image of 'Astrad-
dle on the dolphin's mire and blood / Spirit after spirit' in
'Byzantium').

As far as 'historical idealism' is concerned, Shaw and Yeats
represent a conservative, therefore more obviously Romantic,
attitude. But this kind of conservatism is typical of all three writers
when it comes to elitism, which I have already connected with the
heroic in Romantic philosophy and poetry. Yet, perhaps somewhat
surprisingly, there is not much direct contact here between Shaw,
Yeats, Joyce and, say, Carlyle or Byron. Saint Joan, as I have
claimed, has a good deal in common with the 'world historical
man' of Hegel and, as for her fate, with Nietzsche's superman;
Yeats's fisherman and Irish airman as well as other incarnations of
this basic type are also Nietzschean in their genealogy. Nor are the
contours of the *Übermensch* difficult to recognize in the portrait of
Stephen Dedalus, who, at the same time, takes his motto, 'wandering companionless', from Shelley. But how can it be that despite the obvious links with later and apparently more advanced developments in Romantic thought they call for and warrant the label
'conservative'? The explanation is very simple: *later* in this par-

ticular case is not *more advanced.* It is certainly not *more progressive.* There is something germinal in Carlyle's original concept that anticipates a domestication, I would even say humanization or democratization, of the hero. But that humanization or democratization was not effected by Nietzsche who represents the same excessive individualism as we habitually associate with the high Romantic mode. It was effected by Emerson in his peculiarly American way when he evolved the concept of *representative man,* that is, 'one kind of humanity at its best'.[21] And it was also effected by Marx, whose 'species being' is, in my opinion, a rational, mundane variation on the hero, and also 'one kind of humanity at its best'. Of the characters named, perhaps only Saint Joan answers the above definition within very narrow bounds.

But then my objective was not to condemn these great writers for failing to utilize to the full antecedents which were available to them. Rather, my objective was to confirm what Richard Poirier has only recently proposed: that there is no clear break in cultural continuity between Romanticism and Modernism.[22]

'THE HARMONY OF REALITY AND FANTASY': THE FANTASTIC IN IRISH DRAMA

CSILLA BERTHA

> The harmony or reality and fantasy is the gift of the most
> ancient poetic soul.[1]
>
> — Áron Tamási

> Yet fantasy proliferates. In an age when we are becoming
> statistics and mere consumers, it draws our attention to the
> drama of the inner life.[2]
>
> — Brian Aldiss

Drama is hardly ever considered when theoreticians explore the uses of the fantastic in literature and the arts. While Kathryn Hume is right in saying that 'Some kinds of fantasy are not easily reduced to a physical stage, human actors, and a three-hour time span',[3] the theatre has ample possibilities to compensate for its restrictions of time and space and to incorporate (other kinds of) fantasy. Drama as literature can, like any other form of literature, evoke the fantastic in words, and as theatre-art, it has, in addition, all the theatrical means — visual images, sound effects, movement – to create, in a combined general effect, the terrain for the fantastic. Drama, the great art of illusion, can create not only the illusion of 'life as it is' caught as an audience peeps through the 'fourth wall' into a drawing-room, salon or even a throne room, but also of fantastic events, improbable actions or invisible figures.

The fantastic in drama is as old as drama itself since mimesis is only one dramatic means of expression. Drama, at least partly, grew out of ritual, of imaginative action connecting the natural with the supernatural. Greek drama was only partly mimetic; Shakespeare's bare settings clearly relied on the audience's imagination for creating the stage reality; and oriental theatrical traditions are all based on denotation, symbol, allusion rather than representation. The more the theatre wanted to express 'the drama of the inner life', the more it had to rely on the imagination of the audience that could be inspired by applying non-mimetic modes, means or devices of presentation. This is not to say that all the non-representational means are fantastic, but that fantasy is most intrinsic to the genre of drama itself.

English and most European drama after Shakespeare lost its ritualistic and symbolic features, and by the eigthteenth and nineteenth centuries, when literature became dominantly realistic and naturalistic, the entirely mimetic, social drawing-room drama came to the fore. By the turn of the nineteenth-twentieth century, however, European modern and avant-garde playwrights began to experiment with non-realistic, non-mimetic modes of dramatic presentation, aiming at the expression of deeper, inner realities, cosmic rules, or the eternal validity of psychological archetypes. 'The various experimental forms used in the theatre since the 1890s, symbolism, expressionism, surrealism, and so on, may all be regarded as various attempts to bring fantasy into an active relationship with realism'.[4] The fantastic in drama, as in other forms of literature, can effectively help to bring to the stage, and make visible and tangible, very real but invisible, hidden or inarticulate feelings, events, dramatic tensions; present 'inner landscape[s], one might almost say . . . spiritual landscape[s], which may well have psychological and mythological depths',[5] the working imagination, dreams, unconscious and subconscious processes or spiritual dilemmas; it can also subvert well-accepted meanings, or can be 'an appropriate form of expressing social estrangement'.[6]

Ireland, although part of the western world which 'has traditionally been hostile and dismissive toward the fantastic in most of its manifestations',[7] appears to have had a consciousness and experience essentially different from western culture and thus a more favourable attitude towards fantasy. Whether it is the result of historical circumstances — including the dominance of rural life, a slower rhythm of technical-industrial 'development', a late turn towards urbanization, a long-living oral tradition, an attachment to the intrinsic national and folk culture as a form of resistance to English assimilation — or is rooted in some mysterious national or ethnic spirit that onthologically differs from that of other ethnic groups, the Irish, quite uniquely in Western Europe, have preserved their 'ancient poetic soul' up to the present. They could always

naturally incorporate the fantastic in their literature because it has
been part of the people's way of thinking, part of their reality. Nuala
Ni Dhomhnaill, one of Ireland's most distinguished young poets,
says that, even today, when West Kerry people talk about the sea in
a matter-of-fact way as the 'Land under wave' inhabited by the
counterparts of animals and humans on the land, they are right since
the sea can be seen as 'a projection of a part of our personality that
we have lost — or let slide out of the intellectually credible', or, in
Jungian terms, as the feminine, the unconscious into which we cast
'a fishing line . . . every night when we dream'. She goes on to say
that while the Other World is 'no big deal' for the Irish, 'James
Hillman and these post-Jungian psychologists . . . talk about the
"other world" as if they had just discovered it . . . like Columbus felt
when he discovered America. But that doesn't mean that America
wasn't there before, and there weren't aboriginal Americans living
[t]here — quite happily.'[8]
   A similar feeling of *déjà vu* occurs when reading about postmodern drama and theatre: certain features closely associated with
postmodern consciousness turn out to be basic to most of Irish
literature. One such is irony which, Veronica Hollinger says, 'has
become the privileged trope of postmodern drama'.[9] Another is the
way the fantastic — this 'most conducive [mode] to representations
of the postmodern situation' — features in the theatre 'not as *opposition* to 'reality', but as its new *mise-en-scène).*[10] Nor is the attempt
of postmodern theatre to replace 'verbal language by the language
of spectacle' new — the Japanese Noh and other oriental theatrical
traditions have done that for centuries — and, if Hollinger's
description of Robert Wilson's productions is representative of
postmodern theatre: ('imposing collages of dance, music, song, the
spoken word [as opposed to dialogue], setting, and high-tech stage
machinery'),[11] then Yeats's theatre, as well as several plays of
Denis Johnston and Sean O'Casey in the early and mid-twentieth
century were essentially postmodern, except for the 'high-tech
stage machinery'.
   This is not to say that Irish literature is postmodern, but rather
that the postmodern mind consciously forms attitudes and views
that are immanent in Irish thinking. Thus the Irish, still holding an
organic, mythic view of the world, less rationalistic and more
inclusive than that of most Europeans, work naturally with oxy-
morons—elsewhere possible only in fantasy[12] and in postmodern
consciousness. While the 'mainstream of western thought . . . based

on the Platonic—Aristotelian logic of non-contradiction' operates in 'the orthodox dualist logic of *either/or,* the Irish mind may be seen to favour a more dialectical logic of *both/and:* an intellectual ability to hold the traditional oppositions of classical reason together in creative confluence'.[13] Reality and fantasy, too, act together in such a 'creative confluence' in the way of thinking of the Irish, hence in their literature and drama, also.

Modern Irish drama has, since its beginnings, drawn extensively upon the fantastic. This is one of the reasons why the renewal of drama in English, after its stagnation in the eighteenth-nineteenth centuries, began in Ireland and why it became an important stage in the formation of the whole Western-European modern drama. Irish drama was among the first in Europe to break with nineteenth-century naturalistic-realistic 'well-made' play conventions and to introduce instead more imaginative, mythic, fantastic, legendary, heroic or peasant plays, all feeding on, to varying extent, the archaic folk culture. First, during the Irish Renaissance, the mythic and fantastic folk imagination showed up more directly in drama while later, with contemporary playwrights, the fantastic takes more sophisticated forms.

The playwright of the Irish Dramatic Movement at the turn of the century who most truly acquired and transported onto the stage the deep layers of the archaic folk imagination and mythic worldview, was William Butler Yeats. He succeeded in fitting this set of beliefs into his systematized explanation of the world, a synthesis that he constructed from a variety of eclectic magic-mystic, irrational traditions of thought. As in his philosophy he was concerned with the relationships between the visible and the invisible, the material and the spiritual, so in his plays he most usually dramatized a human quest for the unknown, the unattainable, for spiritual perfection and beauty. And, as in folk imagination the beings of the two worlds communicate with each other naturally, so in his plays the representatives of the physical and spiritual domains appear on the stage with equal dramatic realism.

While in some plays the fantastic offers an *escape* that some character[s] seek — as for example in *The Land of Heart's Desire* (1894) a fairy child enchants the young bride luring her from the boredom of peasant life into the world of eternal beauty and joy —, more often it is a target of a *quest for* higher and more lasting values than ordinary life carries. In *The Shadowy Waters* (1911) the hero is determined to find the home of everlasting love, and physically journeys towards some other world. In both of these plays the colours, the lighting and the music suggest the 'otherness' of the other world; in *The Land of Heart's Desire* green, mystical lights can be seen outside the peasant cottage, and a voice is heard singing as a contrast to the naturalistic setting inside; in *The Shadowy Waters* golden and (the moon's) silver colours and a magic harp's music accompany the chief characters. These are simple theatrical means to signify the fantastic. Dance, a more elaborate device, also occurs quite frequently in Yeats's plays. Yeats associated dance with beauty, perfection and supreme art, and applied it usually at the climax of his plays to express otherwise inexpressible feelings, attractions and great passions. The dance of the fairy child in *The Land of Heart's Desire* casts a spell on the young woman and tempts her to give up physical life. In some later plays, when Yeats used versions of Japanese Noh theatre techniques, he even more freely and effectively used dance, thus removing the stage action still further from mimesis. In *The Only Jealousy of Emer* (1918), a far more complex play, Fand the Fairy, the inhabitant of the Country Under the Wave, embodies men's dreams about unchanging, perfect, eternal feminine beauty, especially when her enchantment culminates in her magic dance, the full effect of which is aided by colours, lights, movement and music.

At the end of *The Dreaming of the Bones* (1919) the young man, in his flight from those who pursue him for having participated in the 1916 Easter rising, witnesses the dance of the spirits of two lovers dead 700 years. The superior beauty of this miracle, the powerful passion and deep tragedy it conveys, reveals, in contrast, the young man's narrowness and insensitivity when he admits that he 'almost' listened to their request and forgave them for their 700-year-old sin.

The ghosts and their dance bring to the stage a glimpse of the heroic past – when passions and remorse were so overwhelming that they have outlived the people by centuries, and when even the unforgivable sin was committed for the sake of love — and contrasts to the prosaic and unimaginative present represented by the nameless young man, restricted and hardened by his nation's tragedy, and closed to spiritual experience. The presence of the supernatural is all the more convincing on the stage because the protagonist is not seeking it. It is not the projection of his dream or desire, nor is it an escape (in fact, he is looking for a much more tangible, physical refuge), but rather an existing part of reality, which he acknowledges but proves to be unworthy of.

Not all Yeats's plays employing other-wordly creatures can be regarded as fantastic, however. Most of them contain fantastic alongside mythic elements, and several are purely or dominantly mythic. Difficult and arbitrary as it may be to separate the fantastic from the mythic, these two are, nevertheless, based on differing outlooks and produce different structures, character-relationships and atmospheres.[14]

The dominantly mythic plays (such as *At the Hawk's Well* [1916], the mythic counterpart of the fantastic *The Shadowy Waters*) dramatize the quest for immortality and completeness, based on the certainty of the shared knowledge and values of the community; the archetypal hero follows the mythic pattern of behaviour and embodies the physical, spiritual and moral ideal of the community. The representatives of the two worlds are conceived as but two levels of the same reality, meeting and fighting in a timeless time. Even though immortality is beyond the reach of human beings, however heroic they might be, a spiritual experience and a deeper, more intense understanding of life can be achieved from the confrontation with the supernatural.

In another fully mythic play, *A Full Moon in March* (1933), the heroes — the Queen and the Swineherd: concrete yet entirely impersonal images of the sublimely pure and the lowly, gross material — act out death and resurrection and through them the achievement of unity and completeness. The ritual action resembles the fertility rites in vegetation myths and is totally removed from anything belonging to ordinary reality.

Yet the twentieth century is no longer a mythic age, as Yeats himself was painfully aware: the age lacks unity, and the human world is at a great distance from the spiritual. That is why most of his plays apply both mythic and fantastic modes since the fantastic expresses uncertainty, the unknowability of truth, 'reduction of being', 'frequent sense of loss' and 'elusiveness'.[15]

A brilliant example of how fantasy, mixed with myth, works on the stage is *The Herne's Egg* (1938). Basically mythic situations such as those of Leda and the Swan and the Fall are enacted with a variety of fantastic means — comic, expressionistic or surrealistic effects, playful, grotesque, sometimes farcical stage figures, objects and gestures — to subvert the ideals embedded in the myths. So Yeats here uses the fantastic in its function of subversion, and with its help he manages to subvert his own earlier ideals in a way that at the same time, also preserves them. In an oxymoron that the fantastic makes possible, the hero is both hero and fool, powerful and helpless, dignified and ridiculous, engaged in a comic and grotesque fight with the supernatural, which is illuminating only inasmuch as it makes him realize his own smallness, and yet also manifests some greatness and strength. All in a highly ambiguous and ambivalent mode.

Yeats's dominantly fantastic plays present individual dreams and desires, the mythic ones collective experiences and ideals. Also, while fantastic elements help to dramatize uncertain longings for the unknown, fears of the supernatural or tragic feelings of human helplessness, myth, with its certainty based upon tradition and collective knowledge, makes the formation of more definite desires for union with the spiritual possible, and allows us to see the human fight with and defeat by the supernatural as part of the cosmic mystery, of the continuous struggle between the antinomies of the world. The plays mingling mythic and fantastic elements unite individual efforts with the collective needs and hopes of the Irish and place all that in the often tragic vision of humankind in this fallen modern age.

Yeats had no immediate disciples yet his impact on Irish drama is so great that nobody could entirely escape his presence. This is true even in cases of rejection or parody, as for example in some of Denis Johnston's plays. Johnston shared Yeats's zest for formal experimentation, but chose very different directions. One of the most experimental early-twentieth-century Irish playwrights, Johnston is often described as an expressionist, but his plays dramatize more subtle emotions, more complex truths and finely ironic judgements, and, perhaps most importantly, a greater life of the imagination than for instance the German Expressionists to whom he is often compared; he 'pushed beyond Expressionism into a surreal form of total theatre in pursuit of a greater complexity of awareness, psychological and moral'.[16]

In his most 'expressionistic' play, *The Old Lady Says 'No!'* (1926), through the figure of the romantic Irish hero, Robert Emmet, Johnston satirizes the whole romantic, even sentimental, attitude to the past as one of the great dangers in Irish thinking. The play is full of inversions, fantastic twists and turns and transformations, as the plot is actually a projection of what takes place in the unconscious of a character. Among the many literary allusions, several turn Yeats's words and dramatic figures inside out, making them their own ironic opposites. The fantastic actions, stage images and transfigurations create both an alienating modernist effect on the stage, and a postmodern feeling of ambivalence, ambiguity and the lack of continuity of character.

A Bride for the Unicorn (1933), Johnston's most fantastic and most unique play, dramatizes a seemingly mythic quest for the Absolute, yet without the notion of the transcendental. The counterpart of Yeats's representations of the spiritual is, in Johnston's play, closer to an abstraction, for the part of the human soul that in Yeats's philosophy was connected to the supernatural, in Johnston's is connected to thought. This rationalized kind of immortality, together with 'the Mystery of Time' and the unresolved contradiction that while 'the Fear of Death [is] so present in our conscious mind, ... our subconscious so clearly repudiates' it since every effort in life brings it nearer,[17] is conveyed to the audience through an extremely rich pattern of fantastic objects, figures, events and transformations. Also, Johnston often reverses the ground rules in both of these plays. This, in Eric Rabkin's view, is 'one of the key distinguishing marks of the fantastic': 'the perspectives enforced by the ground rules... must be diametrically contradicted'.[18] Johnston changes not only the style but also the perspective from scene to scene, and, in *A Bride for the Unicorn,* even the quality of time.

For Yeats's and Johnston's contemporaries who presented aspects of the Irish peasants' lives — such as John Millington Synge, George Fitzmaurice, Edward Martyn, and sometimes Sean O'Casey — the fantastic appeared in their source material as part of reality, and naturally shaped itself into the outlook and mode of their plays. Their characters are usually divided by their relationship to the fantastic: those who prefer the world of fantasy to mundane reality are more sympathetic than the grey, earth-bound, unimaginative people around them (as in Synge and Fitzmaurice), or vice versa, those who are sympathetic human beings, are supported by creatures or phenomena of fantasy, as in O'Casey's late plays.

Central to Synge's plays is illusion and the relationship between illusion and reality. In several of them, fantasy serves — in accordance with one of its main functions in general — to offer a dreamworld, an escape from reality. The world of illusion is usually created only in words but in Ireland the WORD has always had a great, often magical power. The Irish respect what is built up in words; due probably to their long-lived oral tradition the word is

able to create new realities, a whole world of fantasy. According to
Seamus Deane, Synge's plays show how fantasy rivals facts; in
each play a 'story of fantasy ... is, first, rebuked by fact and then, in
the next instant, legitimized as belonging or contributing to a higher
truth than mere fact could ever reach'.[19] Deane further explores this
strange and complex relationship between fact and imagination:

> Mesmerized by an eloquence which begins in illusion but which
> continues after the destruction of illusion, we are forced to concede to
> the imagination a radical autonomy. It insists on its own truth not by
> ignoring fact but by including it and going beyond it. The imaginary,
> overtaken by the real, becomes the imaginative. The dynamic force
> which makes this possible is language.[20]

The whole plot of *The Playboy of the Western World* (1907) is
based on a lie, a deception created by words and their effect on
character and community. When the facts annihilate the lie, its
effect still survives: the liar — or rather the fantasist, since he himself came to believe in his own lie — became able to create a new,
self-supporting illusion, now incorporating his experiences in the
world of facts.

Among Synge's plays it is *The Well of the Saints* (1905) where
illusion and reality clash the most sharply, where the old blind
couple's happy world of illusion is built on the deceptive words of
the people, further coloured in their own fantasy. When they have to
face reality, they are broken and lost, their characters become distorted, and they regain their human attributes only when they lose
their sight again. Escaping from a second and final cure, together
they begin to build up, entirely in their imagination, a new, illusory
world of poetic beauty that no longer feeds on the deception of
others, but on their conscious, deliberately chosen self-deception.
Being an escape from reality, this is no moral victory, yet their
ability to transcend their miserable condition makes them superior
to those bound to mundane ordinariness.

Synge does not attach false values to the escape into a fantasy-
world yet the couple's choice points out the drabness of the unimaginative environment with which the fantasists inevitably come
into conflict. The distribution of values is similar in George Fitzmaurice's fantastic plays: the fantasists are not idealized — some of
them have obvious weaknesses or vices — yet in their conflict with
the ordinariness and narrowness of their environment they certainly

come to represent superior values. While Synge's imaginative characters managed to maintain or renew their illusions, in spite of their
environment, Fitzmaurice's dreamers suffer in addition from the
deception of the supernatural they are in contact with in their
struggle for artistic creation. The old man in *The Pie-Dish* (1908)
can never complete his dish, the work of his life; all the dolls of
Roger Carmody are destroyed by the other-wordly creatures in *The
Dandy Dolls* (1914), suggesting that the artist is at odds both with
his environment and with his own creation: he can never be satisfied
with his work and is never allowed to achieve perfection. The supernatural jealously guards its terrain, including creation and perfection. Only those who approach the invisible in their imagination,
without trying to create objects of perfection themselves, will not be
disappointed in it: Jaymony in *The Magic Glasses* (1913) never
loses his vision of supreme beauty although he is held in contempt
and killed by the narrow-minded people around him.

What divides the characters in O'Casey's late plays is their attitude towards, and the very nature of, the fantastic figures or events
central to each play. If in both Synge and Fitzmaurice the fantastic
is more of an individual experience, showing the imaginative and
creative power of the character, in O'Casey's plays 'the fantastic
components... [are] symbolic representations of abstract concepts',[21] and, as such, they exist even for the restricted and unimaginative. With the other two playwrights the imaginative people had
the potential for spiritual experience, which the others simply did
not have, whereas in O'Casey's plays the relationship qualifies the
characters: the negative ones have a negative relationship with it,
try to deny, ignore or kill it, and are, in their turn, annoyed or
humiliated by it.

The same phenomena, therefore, may convey different meanings
to the sympathetic and to the unsympathetic characters; for example
the superhuman Figure's announcement of flood in *Purple Dust*
(1945) threatens the lives of the comic, arbitrary Englishmen, but
contains a promise of purification and new, free life for the more
vital Irish people. Also, the Cock, with its various tricks in
O'Casey's most amusing, colourful, allegorical and surrealistic
farce, *Cock-a-Doodle Dandy* (1949), is a menace to the narrow-
minded, backward, stupid, and cruel men, but it is friendly and
supportive to the natural, lively young people. The Cock itself — a
combination of the prognostic birds of Gaelic folklore and O'Casey's
own symbol of 'the joyful, active spirit of life'[22] — behaves in a

folktale-like, moral way: it helps the good and punishes the evil. The fantastic figures and events also serve to strengthen the satire: expose hypocrisy and humiliate authoritarianism or dignified behaviour. Thus O'Casey's more objectified and more concrete fantastic figures have greater power to influence life than, for example, Synge's subjective dream-images of individual consciousness, although neither is strong enough to defeat the dark forces of reality.

In the plays of Synge, Fitzmaurice and O'Casey fantasy and the fantastic help character-drawing as well as the presentation of the society and social institutions. The fantastic evoked is always close to some pagan force, while the ordinary is usually connected to the Catholic church, particularly to its clergy, defending the order against which the dreamers or fantasists rebel or from which they escape. Even when we witness a true Christian miracle — as in *The Well of the Saints* — it becomes strangely inverted: curing the blind, instead of giving transcendental experience, opens their eyes to the mundane, factual side of life, and they regain their ability to transcend their physical limitations only when they reject the second cure of the Saint. In his confrontation with the blind, the Christian Saint, although working wonders, appears the more rationalistic.

Synge, by presenting the fantastic as existing in the imagination of the individuals, comes closest to contemporary playwrights, since they, too, are preoccupied with projecting human consciousness onto the stage. Of the rich and diverse ways contemporary Irish playwrights draw on the fantastic, I will comment only on three: as part of folk imagination in the still extant peasant play; as means of revealing psychological depths in essentially realistic plays; and as general stage technique.

Several of John B. Keane's peasant plays depict the danger of cherishing fantastic dreams, of keeping alive fairy-tale figures in one's consciousness, and of mistaking them for reality. As with Synge and Fitzmaurice earlier, here, too certain figures have the ability to build up a whole world in their imagination, and represent a different value-system from that of the ordinary people, preoccupied with mundane cares, especially money or property. In *Sive* (1959) the two travelling tinkers — obviously outsiders to the ordinary community — who are storytellers like the ancient bards or *file,* living consciences and judges, poets and prophets, all at the same time: although unable to change reality, can at least turn tragedy into legend. The relationship between fantasy and reality is more complex in *Sharon's Grave* (1960), where fantasy permeates all reality. In varying degrees it touches the lives of all the characters and influences the plot. The hypnotic power of the evil little hunchback, Dinzie, who — like a rural Cipolla — paralyzes most people around him, hovers between reality and fantasy, and appears rather as a stretching of psychological reality. But Neelus, the dreamer, is obviously considered mad. He is entirely absorbed in his fantasy: in his love for the legendary princess, Sharon. Yet he follows his fantasy not so much to escape from reality as to try to influence it in a meaningful way. Thus, by fulfilling the prophecy of the legend and saving Sharon from suffering in her grave, he saves his real sister from the real danger of being killed by Dinzie. His fantasy gives him the courage necessary for self-sacrifice in reality. The wheel turns full circle: fantasy, first leading away from the real world, turns back, intrudes and helps to bring resolution in it. Life comes to imitate fantasy, but what is equally important: life (that of Neelus's sister and her would-be husband) can go on safely in reality only at the price of Neelus's pursuit of his fantasy.

In the majority of contemporary Irish plays the fantastic does not exist consistently either in somebody's imagination or in certain objects or figures, and it does not come from another sphere or level of existence. Instead, it usually becomes the means to project psychological events or processes onto the stage, to make invisible, hidden or unconscious tensions visible. Even if Bellamin Noel's statement sounds somewhat exaggerated — 'One could define fantastic literature as that in which the question of the unconscious emerges'[23] —, the fantastic mode is exceptionally suitable for psychological exploration.

Brian Friel, Thomas Kilroy, Frank MacGuinness and Tom Murphy, leading contemporary Irish playwrights, each in his unique way employs fantastic means in basically realistic dramatic situations to reveal psychological depths. Murphy is a fair representative of this group. Often in his plays something miraculous happens within a naturalistic framework; in some unexpected, sudden and usually violent action some previously unattainable or unknown possibility or ability manifests itself through which the characters can arrive at a better understanding of their own needs and aspirations and through which they become able to transcend their own selves. The self-liberating action is often verbal — in accordance with the magic power the Irish always attributed to the word. So in *A Crucial Week in the Life of the Grocer's Assistant* (1978) when the protagonist, John-Joe shouts out in the street all the gossip and secrets of the provincial neighborhood, thus violating the rules of conduct in his environment, his act also liberates him and makes him an adult, independent personality overnight. In the *Grocer's Assistant* Murphy works with rather Freudian dream-scenes to emphasize the confused state of mind, the repressed desires and fears of the protagonist, while in later plays the main character often has a double, an alter-ego, who turns out to be a kind of a Jungian Shadow, which, if integrated into the self, is no longer negative and may even invigorate one's creative forces. In *The Gigli Concert* (1984), Murphy's most miraculous and most victorious play, the relationship between the two characters — the forlorn, despairing quack psychologist, J. P. W. King, and the Irish Man, obsessed with the desire to sing like Gigli — is often related to that of Faust and Mephistopheles.[24] Fintan O'Toole points out that this encounter may be most fruitfully seen in the light of Jung's interpretation of the Faust-legend.[25] Jung says that Faust and Mephistopheles struck him as the embodiments of good and bad, spirit and matter, light and darkness: 'Faust, the inept, purblind philosopher, encounters the dark side of his being, his sinister shadow, Mephistopheles, who in spite of his negating disposition, represents the true spirit of life as againts the arid scholar who hovers on the brink of suicide'.[26] Thus, as Jung saw them as two halves of one whole, so Murphy dramatizes through these figures the split personality striving to become an integrated whole again: J. P. W. King makes a pact with this Mephistopheles-figure, his evil, dark side, his 'sinister shadow', who will become the instrument of his renewal. The psychologist gradually comes to identify himself with his client, takes over his obsession to sing like Gigli, and, in the last scene, experiences a true miracle. Having descended to the deepest hell of his despair, exhaustion, abandonment and chaos, he unexpectedly ascends with an unbelievable creative power, and in the perfection of the moment he does sing like Gigli.[27]

In a third group of plays the fantastic does not appear mixed and interacting with realism but *is* the overall mode of presentation. Several plays of Thomas Mac Intyre — 'easily the most experimental of contemporary Irish playwrights'[28] — utilize entirely non-imitative, mostly expressionistic technique: powerful images, symbols, stylized gestures, frozen tableaux, poetic language, song and dance.

Mac Intyre's *The Great Hunger* (1988), a dramatization of Patrick Kavanagh's famous poem of the same title, retains the poem's rather desperate view of Irish peasant life without any illusion or any romanticism. The hero's — and the Irish peasants' — life is not at all idyllic, but neither is it spectacularly tragic, it just slowly wastes away in the struggle for survival among the repressive forces of family and society. The dominating figure of a father or mother occurs frequently in Irish drama, but hardly ever receives such a powerful presentations as with the mother in this play. She is constantly present on the stage — in the form of a wooden effigy. Her son, Maguire, talks to her, occasionally cleans its/her face, takes things out of the drawer built into this statue. Other people also express their relation to her in various serious or playful ways. She, in her immobility and mute acceptance of everything that others do to her, conveys the feeling of her permanence and her magnetic power, life-supporting as well as threatening, better than any well-drawn character could.

Mac Intyre invigorates with inexhaustible wit the images of the poem and enhances both their tragic and comic/ironic impact. For example, to dramatize the poem's opening lines about the 'potato-gatherers' who 'like mechanized scare-crows move',[29] his men pantomime picking potatoes in the fields, and when they hear 'girlish laughter', they try to see where it comes from:

> *The heads of the men dive — Three heads hanging between wide-apart legs — to see. Too late. Slowly they rise from that position and become scarecrows stirring lightly in the wind, scarecrows that swivel and stare vacantly into the audience.*[30]

Then they return to imitating work again.

Such shifts of style from pantomimic to symbolic and back strengthen the fantastic dimension of the events onstage. So does the language: dialogues are replaced by imagistic, metaphoric, poetic language; repetitions of lines; broken, sometimes incantatory, rhythmic speeches. Imaginatively combining essentially poetic means with the visionary and auditory possibilities that the theatre can offer, such plays are capable of a more direct effect upon the senses and instincts and a deeper communication than the conventional theatre: they are able to send messages directly from consciusness to consciousness or even to the unconscious.

The words in Mac Intyre's plays, as in all Irish drama, exercise their magic power to evoke the invisible, either within human beings or beyond ordinary reality. Even his modern (postmodern?) experiments are organically related to this traditional poetic quality of Irish drama, which is probably part of the 'distinctive Irish note' that Hurley identifies in Mac Intyre's plays: 'Tom Mac Intyre's dramatization has also found a distinctive Irish note without being held in thrall to the Irish dramatic tradition'.[31] Mac Intyre appears to carry further Yeats's experimentation with poetic drama as well as his non-conventional theatrical approach and ideas in order to utilize all the verbal and non-verbal, visual, auditory and kinetic possibilities of the theatre that produce the overall effect of 'passionate art, the drowner of dykes, the confounder of understanding, [which] moves us by setting us to reverie, by alluring us almost to the intensity of trance'.[32] Mac Intyre's is a much harsher, more brutal poetry on the stage than Yeats's. Yet it is poetry, and it is very much theatre: theatre which invites the imagination to participate. Thus, the best Irish plays, from those of Yeats, the founder of the Irish national theatre, to the most recent experiments reflect 'the gift of the most ancient poetic soul' that the Irish still share: 'the harmony of reality and fantasy'.

'BOTH HEARD AND IMAGINED': MUSIC AS STRUCTURING PRINCIPLE IN THE PLAYS OF BRIAN FRIEL

PATRICK BURKE

> ...my attitude is this: I look on my manuscript as an or-
> chestral score, composed with infinite care and annotated
> where necessary with precise directions. This is in no way a
> judgement in quality but a statement of character...[1]
>
> — Brian Friel

Friel's emphatic insistence on the significant resemblance between an orchestral score and his play-text — an insistence confirmed in his well-known resistance to insertions in, excisions from or emendations to his texts — is also a pointer to the extent of his musical literacy. Even a casual review of the music specifications in, for example, *Philadelphia, Here I Come!* (1965), *Aristocrats* (1980), or *Fathers and Sons* (1987) leaves one impressed with Friel's close knowledge of such technicalities as key signatures, concerto movements, even bar divisions. And as is obvious from virtually the entire Friel *oeuvre,* such knowledge is not restricted to classical or 'art' music: one recalls such popular tunes as 'Give the woman in the bed more porter!' *(Philadelphia),* 'Oh Susannah, don't you cry for me' *(The Gentle Island,* 1973), 'The Way You Look Tonight' *(Faith Healer,* 1980), 'The Man Who Broke the Bank at Monte Carlo' *(The Freedom of the City,* 1974), 'The Isle of Capri' *(Dancing at Lughnasa,* 1990). A unique instance of Friel's use of Gregorian plainchant, all the more theatrically effective because unexpected, is the very moving ending to the third scene of Act Two of *Fathers and Sons* (1987), in which Vassily and Arina sing out their pain and their faith in the *Te Deum,* after the death of their son, Bazarov.

The most readily perceivable musical strategy in the plays of Friel is that of commentary, most regularly for purposes of irony or pathos, occasionally for dramatic mischief. Uncomplicated instances of this would be Gar O'Donnell's singing of 'She Moved Through the Fair' at the outset of Episode Two of *Philadelphia:* the refrain, 'It will not be long, love, till our wedding day', accords ironically with the loss of his lover, Kathy Doogan, in Episode One and the imminent references to her wedding to a rival in the course of the 'Aunt Lizzy' sequence. Similarly, the emendation of the troupers' anthem in *Crystal and Fox* (1970) bears revealingly on the enigmatic, potentially dangerous, character of Fox himself: the emendations of 'A-hunting we will go' replace 'you' for 'we' in the title and alter the lines 'You'll catch a fox / And put him in a box' to the pointed 'You'll catch *no* fox . . .'. Since the fox connotes predatoriness, defensiveness and wiliness, this change is skilfully wrought and serves neatly as a musical distillation of the play's recurring themes.

More extended and more complex evidence of Friel's skillful use of music is apparent in the dance sequence of *The Gentle Island,* a sequence which follows quickly on Shane's rejection of the unhappily married Sarah's sexual advances. Shane is, at the very least, inhibited in his emotional response by the nature of his own relationship with Peter, his older friend; he has been uneasy, moreover, about what he perceives as the unnatural calm of 'the gentle island' to which they are visitors. The dance sequence serves at once to focus all of those guilty sexual energies and the island's treacherous quietness, as well as to highlight the factors out of which the play moves to its climax, the attempted killing of Shane by Sarah. Shane has repaired an old-fashioned 'horn' gramophone, its long disuse a clear token of the absence of music on the island, and sings along and dances to a recording of 'Oh Susannah', in the course of which activity he is joined with dangerous ambivalence by Philly, Sarah's husband, himself soon attracted to Shane. Friel's unobtrusively skillful dramaturgy is evident in the way the song's words and their seeming self-contradictions bear on the total situation: 'It rained all night, The day I left / The weather it was dry / The sun so hot / I froze to death / Susannah don't you cry'.

In *Dancing at Lughnasa* the Cole Porter song 'Anything Goes' is slyly placed by Friel between the animated discussion by Father Jack and Kate Mundy as to what is socially and morally acceptable in Ryanga, Uganda, where he had ministered for many years, and the very graceful dance of Agnes Mundy and Gerry Evans, the lover of her younger sister, Chris, and father of Michael, the play's narrator. Anges herself is in love with Gerry. Deployed in this way,

'Anything Goes' is thus a mischievous pointer at once to the possibility that polygamy and love children should be socially acceptable (Fr Jack's view) and to the pleasing fantasy, imaged in the dance at which Chris is an onlooker, of a love triangle — which, as we learn from Michael later in the play, the already-married Gerry was entangled in, in any event.

The introductory music and what Teddy in *Faith Healer* describes as 'atmospheric background music' in Friel's plays is quite a different matter. Friel usually leaves the selection of such music to the play's director: for example, the present writer found, in recent productions of *Living Quarters* (1978) and *The Loves of Cass McGuire* (1967) (which he directed in Dublin) that, respectively, the opening of the Slow Movement in Beethoven's *Emperor Concerto* and, perhaps more obviously, the Largo from Dvořak's *New World Symphony,* seemed to support and harmonize with the atmosphere and ambience of the plays. Interestingly, prescription *is* evident in two successive and thematically complementary plays, explicitly in *Translations* (1981) and implicitly in The *Communication Cord* (1983). In the former the transition from Act Two, Scene One, to Act Two, Scene Two, from, in emotional terms, the drunken boisterousness of Yolland and the palpable mutual attraction between him and Maire to the tenderness of the so-called 'love scene', is directly conveyed in musical terms: [Scene One] *'Simultaneously with [Yolland's] final "bloody marvellous" bring up very loud the introductory music of the reel... Retain the music throughout the very brief interval...* [Scene Two] *The following night... The music rises to a crescendo... MAIRE and YOLLAND approach — laughing and running... Fade the music to distant background. Then after a time it is lost and replaced by guitar music...'*[2] That guitar music should be quietly audible throughout the scene, rising *'to crescendo'* at the end when Maire's and Yolland's kiss is intruded on by Sarah, the music thereby becoming a rapid overture to the tragedy of Act Three.

The score which Keith Donald, himself a brilliant saxophonist, wrote (with Friel's approval) for *The Communication Cord* plays a clever musical trick on the audience. It sounds initially like an Irish tune played on that most traditional of traditional instruments, the uileann pipes. The ear then senses that the rhythm is unorthodox, based on five rather than four beats to a bar. Finally, the audience appreciates that the instrument which it is hearing is not in reality an uileann pipes at all but a synthesiser. Such pseudo-traditionalism in

aural terms is cleverly compatible with the overall theme of the play
and is of a piece with the visual pattern of the setting:

> *Every detail of the kitchen and its furnishings is accurate of its time
> (from 1900 to 1930). But one quickly senses something false about
> the place. It is too pat, too 'authentic'. It is in fact a restored house, a
> reproduction, an artefact of today making obeisance to a home of
> yesterday.*[3]

If space permitted, it might be argued that the four plays of Friel
in which music or song is conspicuous by its absence — *The Enemy
Within* (1975), *The Gentle Island, Volunteers* (1979) and *Making
History* (1989) — are also plays in which the imminence of death
and the under-valuing of women are significant features. (Two of
those four — *The Enemy Within* and *Volunteers* — contain, after
all, the only all-male casts in all of Friel's work.) The imminent
deaths in those plays are both individualized (Caornan, the five
'volunteers', Mabel O'Neill) and general (Donegal and Antrim
tribes, terrorist victims, English and Irish soldiers). *Making History* articulates the importance of women most directly in O'Neill's
insistence to Peter Lombard that Mabel, his late wife, be given pro-
minence if Lombard's proposed history of his life and times is to
encompass 'the overall thing'.

If such an argument were valid, it would then follow that those
plays of Friel in which music is a prominent presence would in general tend to be at once celebratory of life and affirmative of
women. In three instances — *Philadelphia, Here I Come!, Aristocrats* and *Dancing at Lughnasa* — this, with varying degrees of
emphasis, is largely the case. The most recent of these, *Lughnasa,*
would appear to be the perfect illustration of my embryonic thesis
in that it centres on women (who for the first time ever, outnumber
the male characters in a Friel play) and contains also their by now
world-famous dance in Act One which both in production and reception in Dublin, London and New York, has been interpreted as
an unambiguous expression of the energetically celebratory. It can
only be so by selective reading of Friel's text which supplies lucid
cues to director and actresses:

> *Very fast; very heavy beat; a raucous sound… They dance and sing
> — shout together; Rose's wellingtons pounding out their own erratic
> rhythm… AGNES and ROSE, CHRIS and MAGGIE, are now all*

> *doing a dance that is almost recognisable... But the move-*
> *ments seem caricatured; and the sound is too loud; and the beat is too*
> *fast; and the almost recognizable dance is made grotesque... With*
> *this loud music, this pounding beat, this shouting—calling—singing,*
> *this parodic reel, there is a sense of order being consciously sub-*
> *verted, of the women consciously and crudely caricaturing them-*
> *selves, indeed of near-hysteria being induced...*[4]

For the dramatist, then, the dance is less a celebration in itself than powerfully indicative of a need, a hunger, to celebrate, an emphasis at least partly confirmed in the dialogue of Gerry and Agnes during their dance referred to above:

GERRY: You should be a professional dancer.
AGNES: Too late for that.
GERRY: You could teach dancing in Ballybeg.
AGNES: That's all they need.
GERRY: Maybe it is.[5]

That existential centrality of dance relates also to Father Jack, the inchoate dance he attempts at the end of the first act, as well as to his eloquent account in Act Two of the dance ritual of the Ryangans in Uganda, in which '...there is no distinction between the religious and the secular'. It relates, too, to the exciting, life-affirming, if dangerous Lughnasa rituals of the backhills people near Ballybeg, whose dancing, in the literal sense, gives the play its title.

Traditional dancing in Irish peoples' homes and country halls (as against its manifestation in, for example, competitions or exhibitions) often represented a domesticated version of the type of ritual just referred to; this is clear in Gar O'Donnell's one-man ceili dance in *Philadelphia*: '...Something lively! Something bloody animal! A bit of aul' Thumpety thump!' The music for his dance is in striking contrast to the First Movement of the Mendelssohn Violin Concerto, which he has just been playing on the gramophone, which, because of its association with his received impression of his long-dead mother, has threatened to overwhelm him. In Episode Three of *Philadelphia* Gar plays the *Second* movement of that concerto in the hope of prompting his father, S. B. O'Donnell, to validate his own precious memory or the day they spent in a blue fishing boat, when Gar was ten:

... D'you know what the music says? *[to S. B.]* It says that once upon
a time a boy and his father sat in a blue boat on a lake on an afternoon
in May, and on that afternoon a great beauty happened, a beauty that
has haunted the boy ever since, because he wonders now did it really
take place or did he imagine it ...[6]

Friel quietly anticipates the failure of such validation, in the following scene of the play, by presenting Gar's father as tone-deaf to
the Mendelssohn: 'I don't hear ... [Gar] playing them records of
his.' It is worth observing, moreover, that Friel's skill in capitaliz-
ing on the musical feeling of the concerto extends to its limitations
of sentimentality and over-ripeness as well as to its strengths, in so
far as its aesthetic limitations reflect character limitations in Gar;
that is, to his blindness to the extent of Senator Doogan's fatherly
concern, of Canon O'Byrne's sensitivity, of his father's love for
him.[7]

The manner in which music as an essential element in a Friel play
characteristically combines the haunting resonances of art music
with more scattered fragments of the popular or vulgar, is best
exemplified in *Aristocrats*. *Aristocrats* constitutes also an exception to my general argument in as much as it is a play where death
does occur, that of the formidable Father, in the very powerful curtain which concludes Act Two. Musically, the play is dominated by
a rich assortment of Chopin waltzes, ballads, sonatas and scher-
zos: for much of Acts One and Three these are played 'live' by
Claire, the youngest of the four O'Donnells of the formerly aristocratic Ballybeg Hall, who is engaged, reluctantly, to be soon married; in Act Two, her Chopin pieces are heard on cassette tape while
the family has a picnic. In *Aristocrats* that music is given dramatic
definition through its association with both the former glories of the
Hall as an arena of culture and refinement, much frequented by artists, writers and prominent ecclesiastics and with the O'Donnells'
deceased mother, presented through memory as gentle, loving,
nurturing, if fragile. The simplest example of that combining is the
ascribing of the title 'The Bedtime Waltz' to the Chopin Waltz in
A Flat Major which Casimir and Alice recall their mother playing in
their childhood, when they hear Claire playing it in Act One. By a
kind of musical shorthand, then, Mother is ultimately figured as the
gentle, nurturing embodiment of the graciousness of the Hall. Opposed to her, finally subjugating her, is that which the now ailing
but once severe Father embodied — social exclusivity, suspicion of

creativity, repressiveness, deference to established authority; as Eamon, Alice's complex husband, defines it in Act Two:

> ...a family that lived its life in total isolation in a gaunt Georgian house on top of a hill above the remote Donegal village of Ballybeg; a family without passion, withou loyalty, without commitments; administering the law for anyone who happened to be in power; above all wars and famines and civil strife and potential upheaval; ignored by its Protestant counterparts, isolated from the mere Irish, existing only in its own concept of itself, brushing againts reality occasionally by its cultivation of artists; but tough — oh, yes, tough, resilient, tenacious...[8]

The unfolding action of the play discloses the measure of the Mother's subjugation by the Father — Alice's alcoholism, Casimir's fantasizing, Claire's manic depression, the well-nigh certain suicide of the Mother herself. That last event is obliquely but beautifully subsumed into the song *Sweet Alice* — 'In the old church yard... / In a corner obscure and alone' — which almost all the characters sing at the final curtain, oblivous to any insistence that they hurry for their bus.

If music illuminates theme in *Aristocrats,* it also illuminates plot and characterization, most evidently at two points in the play. One of these is at the beginning of Act Three, the afternoon of Father's funeral. Stage directions inform us that *'We can hear Claire playing the piano — Sonata No. 2 in B minor, Op. 35, middle section of 3rd Movement (i.e. portion between "Dead March" statements — omit "Dead March")...'* That we are to take the omission of the best known portion of the sonata as reflecting conscious intention on Claire's part is confirmed by her appearance when she enters midway through the act: *'...she is not wearing mourning clothes'*. Through her playing and her appearance Claire is clearly signalling a refusal to mourn, in retaliation, presumably, for her father's 'stifling' of her plans to avail of a music scholarship to Paris which she had won when she was sixteen. And by the ending of the play she has gone even further, resolving 'I don't think I'll ever play Chopin again'.

Eamon and his long-time friend, Willie Diver, are defined in the play as 'local' lads, in contrast to the aristocrats of Ballybeg Hall; indeed, part of Eamon's motivation in marrying Alice was to vicariously experience thereby something of the Hall's fineness. When,

then, during Act Two, a tape of Claire's rendition of the Chopin
Etude No. 3 in E Major is playing on the lawn, after the O'Donnells
have had a picnic, it is appropriate that Eamon sings a popular version of the same tune, 'So Deep is the Night', which was very
popular in the nineteen sixties. It evokes, too, the secular rituals
recalled by Eamon and Willie:

> EAMON: ... Remember dancing to that in the Corinthian in Derry.
> WILLIE: Every Friday night.
> EAMON: The steam rising out of us from getting soaked cycling in on the
> bikes.
> WILLIE: And the big silver ball going round and round up on the ceiling.
> Jaysus... And slipping out to the cloakroom for a slug out of the
> bottle.
> EAMON: And the long dresses — the New Look — isn't that what it was
> called?
> WILLIE: Oh Jaysus.
> EAMON *(to Judith):* Remembrance of things past.[9]

To which Eamon adds, a minute later, 'Plebeian past times. Before
we were educated out of our emotions.' The transmutation of the
Chopin into 'So Deep is the Night' may thus be seen to mirror the
interaction of the Hall with the local Ballybeg community, an interaction defined in terms of character by the short-lived romance
of Eamon and Judith (the oldest O'Donnell sister) and their memories of an idyllic morning after a dance in the Corinthian, in the
course of which they had agreed to marry one another.

Across the whole Friel *oeuvre* we may see how often the 'art'
music of such composers as Mendelssohn, Wagner, Chopin or John
Field (used extensively in Friel's most recent work, *A Month in the
Country,* 1992) is set, sometimes within the same play, against
either traditional Irish 'folk' music or snatches of popular songs.
Such juxtapositioning seems to me to constitute in terms of music a
recurring Friel concern — reconciling fine aspiration and earthy
actuality in so humane a manner that the former does not teeter into
mere escapism or the latter into crass insensitivity.

The Loves of Cass McGuire is, musically, a special case. Here, in
a sense, Friel makes double use of music to facilitate artistic coherence: in an author's note to the 1984 edition of the text, published
by Gallery Press, he both describes his play as '...a concerto in
which Cass is the soloist'[10] and explains his choice of incidental

music from Wagner's *Tristan and Isolde* 'because the *Tristan and Isolde* legend has parallels of sorts in Cass McGuire's story'. Musical structure thus provides a basis of character illumination in *Cass McGuire,* as well as the source of an ironically deployed parallel plot. Under each heading the felt effect is that of *pathos.* As the play unfolds, the concerto soloist Cass is more and more drowned out, as it were, by the other instruments, as she tries to deal with *'the memory sequences that haunt her'.* In a strained conversation with her brother Harry, during which he informs her of his intention to place her in the ironically named Eden House, *'a home for old people',* one stage direction for Cass reads: *'Unable to hold her own line';* that is both a literal and musical cue. A similar inability shows itself in later sequences with her nephew, Dom, and her sister-in-law, Alice, in the course of which physical and mental disorientation move her more and more towards the breakdown we witness in Act Three. By then, unable to 'bear very much reality', she joins, as it were, with two other instrumentalists Trilbe and Ingram, fellow inhabitants of Eden House, in the rendering of their assuaging 'rhapsodies' (Friel's word), even learning to use their refrain: 'But I, being poor, have only my dreams; / I have spread my dreams under your feet; / Tread softly because you tread on my dreams' (W. B. Yeats's 'He wishes for the Cloths of Heaven'). The measure of her defeat, of the loss of her soloist status, is in the play's concluding words, which contrast significantly with her first-act description of Eden House as 'the gawddam workhouse' — 'Home at last. Gee, but it's a good thing to be home'.

The *'parallels of sorts'* between Cass's story and that of Tristan and Isolde in Wagner's opera are reasonably transparent in the play: Cass's nursing of the incapacitated Jeff Olsen corresponds to Isolde's tending of the wounded Tristan, with the Irish woman presented in each instance as an outsider (New York, Cornwall). Prior to their respective involvements with new lovers (Jeff, Tristan), each Irishwoman had had a relationship in Ireland (the Connie Crowley of Cass's reminiscences, Morolt in the opera). The ingratiating *faux bonhommie* of Pat Quinn, the inmate who finally leaves Eden House, is partly indebted to the traitorous Melot of *Tristan and Isolde.* Finally, the plural 'loves' in Friel's title, the reminder therein that Cass's loves also extend to her brother, Harry, and his children, as well as those close friends from her waitressing days on 'the Lower East Side', Slinger and Balowski, is influenced by the movingly presented sisterly and fatherly loves in Wagner's opera

— that of Bramgune for Isolde or Kurwenal and King Mark for Tristan.

The imagery of ships and sailing is prominent in *Tristan and Isolde:* Act One is set on board the ship taking Isolde to Cornwall, while in Act Three her arrival at Kereol is figured musically in Tristan's funeral aria, 'Das Schniff! Siehst du's noch nicht?', as well as in the Shepherd's music when the craft arrives. Friel borrows that imagery to intimate his play's peculiar sense of the restless search for love — Cass's father had 'sailed off when she was a kid', Ingram's bride of two days had 'sailed away forever' in a German count's yacht, and in Cass's dream in Act Three she had been 'sailing home to Ireland'. Her personal 'rhapsody' begins with 'I stood at the stern of the ship' and in her imagined marriage to Jeff Olsen she 'could see the ships 'sailing off to South America... and Ireland... and Glasgow.'

Friel tells us that when he wrote the play in the mid-sixties, he envisaged the rhapsodies of Trilbe, Ingram and Cass 'being played against a musical background; and I chose Wagner...'; the extracts specified come from *Tannhäuser, The Ring* and *Tristan and Isolde.* In some subsequent realizations of the play, notably the Broadway premiere in 1966 (in which Trilbe and Ingram were so beautifully played as not, apparently, to need what Friel calls that 'potent crutch') Wagner's music has been dropped. My own view, based partly on my experience of directing Friel's plays, is that it is a brave director who can choose to dispense with the theatrical resource of music at once atmospheric and evocative, as well as relevant to Cass's life situation, real and fantasy alike.

In Act Three, the counterpointing of Cass's rhapsody by Ingram's reading of the deaths of Tristan and Isolde delicately registers the parallels between their story, their transcendent love, and Cass's, and also the ultimate futility of her love quest in 'the world of verifiable facts' (to quote Friel's programme note). What this play ultimately registers, then, is, in a sense, the differences between a nineteenth-century music drama, in which incomparably romantic music (in both senses) is the necessary expressive medium, and a modern prose drama in which, in a characteristically modernist idiom, confidence — moral, philosophical and linguistic — is radically vitiated. It is the conflict of sensibility between, on the one hand, Wagner and Yeats, and, on the other, Pirandello and Beckett.

'DEATH IS HERE AND DEATH IS THERE, DEATH IS BUSY EVERYWHERE': TEMPORALITY AND THE DESIRE FOR TRANSCENDENCE IN O'CASEY'S *THE SHADOW OF A GUNMAN*

BERNICE SCHRANK

Critics tend to give O'Casey's *The Shadow of a Gunman* (1923), short shrift. David Krause and Robert Hogan, two of the first critics to write about O'Casey's work, treat the play as rough apprentice work, Krause viewing it as a crude early example of O'Casey's tragi-comic art, Hogan dismissing it as structually unsound.[1] Later critics avoid analyzing the play for a variety of reasons.[2] There are, however, four studies of the play that attempt a more comprehensive treatment. Goldstone has argued that the play is a study of the failure of responsibility and commitment.[3] Kosok qualifies this reading by suggesting that O'Casey is more complex, ironic and negative in his presentation of character and theme than Goldstone allows.[4] In two related papers, Schrank further develops this pessimistic line. In the first, she explores various patterns of breakdown in the play and concludes that 'the world O'Casey creates in *Shadow* is in all its aspects hostile to life'.[5] In the second, Schrank examines the uses to which O'Casey puts language in this play and she finds not only that all the characters distort language, but that their unsatisfactory verbal manoevres are a direct response to their hostile and chaotic environment.[6]

In this paper, I propose to study the characters' perceptions of time and their assessment of the possibilities for creative social change in the context of social, economic and political disintegration. There are three distinct concepts of time at work in *The Shadow*. The play as a whole is committed to historicity: O'Casey knows where Ireland has been, where it is, and what may become of it. In short, he dramatizes a world that has a past, a present and a future. His view of the historical process is, as I have argued elsewhere, deeply pessimistic. One of O'Casey's most painful ironies in this play is that the worse the objective situation of his characters becomes, the more urgent the need for amelioration, the less likely they are to respond positively. Rather than taking a reasonable view of the relationship between past, present and future, the characters either contract time into the narrowness of total immediacy, or they expand time into the etheral realms of religious and literary immortality. These attempts to transform objective, historical time into private subjective strategies fail, and the characters are overwhelmed by external events, the force of which they must acknowledge even as they are confirmed in their impotence to alter them.

Chaos characterizes the world of *The Shadow of a Gunman* both in terms of the personal lives of the characters, and also in terms of the political and economic reality with which they interact. In the lengthy stage directions, O'Casey tells us that Seumas's room, the setting of the entire play, conveys an air of *'absolute untidiness, engendered on the one hand by the congenital slovenliness of Seumas Shields, and on the other by the temperament of Donal Davoren, making it appear impossible to effect an improvement in such a place'.*[7] As O'Casey explains, the disordered external setting corresponds to the psychological peculiarities of the characters. But the disordered room and all the activities that are enacted in it are a major indicator of the economic deprivation and the social dislocation of their lives. Seumas's room offers no refuge from the terror and instability of the external world.

It is only in a general way a 'home'. For a start, he shares it with Donal, a transient of no fixed address. Moreover, Seumas and Donal are threatened with eviction because, between the two of them, they cannot pay the rent. But even were their rented space more secure, the kind of existence engendered by the forced intimacies of poverty is confusing and disruptive. Tommy Owens, Mrs. Henderson, Mr. Gallagher, Mr. and Mrs. Grigson, and, for that matter, Minnie Powell, all force their way into Seumas's room and Donal's life, demanding attention, interfering with his work, and destroying any possibility of privacy and domestic tranquility. This situation is, of course, not peculiar to Donal, but is endemic in the tenements, as Mr. Gallagher's complaints about his abusive neighbours makes clear. There is rich irony in the fact that as Mrs. Henderson and Mr. Gallagher elaborate on their problem, they in essence perpetrate on Donal what they object to in their own neighbours. Clearly life lived at such close quarters moves between petty irritation and enduring frustration. Without the possibility of earning adequate income, and thus without decent homes, these people cling to the fringes of existence. Superimposed on their poverty is the long nightmare of the 'troubles'. Nationalist attacks and Black and Tan reprisals inflicted on an unprotected civilian population make the already desperate conditions of the tenement dwellers absolutely intolerable. What is worse, the random violence of Irish patriots and English soldiers alike stand in no clear relationship to the chronic poverty at the center of *The Shadow*. Despite the lip service various characters pay to the political ideals of the Nationalists, *The Shadow* dramatizes the disjunction between Nationalist activities and the economic needs of the characters.

The characters respond to the cumulative violence of poverty and political terror by a series of manipulations of their time sense, manipulations which offer them temporary personal comfort, but which fail to generate any long-range solutions to ameliorate their situation. In different ways, Tommy Owens, Adolphus Grigson and Minnie Powell live in the intensity of the moment, attempting to blot out the brutalities of their lives through emotion or alcohol. Seumas turns to otherworldly salvation for transcendence, and Donal uses the hope of literary immortality to try to overcome and rise above the surrounding disorder. While these mechanisms for coping reveal bursts of brightness, wit, humour, sensitivity and bravery in the characters, none of them addresses the destructive realities of their lives. In political terms, these attempts to transcend historical time are escapist in nature, and their overall effect (whatever their intention) is to perpetuate the processes of disintegration already at work in the play.

As a result, in *The Shadow,* the dramatic whole is an aggregate of small dramas of temporal evasion, of failed attempts at transcendence. For example, in Tommy's patriotic effusions in Act I and Dolphie Grigson's in Act II each has a routine designed in part to impress Donal, the supposed gunman on the run, with the dimensions of his heroism. In part, too, their outbursts of bravado are designed to obliterate (if only for the duration of the performance) the pervasive atmosphere of terror, no doubt exacerbated in their own minds by the presence of the supposed gunman, Donal. Of course, when reality overtakes them and the Black and Tans break in the door, Tommy is nowhere to be found, and Mrs. Grigson reports that Dolphie met the challenge by cowering in his bed. Although both Tommy and Dolphie are braggarts and hypocrites, they cannot be dismissed as inconsequential. In the highly politicized context of *The Shadow,* such diversionary attempts at transcending reality actually perpetuate the status quo. What is worse, by their gestures and phrases, they give credibility to the kind of impulsive patriotic behaviour that sends Minnie to her death.

Although Minnie's behaviour, particularly her heroic gesture in taking responsiblity for the bag of bombs, appears in stark contrast to the cowardice of the male characters, she nevertheless shares with Tommy Owens and Dolphie Grigson the need to live in the immediacy of the moment, devoid of a sense of future, and, because we have no evidence that she considers events retrospectively, devoid also of a clear sense of the past as it impacts on the present. Minnie's sudden affection for Donal is in part fuelled by the troubles (after all she thinks, wrongly, that he is a gunman) and in part by an attempt to fill her consciousness with pleasant romantic possibilities. Her willingness to take the bombs is an adrenalin charge to the brain, an instantaneous response to the immediate pressure of the troubles and to her feeling for Donal, a response which is meant to deesclate the threat of the Black and Tans to Donal at no cost to herself because, she reasons, the Black and Tans will be lenient with a woman.

Unlike Tommy's and Dolphie's performances, Minnie's actions have both positive and negative valences. Her bravery and decency are sterling qualities; but unaccompanied by a grasp of the political and economic realities of ther situation, those qualities are squandered in the service of illusion (Donal is not a gunman; the Black and Tans arrest women as well as men) and they do nothing to alter the chaos that overtakes and destroys her. While she dies in crossfire between Nationalists and Black and Tans, an apparently 'accidental' victim, she contributes to her own victimization and to the overall collapse by her willingness to act impulsively but uncritically.

Seumas's situation is in many ways more enlightened than Minnie's. He is the most articulate anti-Nationalist in the play, a man of great rhetorical skill whose set piece, 'I don't want the gunman dying for me', is the most often quoted and referred to statement in the play. He is shrewd and telling in his observations about Minnie, a 'Helen of Troy come to live in a tenement'. (p. 130) He cuts through to the essentials of the Donal-Minnie relationship: 'You think a lot about her, an' she thinks a lot about you because she looks upon you as a hero — a kind o'Paris ... she'd give the world

an' all to be gaddin' about with a gunman'. (p. 130) He is brutal in
his deflation of Donal's poetry 'If I was you', he advises Donal, 'I'd
give that game up; it doesn't pay a working-man to write poetry'.
(p. 127) Ignoring the fact that as an unsuccessful peddlar, Seumas is
in a weak position to offer advice on what constitutes a secure
living, he pursues Donal's romantic impulse relentlessly. With the
kind of romantic cliches Donal might use, Seumas turns Davoren's
poetic vocabulary into parody and seriously challenges the aesthetic theory on which it rests.

> I don't know much about the pearly glint of the morning dew, or the
> damask sweetness of the rare wild rose, or the subtle greenness of the
> serpent's eye — but I think a poet's claim to greatness depends upon
> his power to put passion in the common people. (p. 127)

Seumas's perception of engaged art flies in the face of Donal's
ivory tower notions. Inasmuch as Seumas recognizes the need to
relate art to life, and, in his pungent criticism, he shows the observing eye of a person deeply committed to the peculiarities of
life, he appears to be a realist and for that reason alone the intellectual superior of the other characters.

Nevertheless, Seumas's perspective is oddly truncated and distorted by his recent recovery of religion, (he is, he assures Donal, a
daily communicant) and his continued reliance on superstition. His
response to economic insecurity and to political terror is to replace
any notion of struggle in the here and now with a belief in personal
salvation in the hereafter. His newfound religiousity accommodates
itself wonderfully well to his equally strong belief in a spooky
netherworld full of strange noises. He finds it easier to blame all
difficulties (including Minnie's death) on a missed Mass and on the
tapping on the wall rather than on any personal inadequacy. That
Seumas so easily equates the superficially different demands of religion and superstition makes its own ironic comment on the depth
of his religious professions. Moreover, his unwillingness to accept
any measure of responsibility for unfolding events indicates that,
for Seumas, religion and superstition are forms of fatalism that
have, as corollaries, ethical neutrality and political quietism.
Traumatized by political and economic troubles, Seumas seeks
transcendence in a renewed Catholicism. But in so doing he furthers
the pattern of breakdown in the play.

In the evasions of history implicit in the behaviours of Seumas

and of Minnie, O'Casey illustrates the power of the dominant ideo-
logies, religious as well as political and cultural, to absorb and un-
dermine precisely those qualities of mind and spirit that ought to
become the resources for a more positive restructuring of society.

As a would-be poet, Donal is the character who might be expected
to possess the intellectual and spiritual potential to produce new and
better insights. Donal's claims are indeed grand. With a bravado un-
sustained by what follows, Davoren pointedly assures Seumas that he
leaves the 'fear of death to the people that are always praying for
eternal life', that is, to Seumas. After all, he continues in the same
smug manner, ' "Death is here and death is there, death is busy
everywhere" '. (p. 133) No sooner does Davoren quote this line, a
line which in this context appears romantically overblown, then he
hears a volley of shots outside that restore him to a nagging fear-
fulness. But it is not only the troubles that terrify Donal. He is also
overwhelmed by thoughts of his own mortality. As a release, he
turns to poetry and its promise of literary immortality.

Unlike Seumas's aesthetic of an engaged art, Davoren values
poetry in direct proportion to its irrelevance to the everyday concerns of ordinary people. In a burst of pride and petulence, he articulates aesthetic principles which the entire play undercuts:

> Damn the people! They live in the abyss, the poet lives on the moun-
> tain-top; to the people there is no mystery of colour: it is simply the
> scarlet coat of the soldier; the purple vestments of a priest; the green
> banner of a party; the brown or blue overalls of industry. To them the
> might of design is a three-roomed house or a capacious bed. (p. 127)

Through poetry, Donal hopes to sidestep these (to him) petty temporal concerns.

But Donal's theory is flawed. The people are not as Donal
describes them. He is blind to the verbal skills embedded in the
rhetorical acrobatics of Tommy and Grigson. He is unappreciative
of Minnie's vitality and sensitivity to beauty. He ignores the educated intelligence of Seumas who recognizes and identifies Donal's
literary quotations.

Further, Donal's poetry is not as he envisions it. He does not
appear to notice that his own efforts do not celebrate the richness of
life. Rather, in second-rate imitation of Shelley, Donal's words
commemmorate life's dying fall. These are Davoren's first words
and the first words of the play:

Or when sweet Summer's ardent arms outspread,
Entwined with flowers,
Enfold us, like two lovers newly wed,
Thro' ravish'd hours —
Then sorrow, woe and pain lose all their powers,
For each is dead, and life is only ours.

           (p. 94)

I have argued elsewhere that 'ours' in the last phrase, 'life is only ours', puns unintentionally on 'hours' and that the pun reveals Donal's preoccupation with the, for him, meaningless passage of time. Although poetry is his strategy for transcendence, it ironically expresses his concerns about mortality, and it does so in such tired language as to guarantee its forgettability. Donal will need more than his kind of poetry to join the company of the literary immortals.

Finally, Donal's aesthetic theory is flawed by the fact that he is not divorced from either 'the people' or from their historically derived circumstances. The entire play is a demonstration that there is no isolated reality on a mountaintop, but a series of interconnecting ripples emanating from the behaviour of the characters as they intersect with history.

However, Donal, unlike any other character, does achieve a moment of truth precipitated by the death of Minnie Powell. Despite the formality of Donal's concluding speech, he responds to the event with greater moral and artistic insight than he has previously shown.

DAVOREN: Ah me, alas! Pain, pain, pain ever for ever! It's terrible to think that little Minnie is dead, but it's still more terrible to think that Davoren and Shields are alive! On, Donal Davoren, shame is your portion now till the silver cord is loosened and the golden bowl be broken. Oh, Davoren, Donald Davoren, poet and poltroon, poltroon and poet! (pp. 156-7)

In this speech, literary allusions, biblical cadences, alliteration, repetition and parallelism create complex decorative and distancing effects. Donal's verbal dexterity allows him to detach himself from the emotional consequences of Minnie's death and to pass increasingly harsh moral judgement on his own not insignificant failure.

There is considerable strength in Donal's final statement. Nevertheless, it circumscribes its moral concerns by its sheer virtuosity. Donal's claims in this passage are aesthetic as much as moral; he is a self-proclaiming 'poet' in addition to being a 'poltroon'. In making such claims, Donal underlines the artfulness of his language, far better demonstrated in this prose routine than in his highly derivative and inferior verse. Moreover, the use of 'poltroon' as the second term in the first alliterating pair ('poet and poltroon', he says) strongly suggests that his choice of 'poltroon' was determined in large part by his artistic need to find an alliterative balance for the 'p' in 'poet'. Thus, Donal is a 'poltroon' because he is a 'poet'.

It is nevertheless true that, when Donal repeats the alliterative phrase, he transposes the terms so that 'poet and poltroon' becomes, in the second version, 'poltroon and poet'. In doing so Donal appears to recognize that he has become a 'poet' (defined by this context as a skilled word user) because he is a 'poltroon'. It is not his previous practice of versifying, but his cowardice in allowing Minnie to take the bag of bombs that produces his best verbal effects.

The improvement in Donal's use of language at the end of the play rests on his confrontation with the force of history as it affects 'the people', in this case Minnie Powell. Donal finds an authentic voice by descending from the 'mountain-top' (that is, from his ivory tower aestheticism) into the 'abyss' of history and articulating the passage.

O'Casey calls *The Shadow of a Gunman* a tragedy. It is certainly not Aristotelian tragedy. Rather, it is a tragedy of failed opportunity. The play is saturated with a sense of crisis; what appears to be needed are characters of sufficient insight and understanding to transform the pattern of disintegration into a design for positive economic and social renewal. But even granting Donal's growth, such characters do not exist at a sufficiently high level of consciousness. Whatever opening for radical change the combined outrage of the 'troubles' and poverty creates is dissipated by the force of circumstance and the limitations of character. However much Donal's final words show growth, it is unclear whether he can translate them into decisive action.

THE WAYS OF TWONESS: PAIRS, PARALLELS AND CONTRASTS IN STEWART PARKER'S *SPOKESONG*

MÁRIA KURDI

After having spent a few years teaching in the United States, the late Stewart Parker (1941–88) returned to his beloved Belfast in 1969, the same week when the Troubles began. It was during the time of bombings and killings, but also when in spite of everything, many 'succeeded in living normal lives, in rearing their children, doing a good job of work, being considerate neighbours, useful citizens'[1], that he matured as a playwright. His first stage success was *Spokesong* in 1975, a play reflecting on secterian violence in its own characteristic way. Measured against the backdrop of contemporary Irish drama in general, it apparently belongs with works which are marked by 'a far greater amount of experimentalism than was the case in former decades, and with it [by] a greater iconoclasm.'[2] Among the plays addressing the problems of the political crises and impasse, quite a few employed a comparatively direct, documentary or even naturalistic approach, including John Boyd's *The Flats* (1971), Bill Morrison's *Flying Blind* (1977), Graham Reid's *The Closed Door* (1980), and Martin Lynch's *The Interrogation of Ambrose Fogarty* (1982), to name just a few. Others chose unrealistic, often metaphorical, ways of referring to the Troubles and its bearing on individual lives. Parker's *Spokesong* has affinities and shares certain features with this second group, where one can find Brian Friel's *The Freedom of the City* (1973), David Rudkin's *Ashes* (1974), Frank McGuinness's *Carthaginians* (1988) and so forth.

In the author's words, *Spokesong* 'tries to isolate what is at the heart of the turbulence in Ireland at the moment. But I decided against writing a play about Protestants and Catholics... That would only be dealing with the surface, anyway. I wanted to go underneath all that and look at the core'.[3] Elsewhere he added that when writing the play he aimed 'to construct a working model of whole-ness by means of which this society can begin to hold up its head in the world'.[4] Set in both the present and the past, the action takes place in and out of a bicycle shop situated in a house divided against itself, located in a divided town in a divided land. Whole-ness seems to be achievable only by going beyond the immediate, the whole thus growing out of the hell-hole of brutal reality. There-fore the play grasps and presents a complexity of facts and feelings which run parallel or counter to each other, maintaining creative tension and dramatic suspense at the same time.

Spokesong strikes its audience as highly and captivatingly theat-rical. Borrowing the words of its author again, it well deserves description as a product of 'an unconscious impulse to express the most ancient element in playacting — the instinct for play itself'.[5] Its very title is a funny-sounding compound of a pair of one-syllable words suggesting the fusion of prosaic reality and transcending music, reinforced by the fact that 'spoke' has two distinct meanings. The thus foregrounded use of puns and rich verbal ironies remains characteristic throughout. That the play is intrinsically a play be-comes noticeable as early as in the first scene. A figure called the Trick Cyclist appears in a variety-act uniform riding a unicycle and singing the happy 'Daisy Bell' song, after which he transforms himself into a public servant interviewing a man called Frank Stock. In the ensuing dialogue Frank, who is a spokesman because he repairs bicycles, turns out to be an inspired advocate of and spokesman for the rediscovery of the 'faithful bicycle'[6], over against plans for building one more motorway for vehicles with in-ternal combustion engines. The physical unreality of the scene suggests its taking place in mental and emotional terrains, in the form of a constant debate with the hostile powers of the world. This metaphorical action is followed by an earthly one: the first meeting of Frank and schoolteacher Daisy in the former's bicycle shop. The juxtaposition of the two scenes introduces two planes, one in the mind where desires are conceived and travels elsewhere are pos-sible without limit, and the other in everyday reality.

Calling into being alternative worlds, the 'central, dramatic ten-sion' in Parler's play is 'between what a man feels life ought to be and the thwarting, hostile reality of what is'.[7] Used both physically and metaphorically, it is the bicycle that establishes a connection between the ideal and the real. As part of the folklore of Belfast, where John Dunlop invented the pneumatic tire in 1887, the bicycle is related to both the city and its people. As opposed to the discontinuous history of the six counties it has, according to Frank's triumphant assessment of it, one which displays an ongoing fulfilment of human visions ever since wheeled vehicles started to be used in Lower Mesopotamia in 3,500 B.C. Daisy, his listener, is a teacher of history, whose reference to Belfast teenagers' historically developed expertise on guns and explosives easily forms an ironical counterpoint to Frank's idealism.

Throughout the beginning of the play Frank's 'bicycle-philosophy' gradually unfolds. He idealizes it because 'So far as personal transport goes — the bicycle was the last advance in technology that everybody understands'. (p. 19) For him, it is the embodiment of a set of human values like harmony, peace, and fraternity; even Christ can be thought of as riding a bicycle. He declares its superiority to the automobile, in which bombs can be planted, and to the aeroplane, which makes the passenger feel helpless and estranged. Frank's dreamworld of all mankind peacefully riding bikes is contrasted by the traps of 1970s reality, which gradually envelope his Victorian shop in the rest of the play. First the audience hears about the City Redevelopment Plans menacing small properties like his; then, with the reappearance of his foster brother Julian it becomes obvious that the cruel fratricide of Northern Ireland confronts Frank's and others' way to individual, bicycle-symbolized freedom. In addition, the explosion of bombs and the death of innocent citizens, such as a petshop owner, loom large in the background.

Julian's character is directly opposed to that of Frank whose naively good common wheel plans and general humanism are a far cry from the former's cynicism, lack of consideration and hatefulness which he calls a sense of reality. In the end, however, Julian's 'reality' proves to be nothing else but corruption and consequently Daisy, unlike her namesake in *The Great Gatsby* who turns away from the dreamer, remains with the idealist Frank. The lovers mount their tandem in faith and merrily wheel out of the play, but not without the awareness that their happiness is privately owned, while the city is still the same. Daisy's remark to the effect that changes have to be made seems to bear reference not only to the shop and its business but to the larger scene as well. The audience, on the other hand, might easily be reminded of the fate of Nagg and Nell in *Endgame* by Parker's greatest master, Beckett, who lost their shanks while on a ride on their tandem and became reduced to ashcan-entombed human wrecks.

On a more concrete level, Frank's and Daisy's brittle happiness is undercut by the callous robbing of the till by Julian and the Trick Cyclist. The latter's merry song is about Daisy Bell as at the beginning, but its sweetness is not able to dispel the poison of mixed feelings in the air. According to Parker, the play 'ends on an ambiguous note, but not a pessimistic one'.[8] Even strong believers like Frank, whose bicycle-religion suggests the transcendability of sectarian opposition, have access only to hardearned private solutions while public reality remains an unconquerable stone 'in the midst of all'. The common wheel of a bicycle cannot guarantee a different ending for a divided commonweal, as it would demand more energy and co-operation than what two people can provide. With 'two brothers fight[ing] over the inheritance of a bicycle shop'[9] where one owns the house and the other runs the business, Parker creates a metaphorical reference to the divisions in Northern Ireland carrying the threat of hostility and violence. Julian is not merely a Cain-like figure but a warning that out of the union of Catholic and Protestant — as his parents are described — a very bad mixture may come.

The above parallels and contrasts of the ideal and the real are elaborated and enriched in scope by the shifts between the present and the past. The actions and conversations recalled from Frank's grandparents' life echo what is going on in the present, they are virtually evoked by it. There is a strong sense of the past being experienced subjectively. According to Frank's memories, the duet between him and history-teaching Daisy was preceded by bicycle-fanatic Francis wooing a hard-headed girl named Kitty who wished that Ireland and womanhood would gain sovereignty in one process. Loyalist and Nationalist they are, but united by the bike. In the past the universal acceptance of the common wheel was also questioned but for different reasons: Victorian morality had its objections to it. Nevertheless, it contributed to women's emancipation. In the Great War the bicycle was used for military purposes, so Francis's idealism was also subject to the blows of reality and history. Differently though again, as the story of the Army Cyclist corps, for whom 'it is imperative that the cyclist should not allow his machine to fall intact into the enemy's 'hands' (p. 49), is told with so much amusement. The parallels between past and present reinforce the transcending nature and role of ever-cycling ideals which help people find the centre of their lives and keep above the tide of distress. At the same time, the continuity of human life is emphasized in spite of all drastic historical changes.

The scenes from the years gone by, appearing in Frank's mental theatre, enact his obsession with the past and its old-fashioned values. He is reliving and reinterpreting the past of his own bicycle-loving family, which gives him moral strangth and rectitude despite his daily experiences of an unstable present and future. The ideal in the play is inseparable from the nostalgia for past values. Frank's nostalgia, however, is not totally blind: after the first evoked scene between Francis and Kitty there is a direct switch to Frank, who muses on their doings. Much later, in utter distress amidst the encircling mud of sectarian violence, he speaks directly to Francis and claims that 'It is not just the same as it was for you. There's no simple enemy. There's no Back Home. No Boche. And no Blighty' (pp. 64-5). The grandparents are forced to recede when the impending but ultimately unrealized betrayal of Daisy has further distressed Frank, who finds his new solace in the bottle and the company of the Trick Cyclist. He is at his lowest, acknowledging personal defeat: 'Say what you like . . . the bicycle has a great past ahead ot it . . . I came to be a pacifist, a philosopher and a lone wolf by the age of seven'. A pun serves to sum up his sense of helplessness: he describes himself as a static and ineffectual 'bouncer' opposed to the mobility of 'breakers' (pp. 70-1).

With his doggedly optimistic eulogies about an old-fashioned vehicle, his long-lasting trust and ever-renewed daydreaming followed by a spectacular collapse, Frank is also seen as considerably comic. Set against the cynicism of Julian, however, this proves to be a more human, and therefore superior, quality. In a powerful dialogue of the two, Julian tries to ridicule the feelings of his half-brother but turns out to repeat slogans of destructiveness, even terrorism. It is the idealistic Frank who points to a workable use of the past for the sake of life in the present:

> JULIAN: Look at yourself. Hunkered down in this . . . blocked-up latrine of your own memories. That's what memories are, big brother, that's what the past is, history, the accumulated turds of human endeavour. I don't like it, I'm a cleanly fellow. It has to come down, the whole edifice, brick by brick. Wiped. Flushed.
>
> FRANK: Have you not learned anything at all? You *are* your own past, kid. You're the sum total of its parts. Hate it and you hate yourself. No matter how calamitous it may have been, either you master it or die (pp. 60-1).

Action is discontinuous in *Spokesong*.[10] The shifts between the past and the present, imaginary and real scenes, songs and dialogues build up a mosaic structure. In the two-act composition of the play an essential design of twoness can be observed. Scenes refer to each other, or strengthen or undercut meanings by their juxtaposition. It is an early case in point when in the middle of Act I two comparable scenes show Julian with Frank and then talking to Daisy. The changes in his behaviour introduce him not only as a cynic but also as a turncoat. On the other hand, the differences here are also attributable to Julian's being seen by two diferent people. For Frank he is a troublemaker who destroys the remaining peace of the present, while for Daisy he is a newcomer bringing excitement. Themes constantly appear in two lights, for instance when, at the end of Act I, history teacher Daisy and Frank disagree about the meaning of history. His way of looking at it is genuinely subjective: 'I don't see the truth in battles or the lives of the celebrated megalomaniacs. That's not the important history either. I see it in all the things that ordinary people do with their time' (p. 35). This view is strongly questioned by the intrusion of Daisy's reference to a hard-boiled fact of contemporary reality: 'My father's one of the neighbourhood gangsters' (p. 36). The juxtaposed scene recalled from the past leads the Trick Cyclist on stage clothed in an Irish Guards major's uniform of the Boer War. He is the father of Kitty, hostile to the union of his daughter and Francis. Once again, the bicycle image and the freedom associated with it is challenged by authority figures, in this case represented by the two fathers.

At the beginning of Act II wars in the past and in the present are set against each other, along with people's varying attitudes to them. Francis's dislike of violence and instinctive search for self-defence while serving in World War One Army Cyclist Corps is flanked by a scene following the explosion of a bomb in the present. The Trick Cyclist, this time as leather-jacketed Duncan, Daisy's father, capitalizes on the fact that ordinary people can be frightened into paying for the privilege of having their premises left intact. Violence and war reappear in the later mention of a bomb which killed Frank's parents. In Kitty's words: 'They were killed by a German bomb. If Ireland had been a united country it wouldn't have been dropped' (p. 54). The latter part of her statement rings also true of the preceding scene, with its explosion in the present. Nevertheless, a parallel idea blunts the appeal of Kitty's nationalist explanation: it was a cat's eczema, according to old Francis, that helped to change the family's history. This renewed turn to the importance of the bicycle disguises Frank's desperate reaching out for comfort in the past and its inheritance, because of his first-hand experiences of terrorism topped by Julian's having sold his shop to be turned into terrorist headquarters. The imagined family scene helps him to momentarily accept his present in terms of the past: 'Love, war and the bicycle... the gist of their lives... mine too. My love, my war, my bicycle' (p. 56). But violence returns in the next mosaic where Daisy's story about the schoolchildren's terrorist deeds is told to justify her decision to clear out for good and leave Frank homeless in more than one sense. Finally, after darkness has almost won, a miraculous ending lifts Frank and the play out of their staggering deadlock: circumstances awakened Daisy to see through Julian and come back to Frank.

The design of dualities and contrasts is reinforced by Parker's choice of names. Francis/Frank recall the legendary Francis of Assisi, a saint of peace and kindness especially devoted to nature. The figure opposed to them, Julian, bears the name of Julian the Apostate, the Roman emperor whose 'policy was to degrade Christianity and promote paganism by every means short of open persecution'.[1] With regard to women, the bicycle-liberated Kitty is the namesake of her historical contemporary, Katharine O'Shea, Parnell's mistress. Daisy, on the other hand, wears a rather common name borrowed from the extensively quoted folksong 'Daisy Bell'.

The play mentions two writers of the late nineteenth century side by side, both universally known but for admittedly different reasons. One of them, Arthur Conan Doyle, is relevant as the writer of a story entitled *The Solitary Cycslist.* His memorable creation, detective Sherlock Holmes, is a defender of law and order. The other literary giant, Oscar Wilde, represents art and eccentric freedom. The spirit of his drama is recaptured by 'an obvious Wildean wit' that the female characters display.[12] Rich in literary allusions and intertextuality as it is, Parker's play quotes the poet Wordsworth twice. In his rehearsal for the public inquiry, Frank uses the line 'Earth would not have anything to show more fair' (p. 28), from 'Lines Composed Upon Westminster Bridge, September 3, 1802' as an argument for a world of bikes with clean air and energy conservation. When his early enthusiasm is deflated by the accumulation of negative experiences, and he has taken to drinking in the company of the Trick Cyclist, he distorts a Wordsworthian title ('Ode: Intimations of Immortality' from 'Recollections of Early

Childhood') along with starting to destroy himself, saying: '... let me tell you about this beautiful old shop ... herewith, An Ode! Intimations of Negativity in Late Childhood' (p. 71).

The omnipresence of the bicycle and especially its final metamorphosis into a tandem, 'a new model' (p. 73) lends the play an atmosphere of wishing for harmony and peace. After all, the two wheels of a bicycle can do their job only in unison if any kind of progress is aimed at. This all-pervading metaphor becomes a constant reminder of basic human needs. On the other hand, a different vehicle is ridden by the Trick Cyclist, 'who combines the role of song-and-dance man with a number of other ones'.[13] With his unicycle he is an everyman figure who unites both good and bad features. His appearance as gangster, political hoodlum and major in a long and disastrous war, however, suggests that his variety act singing and dancing sweep merely the surface; the core is more on the side of corruption. Both his name and his vehicle are related to tricks, the opposite of honesty and frankness. In the last scenes, as Frank's companion in self-destruction and that of Julian in plundering the till, he acquires satanic features. The desperate Frank describes his loss of faith with the words: 'God's a bad trick cycling act' (p. 72).

Is the Trick Cyclist the lurking evil in man whose bicycle-happy songs fill the air only to generate false beliefs? There is no clear answer. At any rate, his in-and-out presence in the play parallels and also contrasts with that of the bicycle, since he is more than one of the characters, a symbolic figure, like the bicycle which serves as more than a means of public transport in the play. His roles reflect on the latter in several different ways, the overall effect being one of complexity, the defiance of maintaining the belief in easy solution despite desires and idealism. Evil may emerge where it is least expected. The conclusion can be drawn that the Trick Cyclist emboides features which are latent in the human being, therefore he appears in different guises and roles, both appealing and reppeling. But his unicycle is by no means a common weal, perhaps thus also referring to man's essential loneliness and, lamentably, selfishness.

Spokesong is a serio-comic play in which a lot of singing is used to assert individual as well as communal feelings, similarly to other 'Troubles-plays' like Patrick Galvin's less significant *We Do It for Love* (1975), where the central metaphor is a Merry-Go-Round. This feature, however, does not transform Parker's play into a musical. The richness of its effects includes charm and vivid humour, the latter mostly produced by the puns and colloquialisms of its language, as well as some vague sense of fear that all the mirth is so brittle. Artistic and at times falling into pieces, *Spokesong* puzzles the audience by its theatrical double-dealing. It shows the wholeness of being both funny and disturbing, promising and distressing in which nothing has a uniform face. Through thick and thin, however, the object and metaphor of the bicycle, with its harmoniously running wheels gives a frame to the fluid matter which is fragile and strong equally. The protagonist's, Frank's job, at the same time, is putting pieces together. In this respect he can be compared to Wilson John Haire's The Buck Lep, a figure with a lot of humour and helpfulness who works as a (rebuilding) mason in the author's 'Troubles play', *Bloom of the Diamond Stone* (1973).

Spokesong reflects on the Troubles from a unique point of view, delicately presenting two planes at the same time: one is the level of desires for harmony, love and peace, while the other is that of inconsideration, thirst for vengeance, and hatred. That the two have possible meeting points and sometimes even overlap, is underscored by Daisy finally dismissing Julian with the words: 'You are a worse clown than your brother. You're pathetic' (p. 69). The city development plans, while endangering the future use of the bicycle, mean construction against the damage of explosions. Through its absurdities this funny play emphasizes the abnormality of the situation in Northern Ireland, but does not leave the audience with the feeling that violence and destruction rule uncontested. Parker's greatest plays focusing on his homeland, following *Spokesong* by years when he was more aware of what the 'great flat thick slab of granite' (p. 58) in Daisy's description about the province was, are not wholly dark either. In *Northern Star* (1984) the deterministic view of history is tempered by images of hope and freedom. *Pentecost* (1987), which 'is about healing rifts'[14] ends in human reconciliation under a clear sky. Due to the author's 'basic dynamic outlook'[15] and treasury of theatrical devices, on Parker's stage transcending values are likely to shine through even the darkest moments, and the surrounding hostile reality never seems strong enough to obliterate dreams of wholeness and the wish to play.

ANCIENT LIGHTS
IN AUSTIN CLARKE
AND THOMAS KINSELLA

MAURICE HARMON

Two modern Irish poets, Austin Clarke and Thomas Kinsella, are particularly associated with the long poem. Austin Clarke wrote several long poems — 'The Loss of Strength', 'The Hippophagi', 'Martha Blake at Fifty-One', *Mnemosyne Lay in Dust,* 'The Disestablished Church', 'Orphide', 'The Dilemma of Iphis', 'The Healing of Mis', and 'Tiresias'. He wrote several other poems of considerable length, such as 'Ancient Lights' and 'A Sermon of Swift' and all of these in the last twenty years of his life. They form the major evidence for his growth and development during the period of 1955 to 1974 when he re-emerged as an important poet. Thomas Kinsella has also written several long poems. — 'A Country Walk', 'Downstream', 'Nightwalker', 'Phoenix Park', and 'The Good Fight', and since 1972 he has been at work on a series of poetic sequences that are part of one long sequence.

Austin Clarke's later, long poems are preceded by 'Ancient Lights' in which he declared his liberation from the restrictions of the Irish Catholic church. Its title is a legal term that guarantees the individual's right to light. Just as your neighbor cannot erect a highrise building beside your house, thereby denying your right to light, so neither church nor state, nor personal trauma nor mental instability, can deprive the poet of his right to the light of imagination, his freedom, his right to think and write. The poem concludes with a defiant ritual of liberation.

> my fears
> Were solved, I had absolved myself:
> Feast-day effulgence, as though I gained
> For life a plenary indulgence.[1]

Light floods into the poem signalling the self's absolution and release.

Ironically, soon after Clarke announced his newfound feeling of liberation, he suffered a serious heart-attack that curtailed his physical movements. But if he was physically impaired, he could be imaginatively srong. If he could no longer range freely throughout the countryside, he could remember, recreate and reflect on himself and on the circumstances and events that had shaped him. He had always known that he had been seriously affected in childhood, adolescence and early manhood, by an exaggerated fear of sin and damnation, by the failure of his first marriage, by nervous breakdown and depression. Much of his writing, prior to 1955, had dealt indirectly with these issues. When he had looked at them more directly in his novel, *The Singing Men at Cashel* (1936), and in his collection of poems, *Night and Morning* (1938), the result had been a catastrophic descent into silence. Now, after 1955, in one long poem after another, with growing strength and confidence, with deepening powers of observation, and increasing directness and honesty, he embarks on the course of self examination that leads him to the traumatic centre where the horror of his incarceration in St. Patrick's Psychiatric Hospital, and its attendant causes, could be faced and recreated. Thereafter, the long poems revel in freedom from restraint. Poems like 'Orphide' and 'The Healing of Mis', at the end of his life, are much less anguished and burdened than those at the beginning of this final phase, such as 'The Loss of Strength', 'The Hippophagi', or the climatic *Mnemosyne Lay in Dust.*

'The Loss of Strength' reflects on the poet's diminished physical powers and relates them to more general losses of energy and coherence in history, religion and culture, so that the personal and the national become mirror images of each other. But in addition to being an elegy about loss the poem is an *apologia* for the poet's life, for choices made, for his imaginative and intellectual decisions. All of the long poems have this justifying, explanatory element. They confess and reveal, they examine and uncover what has been central and do so with growing confidence and penetration, but they are also saying that here are the ingredients of life, these are the issues, these are the circumstances and out of these and through these the poet writes. They are what he is. In the final analysis the poems are manifestoes. The flexibility of language and organization in 'The Loss of Strength' declare that the poet's inner life, of the mind and

of the imagination, has not been impaired. There is both regret and
confidence.

> I climb among the hills no more
> To taste a last water, hide in cloud-mist
> From sheep and goat. The days are downpour.
> Cycle is gone, warm patch on trousers.
> All, all, drive faster, stink without,
> Spirit and spark within, no doubt.
> When hope was active, I stood taller
> Than my own sons. Beloved strength
> Springs past me, three to one. Halldoor
> Keeps open, estimates the length
> To which I go: a mile to tire-a.
> But I knew the stone beds of Ireland.

'I climb among the hills no more'. The mood is personal, remembering former freedom, lamenting present loss. His sons now have
the energy he once had. But the last line firmly makes its claim: 'But
I knew the stone beds of Ireland', that is, the places where Irish
saints slept in the Christian medieval period. With a touch of self
mockery he re-enacts the days when he, too, could roam freely and
imaginatively, on his optimistic quests: 'Beclipped and confident of
shank, / I rode the plain with chain that freed me'. These journeys
were not only searches for the legendary and the mythological, they
were journeys of release from the restrictions of home and church,
school and city, from the rigid, post-Tridentine rules and regula-
tions of the Maynooth catechism. In the peace and solitude of remote places, he could find mental ease. He remembers and justifies
the attractions of Irish mythological and prehistoric material but
laments that the connections between man and the marvellous have
been weakened. This is another aspect of the poem's theme of loss.
Not only has engineering harnessed rivers and reduced their powerful flow, but the church, in a parallel metaphorical way, has
impeded the flow of human sexuality. In the combined process the
supernatural, associated with figures from mythology, with the
spiritual, and with medieval Ireland, has been made ordinary. The
result is detrimental to the power and flow of the imagination. In
modern Ireland celibacy, another form of restraint, is dominant.
Churchmen condemn the senses, religion gains adherents, and
sexuality is under suspicion. Ironically, Clarke returned from exile

in order to be close to what fed his imagination. Just as the crafts-
men and scholars lived within their confined world and radiated
their influence, so Clarke could live on a small scale and expand
imaginatively. He saw 'God's light through ruins', finding the light
of imagination in the world of Celtic Romanesque Ireland. That
medieval church was intellectually independent, self-reliant and
adventurous unlike the church in modern Ireland which is restrictive. The poet's task is to fill the void, to make up for various
deprivations that the poem relates.

His use of historical material relates directly to himself. In
twelfth century history it is the reform of the monasteries that is
important, not the coming of the Normans, because those reforms
established the diocesan and parochial system that remained in
force until Clarke's own time. In similar fashion modern Ireland
saw the introduction of many continental orders. History repeats itself: the reforms of the twelfth century that put an end to a church's
independence resemble those in the twentieth century that made
Ireland passive and timid. The freedom won in 1916 is of dubious
value when it results in the kind of middle-class Catholic society
that limits individual freedom. The poem ends with further images
of loss and restriction, but the poet's faith is in himself, in the power
of the creative imagination. Ironically, a poem about loss, shows in
the skill and control with which it is written, how valid that faith is.

'The Hippophagi' concentrates on the first twenty years of
Clarke's life. Cruelty to horses is a metaphor for insensitive, uncaring action, particularly when it emanates from or is condoned
by church or state. Stanzas about Clarke's boyhood are details in the
emergent portrait of a life impinged upon by cruelties. The emphasis is more explicitly sexual, since the church both preaches against
sexual activity and, ambivalently, uses confusing sensual language
in some of its devotional material. Religion, like sex, caused a
'swoon of sense'. Each produced or were expressed through similar
feelings, yet one was holy, the other sinful. Religion was also senti-
mentalised. In watered-down lives saints were turned into pious
models and finders of lost objects.

Disappointment with Christianity runs through the poem. The
horse disappeared from the streets of Dublin. So, too, has God's
love. The destruction of Sodom and Gomorrah parallels man's
destructive power in the twentieth century. Cruelty is a paradigm
for a society in which all the children of the nation are not treated

equally. Given the existence of stultifying repression poetry is the counter-force, the means of personal liberation and redemption. There is a sense in which 'The Loss of Strength', 'The Hippophagi' and the lyrics and satires that surround them, all lead to Clarke's major poem, *Mnemosyne Lay in Dust* (1966). Unlike its more objective predecessors, *Mnemosyne* is a psychological narrative dealing with the trauma of mental collapse, institutional treatments, and recovery. It dramatizes the state of barrenness to which Maurice Devane has fallen and gives an extraordinarily vivid account of the processes of recovery. Devane is confronted with the horror and confusion of his psychological state and the horror and confusion of his curative trauma. He suffers severe depression, paranoia and loss of identity. His dream of Mnemosyne in dust takes place in a context of helplessness and terror. Instead of the marble stairs and the sexual promise of a previous brothel dream, he is forced to climb 'spiral steps / Outside the building'. In 'a cobwebbed top-room', littered with 'bric-a-brac', and in a moment of heightened sensation he arrives 'stumbling / Where Mnemosyne lay in dust'. It is a devastating discovery, a confirmation of the 'Olympic doom' that propelled him forward. Images of waste, abandonment, and disorder define the circumstances. The dream externalizes his sense of loss and deprivation. Mnemosyne, goddess of memory (and Jupiter's consort), is also the mother of the muses. Her significance is therefore comprehensive. When she lies in dust, the sources of creativity have dried up.

> Always in terror of Olympic doom,
> He climbed, despite his will, the spiral steps
> Outside a building to a cobwebbed upper room.
>   There bric-a-brac was in a jumble
> His forehead was distending, ears were drumming
> As in the gastric fevers of his childhood.
> Despite his will, he climbed the steps, stumbling
>   Where Mnemosyne lay in dust.

Recovery involves facing up to subconscious fears and needs. His dreams and hallucinations often contain hidden fears and guilts. His hospital experience is in effect a descent into the Otherworld, a therapeutic engagement with personal pain and hidden shames, from which he eventually emerges to the realities of Dublin life. In Swift's 'Mansion of Forgetfulness' Devane is cut off from and unable to cope with everyday life. He is cut off not only because he is locked away but because he is unable to deal rationally with experience.

In other poems Clarke exposes cruelty and insensitivity, in *Mnemosyne* he recreates the humiliation and cruelty meted out to those who are victims of the aggressive and terrifying treatment in the asylum. It is one of the frightening ironies that the medical attendants and the warders are themselves sources of terror and it one of the poem's major paradoxes that the terror they induce is curative. Devane's claustrophobic descent into the void of lost memory is a defilement of body and spirit. Harpies, together with images of darkness, descent and suffocation, attend his entry to the asylum. The progress is an archetypal descent and return, an allegory of death and rebirth, the winter of loss followed by the summer of renewal; the disoriented imagination replaced by the creative imagination. The central element is the creative force of sexuality, lost and then recovered. In the Dionysian procession of Devane's vision it is the power of his creativity that is worshipped. In Hindu mythology, also part of his dreams, the ritual of sexual intercourse symbolises the creative union of opposites. To be cured is to be capable of love. To be cured also means to be made capable of a creative relationship with the world. Mnemosyne is recovered in the person of her daughter, Erato, for it is love that has been absent and that must lead Devane out of the garden of forgetfulness back to reality. The resolution brings him back to what he knows, to what he can see and understand. In his recovered state his senses do not lie, he is not disoriented, no longer suffers from hallucination, no longer tormented by the Jungian shadow figures that externalize his secret guilts. Self-confrontation is part of the process of renewal. Devane must use his mind, must activate his memory, in order to face up to his identity and face up to his psychological needs. To kill your father is to experience a radical sense of loss and alienation, and to be confronted with the infertility of Mnemosyne. Now, 'Rememorised', Devane enjoys the power of abstraction. He walk calmly into Dublin and is capable of that kind of rational, creative literal engagement with experience that characterized Clarke's writing from 1955 until his death in 1974.

A pattern of contrasting images embodies Devane's progress from crippling collapse to creative recovery. On the one hand are all the references to impeded movements that include not only his incarceration but sensations of choking, suffocation, throttling, and sexual frustration. Closely associated with them are references to victimization, aggression, the loss of consciousness, defilement, the loss of control over bodily movements, functions and directions, perceptual distortion, the failure of memory, and the mind's inability to function normally. On the other hand are all the references to unrestrictive activity, references to pleasing sounds, attractive smells, children running, peaceful settings, sun, sleep, all the references to the familiar and ordinary in Dublin, and all the sexual allusions. What Devane suffers in the asylum is alleviated and eventually overcome by what he can recall, value and anticipate.[2]

The purgation of private pain enabled Clarke to write more freely about sexuality. Sexuality is the central issue of the final collections which contain six long poems — 'A Sermon on Swift' and 'The Disestablished Church' published in the collection *A Sermon on Swift* (1968), 'Orphide', 'The Dilemma of Iphis' and 'The Healing of Mis' published in *Orphide* (1970) and *Tiresias* (1971). Their relaxed mood relies on a philosophical position reiterated in 'A Sermon on Swift' where Clarke recalls Swift's poem 'The Day of Judgement' in which Swift 'Damned and forgave the human race, dismissed / The jest of life'. That judgement granted universal forgiveness. In his *De Divisione Naturae* Eriugena also formulated a non-judgemental view of man, arguing that since man was part of God from the beginning he would return to God at the end. This moral detachment represents Clarke's final outlook. Like Swift, he has became a 'chuckling rhymester' and freed himself from Victorian narrowness and jansensistic Catholicism. In 'Ancient Lights' he absolved himself; in *Mnemosyne* he purged his mind; now he believed in "Eternal Absolution" and was able to delight in the physical. The erotic poems form a happy conclusion to a life-time's experience of repression and fear. 'The Healing of Mis' is representative; it is a parable of personal recovery. Mis goes mad when she sees her father's dead body. Fleeing into the mountain she becomes a wild creature, but the harper, Duv Ruis, wins her back to sanity through the combined power of music and sexual intercourse. His washing of Mis is a sluicing away of accumulated filth in preparation for the sacrament of sexual healing. At the same time Mis is tormented by 'curious dreams' of volcanic eruption, labyrinthine corridors, a 'subterranean / Maze', and paternal incest. The images resemble those Clarke has often used to describe his own mental collapse. Duv Ruis succeeds in liberating Mis; her scarred

mind is healed, her body is made beautiful. In the medieval romance a beautiful woman often entices a mortal youth to the Land
of the Ever Young, in this romance the mortal youth brings the de-
mented woman back from the otherworld of insanity and isolation.
The similarly with *Mnemosyne* is clear. This is another version of
descent and recovery but told in terms of erotic pleasure.

'The Disestablished Church' is about the consequences of the
disestablishment of the Protestant Church in Ireland but, more
generally, it is about the failure of religion. Religion itself has been
disestablished, its place taken, in Clarke's work, by a liberating,
non-judgemental philosophy. Once again, as in 'Ancient Lights',
Clarke recalls the moment of release and the fact that he did it on
his own.

> No angel rolled back the faraway boulder.
> A light shone out from misery.
> The hand that spared me was its own.

He escapes from the tomb of restriction, cruelty and darkness. Now
he celebrates that release and its philosophical basis.

> All human beings will be released.
> The clarabella, clavecin,
> Are not more sweet to hear in the bout
> Of melody when the notes are single,
> My little spoon at last was singing —
> Impudent handle was unbowed,
> For consciousness is as we deem it.

'All human beings will be redeemed'. 'Consciousness is as we
deem it'. The reference to 'spoon' or 'stirabout', that is, porridge,
mockingly define the restrictive contexts from which Clarke struggles
free. Just as the 'child of grace' in 'Ancient Lights' could frighten
off the fabled bronze bird, so here the 'little spoon' achieves its
liberation and is impudently 'unbowed'. The sexual implications
hardly need to be mentioned.

The historical association for the imagery of porridge and personal faith is clear. The Church council at Valence declared that
Eriugena's philosophy was 'pultes Scotorum', that is 'Irish porridge'. By calling it 'stultes / Scrotorum', as Clarke mischievously
does, he is able to describe the stultification that results from

oppressive teaching and cruel punishment. At the same time he slyly argues that Eriugena had scrotal power, had the courage of his convictions, that his ideas were fertile. 'Spoon sang the grace', not just grace at meals, or Divine grace, but the absolution recorded in 'Ancient Lights', the 'Eternal Absolution' of Swift's 'Day of Judgement', the universal redemption of Eriugena's philosophy.

The Protestant Church has been disestablished. The Catholic church has lost direction. Too great a vine, Clarke tellingly observed in 'The Loss of Strength', can sour the best of clay. A church grown wealthy and complacent feeds off the people, instead of serving them. In the final poems paganism becomes an alternative religion celebrated in the poetry of erotic desire, sensuality and unashamed sexuality. It receives its philosophical justification in Eriugena and Swift and in Clarke's declaration of faith in a merciful God, not the God of the Old Testament who had disturbed his youth.

Thomas Kinsella is also concerned in his long poems with the interaction between the individual and the past and between the individual and his immediate environment. In 'A Country Walk' the walker achieves a greater personal awareness through his perceptions of the historical and contemporary associations of a particular place. 'Downstream' is a journey into the underworld of horror and death. Horror is associated with the violence of the second world war. It was a time of nightmare: by day the 'barren world' was lit by conflagration caused by 'swinish man'; by night the walker dreamt of human evil

> the evil dreams where rodents ply
> Man-rumped, sow-headed, busy with whip and maul
>
> Among nude herds of the damned.

The final stage of the journey discloses an ambiguous blend of good and evil, white and black, bird and beast.

> The phantoms of the overhanging sky
>   Occupied their stations and descended;
>   Another moment, to the starlit eye,

> The slow, downstreaming dead, it seemed, were blended
> One with those silver hordes and briefly shared
> Their order, glittering.[3]

That vision of a universal design is momentary. The reality at the end of the journey is a barrier of rock that blots heaven from view. Its 'varied barrenness' remains fundamental to Kinsella's outlook, confronted again with 'Nightwalker', in 'Finistere', in the barrenness of *Notes from the Land of the Dead*. The sterile and depressive universe, first outlined in 'A Country Walk' then conveyed starkly in 'Downstream', is something that Kinsella has had to absorb into poetry.

Both 'Nightwalker' (1967) and 'Phoenix Park' (1968) are more ambitious and more comprehensive than 'A Country Walk' or 'Downstream'. In 'Nightwalker' Kinsella begins that critical investigation of himself and of the past that has occupied him ever since. Destruction, cruelty, deprivation are both Irish and universal, experienced locally in the areas of education, nationalism, political change, cultural loss, and universally in imagery of massive destruction. In 'Nightwalker' the depressed sensibility directs the intelligence in sharp scrutiny of what it means to be Thomas Kinsella at this particular time. Just as Austin Clarke's long, autobiographical poems bear witness to what it was like to be Austin Clarke in his period, so 'Nightwalker' bears witness to Irish experience in Kinsella's time. The central event for Kinsella was the political acceptance of the First Economic Programme under which the ethic of commercial success became primary. The intrusion of foreign capitalists, welcomed by a new Government policy of tax concessions and subsidies, is destructive of older values. Kathleen Ni Houlihan has become a prostitute who welcomes the capitalists and sells herself cheap.

> Lend me your wealth, your cunning and your drive.
> Your arrogant refuse;
>   Let my people serve them
> Bottled fury in our new hotels,
> While native businessmen and managers
> Drift with them, chatting, over to the window
> To show them our growing city, give them a feeling
> Ot what is possible; our labour pool,
> The tax concessions to foreign capital,[4]

Just as Yeats found evidence of a destructive barbarism close at
hand in the Anglo-Irish War and the Civil War, so Kinsella finds
evidence of cultural barbarism within his own experience. The
poem advances successive examples: Dublin as a necropolis, the
Government still controlled by violent men, the country born out of
violence, education inadequate to the true nature of experience, a
language lost, a culture destroyed. Listed so tersely, the poem
seems excessively negative, but it is not a poem of rejection. The
walker is observer, victim and product. Just as Austin Clarke
accepted the disabilities and hindrances of Irish life and culture as
those factors which had marked him and from which he could write,
so Kinsella declares his involvement and acceptance. 'Clean
bricks', he says, 'are made of mud. We need them for our tower'. As
in the case of Clarke the creative imagination enters into the mud,
into the threatening reality, into the conditions of everyday life and
from that encounter makes poetry. In a depressive environment his
consciousness is the creative centre, perceiving clearly, without
romantic distortion, analysing, understanding, facing at the poem's
end a direct confrontation with sterility and disappointment. In
Kinsella's informing philosophy one must see clearly and out of
that seeing create one's poetry. He believes in the creative imagination and in the supportive power of love. These twin beliefs are
joined in the long poem, 'Phoenix Park'.

Addressed to the poet's wife, 'Phoenix Park' is a kind of love
poem. Since they have to leave Ireland, questions of permanence,
change and renewal naturally arise. It is also a poem about the
making of poetry. Eleanor is an example of how to respond positively to change and the risks attached. For her acceptance and per-
sistence are instinctive. For him, they require rational justification.
Therefore, the poem is an argument. It seeks to demonstrate what
she instinctively is and what he believes. Unlike Clarke, Kinsella
has never been preoccupied with problems of religious belief. That
is partly the result of temperament, partly the result of growing up at
a different time. Clarke was the product of the post-Tidentine,
casuistical church, the product of its devotional revolution, the
product and the victim. For him that kind of religion and its traumatic consequences were inescapable. Until he could confront its
impact and measure its consequences, he could not be a free man.
His long poems are a series of readjustments in that process of definition, a series of adjustments as he brought himself closer and
closer to the experience. Thomas Kinsella's training was not based

as rigidly on religious teachings. When he felt its unimportance he simply put it aside. Emotional devastation in his case is however as important as it was for Clarke and it does not seem to have been brought on by any single cause. He points in 'Downstream' to the discovery of the evil that human wills can devise and carry out. The 'Old Harry' poem luridly outlines the consequences of Harry Truman's decision to drop the atomic bombs. Significantly, as in Clarke's *Mnemosyne,* the result devastates the imagination. Kinsella's perception of evil is allied with his feeling about the precariousness of existence. 'Phoenix Park' clarifies his understanding of evil, the threat to existence, to love and to poetry. It also reveals how poetry and love together can transmute evil. That process rests on the 'positive dream' of 'undying love'. The human spirit lives on the brink, reaching out into the void, reaching inward into the abyss, until everything that can be experienced has been assimilated. The metaphor that runs through the poem is life taken as a body, a substance to be eaten and made part of one's flesh. Life is consumed and the process fulfilling: 'ordeal / Succeeding ordeal till we find some death' ... 'that state of hungerless no dream'.

Together 'Nightwalker' and 'Phoenix Park' mark a decisive moment in Kinsella's development. In one he defines the political circumstances within which he has been shaped and matched his sensibility with it. In the other he provides the philosophical framework on which he intends to work. One points inward to the hidden areas of the self. The other concludes by signalling the psychic sources from which future work will come. The descent to the land of the dead in *Notes from the Land of the Dead* is a descent into the underworld of the self, a journey 'out of my mind', a turning 'to things not right nor reasonable', to an area or state where 'Time, distance' mean nothing. The metaphor of descent, or of falling, permeates the book. It involves a lapse from normal references of place and time, it leads to the liberation of inarticulate feelings and desires, to meetings with figures from the familiar past, to the nightmare world of darkness and mystery. But as in Clarke's archetypal descent into bitter experience, the end result is restorative and redemptive. The metaphor of the fall signifies a radical and absolute exploration. In the abyss embryonic stirrings and formations, tiny drops of moisture, sounds of rustling, indicate potential within the dust. Evocations of the myth of Persephone and of the arrival of peoples on the coast of Ireland, symbolic conjunctions of small boy and grandmother, and in later sequences the transformations of the barren rock into the womb, the invigoration of the standing pillar, of rock or of wood, until it gives birth, the persistent, recurrent examinations of individual figures and of particular places and experiences, all express the unifying drama of exploration in which the fundamental pattern is as it was in 'Phoenix Park'.

> There is no end to that which
> not understood, may yet be noted
> and hoarded in the imagination,
> in the yolk of one's being, so to speak,
> there to undergo its (quite animal) growth,
> dividing blindly,
> twitching, packed with will,
> searching in its own tissue
> for the structure
> in which it may wake.[5]

The magalithic voyagers in 'Finistere' reiterate the theme. Their journey through the salt chaos of the ocean is a voyage towards birth, an underworld journey in reverse, towards the creation, once again, of a megalithic civilization. It is also a celebration of Kinsella's fundamental artistic belief, an affirmation of man's insatiable hunger. The voyagers respond to an inner 'unrest'. They settle and are unsettled. Some force outside them compels them forward. In an inspired act Kinsella imagines that the patterns incised on the stone slabs at Newgrange are their attempts to represent the force that drives them.

> whose goggle gaze
> and holy howl we have scraped
> speechless on slabs of stone
> poolspires opening on
> closing spiralpools
> and dances drilled in the rock
> in coil zigzag angle and curl
> river ripple earth ramp
> suncircle moonloop...
> in whose outflung service
> we nourished our hunger
> uprooted and came[6]

Then in a startling act of identification and confirmation of the poem's theme he creates Amairgen, the first poet, stepping on shore with the people, singing his hymn to creation and finally reaching forward into the sinking sun, to that light that, first seen on the western horizon, made the people set out from Finistere to journey to Ireland, to find there the earthly paradise that became the land of the dead, place of death and renewal, where Cessair brought his people, where Fintan survived the Flood, where cave becomes womb, where death leads to life.

A similar magical moment occurs in the poem 'His Father's Hands' when the carpenter's bench, turned on its side years after it has been abandoned, yields its 'extraordinary' birth

> Extraordinary ... The big block. I found it
> years afterward in a corner of the yard
> in sunlight after rain
> and stood it up, wet and black:
> it turned under my hands, an axis
> of light flashing down its length,
> and the wood's soft flesh broke open,
> countless little nails
> squirming and dropping out of it.[7]

Perhaps more than anything else the poetic sequences that began in 1972 are about origins, aspirations, achievements and endings, the graph of human growth, with all the inevitable moments of optimism, often qualified in the light of actual or maturer understanding, and the inevitable moments of failure. *Notes from the Land of the Dead* (1972) returns to the setting of 'Baggot Street Deserta', that room to which Kinsella went to read and prepare himself for the task of becoming a poet, where he and the composer Sean O'Riada listened to music, that point in his life — bleak and uncertain — before the arrival of love and fulfillment. Love, too, that kind of feverish passion that attends an early love affair, is replaced in a later poem, in the Wormwood sequence, in 'Phoenix Park', in several individual poems within the later sequence, by a different kind of trust and a different kind of requirement — the need for an ongoing, changing, enduring relationship, in which the beloved is both particular and emblematic, a sharer in the daily grind and in its temporary triumphs, a figure in the metaphysical design, one within a whole series of women figures from grandmother to goddess, both beautiful and grisly. *Notes from the Land of the Dead* also indicates the numerological system on which the later system is built — 'the five wounds of Christ / I struggled toward, by the five digits / of this raised hand'. If love is seen within a specific pattern, so too are other figures and other relationships. Sean O'Riada with whom Kinsella shared an initial youthful enthusiasm is a frequent figure. *A Selected Life* (1972), an elegy, introduces the alert musician, evokes his life and music, and then consigns him to the earth. *Vertical Man* (1973) recreates him as the fellow artist within the terms of the creative struggle, the strain, the momentary success, the fresh beginnings.

> That for all you have done, the next beginning
> is as lonely, as random, as gauche and as unready
> as presumptuous as the first,
> when you stripped and advanced timidly
> toward nothing in particular.[8]

In O'Riada's case the achievement was considerable — 'you may startle the heart of a whole people' — yet he too has to struggle towards each new beginning, although there is a 'kind of residue' ... 'a maturer unsureness'. In this poem, also, Kinsella outlines the structure of the entire Peppercanister sequence.

> At the dark zenith a pulse beat
> a sperm of light separated wriggling
> and snaked in a slow beam down
> the curve of the sky, through faint
> structures and hierarchies
> of elements and things and beasts. It fell,
> a packed star, dividing
> and redividing until it was a
> multiple gold tear. It dropped
> toward the horizon, entered
> bright Quincunx newly risen,
> beat with a blinding flame and dis-
> appeared.[9]

'The Good Fight' (1973), a philosophical poem about justice, good Government and the sources of decision, also reveals the pattern of hope, relapse and renewal. John F. Kennedy and Plato argue that all reasonable things are possible. The poem recreates the politics of the New Frontier, another optimistic time, like that of Kinsella and O'Riada in Baggot Street, like Europe before the first world war. Yet disaster strikes. Oswald, the outcast, determines to make his mark, to find himself through the gun. The poem insists that 'all *un*reasonable things / are possible. *Everything* that can happen will happen'. This truth is verified in the poem, which is post-Plato and post-Jung in its perceptions. Unreason and the dark forces within the psyche make Platonic doctrines inappropriate. Only the artist, as Kinsella suggests through the figure of Robert Frost, can hope to discover some kind of order within the irrational and inexplicable, but we also hear the tone of ironic deflation.

> it is we, letting things *be*
> who might come at understanding.
> That is the source of our patience.
> Reliable first in the direction
> and finally in the particulars of our response,
> fumbling from doubt to doubt,
> one day we might knock
> our papers together, and elevate them
> (with a certain self-abasement)
> — their gleaming razors
> mirroring a primary world
> whose power also is a source of patience
> for a while before the just flesh
> falls back in black dissolution in its box.[10]

The poetic sequence, as these specific examples may indicate, moves back and forth in time, refocusing on particular places, events and people: home, school, Baggot Street, parents, family, teachers, friends, and in the background are historical and mythological examples of similar processes: the arrival of peoples in Ireland, the settling in, the way in which the land responds to their cultivation. Over and over we find these signs of the reward for careful attention, for disciplined application: things root and become transfused with life, death yields to life, the union and communion of man with nature becomes fruitful, the carpenter's bench flashes with spermatazoic life, the standing pillar takes on human force, love is destructive but fulfilling, the generation of positive disgrace becomes capable of achievement.

The repetitions in this poetic sequence, and indeed as we increasingly see, within the entire Kinsella canon, are repetitions in which a particular subject is made part of the life of the particular poetic sequence in which it is found and part of the life of the entire later sequence. It functions within a particular context and at the same time, because it occurs elsewhere, it has a significance beyond its immediate context, its force is both particular and general. Elsewhere it may appear in more expanded or more concentrated form, or be realized in a different style, seen within a different imaginative perspective. And this condition of singularity and complexity, of oneness and multiplicity, of isolation and participation, attends each one of the poetic sequences that is part of the ongoing poetic sequence. Increasingly, as the poetic sequence emerges, the organic patterns of theme, image, and tone clarify themselves with their contrasting motifs of the grand and the ordinary, their links back and forth in time, both personal and historical, their persistent philosophical concern.

Thomas Kinsella does not write the complete poem in the traditional sense. The unity he seeks is larger, even larger than the unity of a particular sequence. As these sequences appear it is clear that a total work is accumulating. There is an accomodating openness at work, a precise sureness of touch in specific detail, a stylistic flexibility, an ability to control the rhythms of line, structure and form, an ability to keep going, and a trust in the availability of creative readers to complete the act of communication.[11]

Both Austin Clarke and Thomas Kinsella deal with the plight of the individual at a particular time and place. Remarkably both men have a burdened, depressive sensibility, the one because of distorted religious training in his early life and because he had to live at an ingrown and intolerant period, the other because of a temperment that viewed life in terms of its tragic brevity and destructiveness. Austin Clarke struggled for a long time to free himself. Realizing that the drama of the individual conscience is also the drama of the race, that he was not unique or abnormal, that the pressures that had afflicted him also operated on his contemporaries, he took on the task of exploring and clarifying the pressures and events that had shaped him. That one so beaten by life could challenge the fabled bird, could take on church and state, and could make poetry out of that engagement, was the discovery that drove him forward with increasing skill and success.

Similarly Thomas Kinsella has advanced along the path of intense and purposive investigation of personal and psychic realities. At the heart of that investigation is the tension between his perception of life's negative elements and a belief in the positive value of art itself. At bottom his poetry not only affirms that ongoing, evolutionary, creative power, in poems like 'Finistere', in recurrent illuminations of the creative process itself, but in itself, in its tenacious, deepening and interconnecting nature it bears witness to creativity. In the end and in a most satisfying way both poets affirm the indestructable, life-enhancing power of the creative imagination.

Both accept the harsh realities in themselves and in their surroundings. As Clarke says 'there is nothing left to sing / remembering our innocence'. Innocence and the kind of song that would express it are inappropriate to adult experience. When innocence has been blighted, when the world about seems barren and destructive, the poet has to enter into the underworld of evil and out of that encounter has to return renewed and able to write. Kinsella makes the same point in 'Phoenix Park'; the language of the poet avoids fluency and playfulness; it is spare, plain, unglamorous. The notion of poetry as melodious consolation is avoided. Both poets treat the self as victim, but also as active consciousness, alert and responsive in an environment that threatens to suffocate and diminish them.

At the deepest level both Clarke and Kinsella write about the writing of poetry, but not in the playful manner of some contemporary poets. They come at the idea through successive examinations of the ways in which the creative process either works or is inhibited. Clarke's concern about physical decline, about repressive, stultifying systems of education, about jansenistic religion, about uncaring societies are fundamentally about conditions in which the creative self works or may not work. The loss of *Mnemosyne* is the loss of fertility; the images of terrified flight in the labyrinth of the irrational express the state of disorder in which the imagination cannot function. In Kinsella a whole poetic career descends into the dark nutrient sources of creativity where he discovers significant intimations of a way forward. His long poems give one version of this, but it is in the ongoing Pepercanister sequence that one best follows the symphonic realization of his exposure to the hidden sources of creativity.

POETIC OUTRAGE: ASPECTS OF SOCIAL CRITICISM IN MODERN IRISH POETRY

EOIN BOURKE

The young poet Kieran Furey gives a reasonably accurate assessment of the poetic situation in the Republic of Ireland today when he contends:

> I think that Irish poetry deals too much in abstracts, and not enough with the realities of political, economic and social life at home and abroad.[1]

Why this is so has perhaps to do with the legacy of W. B. Yeats, who is more often than not referred to solemnly as 'Ireland's national poet'. Most well established poets and critics since Yeats seem to have imbided Yeats's dictum, pronounced at the turn of the century, that poetry is not a criticism of life but rather a revelation of hidden life.[2] Those who have consistently attempted to write what Yeats disparagingly called 'poetry of the point of view' and what Bertolt Brecht approvingly called *'Gebrauchslyrik'* have either been ignored, like Kieran Furey, or severely censured, like Austin Clarke. When in the forties and fifties Clarke geared his considerable poetic craft to highlighting the baleful effect of the Catholic Church's domination of Irish social and political life, he was attacked not only by zealots for being godless but also by aesthetes for being too topical. Augustine Martin accused him in 1965 of lapsing into 'mere controversy'[3] and Donald Davie roundly condemned the same tendency:

> This refusal to universalize the themes, so far as to let into the secret those who happen not to be Irishmen of a particular generation, seems nothing short of perverse.[4]

Poetic vision, they seemed to think, had to be synoptic, poetic truth all-embracing, poetic moments timeless, or else they would not qualify as poetic. It is a conventional view of poetry, in keeping with another early statement of Yeats to the effect that literature 'dwindles to a mere chronicle of circumstance ... unless it is constantly flooded with the passions and beliefs of ancient times'.[5] It is moreover an expectation of poetry shared by other cultures, as borne out by Johannes Klein's dogmatic statement in his *History of German Poetry* that for poetry a political message is unsuitable because it is not sufficiently broad or human(!). It presupposes partisanship, he says; it is tied to the moment and can therefore make no claim to validity.[6] But whereas, despite such conventions of reception in the Federal Republic of Germany, there occurred in the sixties a great breakthrough of poetry as a vehicle for socio-political commentary,[7] nothing similar has happened in Ireland.

One reason for this general dearth of socially critical discourse in the Republic of Ireland is the unspoken consensus — fuelled assiduously by politicians glad of any opportinuty to divert attention from their own shortcomings — that the problems of the Republic will have to await a solution until the 'Northern Question' is somehow solved. When the Northern 'Troubles' came to a head in 1968, they engendered an impressive body of poetry on that subject by both Northern and Southern Irish poets. But as Fintan O'Toole has pointed out in a recent pamphlet, 'not only has the *Southern* Question not been answered, it has not, officially, been asked'.[8] Because of the Northern Irish situation, because of the Irish Limbo of being caught somewhere between colonialism and post-colonialism, there has been a marked intellectual lethargy with regard to specifically Southern problems, although, in O'Toole's words, 'socially and economically, the Republic of Ireland is more divided, has alienated more of its population, even to the extremes of exile, and is a worse failure as a political entity than almost any other in Europe.'[9]

And yet there are, as the title of this paper suggests, *elements* of social criticism strewn liberally throughout the corpus of Irish poetry, peeping out here and there from between the would-be perennial truths and, ironically, often proving all the more memorable for their historic specificity and erstwhile topicality. Even Yeats used verse for social commentary in apparent contravention of his own aesthetic programme. Most Irish schoolchildren are acquainted with the marvellous lines by Yeats —

> What need you, being come to sense,
> But fumble in a greasy till
> And add the halfpence to the pence
> And prayer to shivering prayer, until
> You have dried the marrow from the bone?
>
> ('September 1913')[10]

— even if they are not always aware of the historical context. The lines addressed the newly emerging Catholic bourgeoisie of Ireland as embodied in the Dublin capitalist William Martin Murphy, a parvenu class that manifested the particularly odious combination of ruthless profiteering, graft politics and religious sanctimoniousness, the same class that Patrick Kavanagh was to impugn three decades later with the lines

> Respectability that knows the price of all things
> And marks God's truth in pounds and pence and farthings.
>
> (The Great Hunger)[11]

This new class was in a very real sense a product of the partition of Ireland in 1922 insofar as the division facilitated the creation of a conservative Protestant landowning plutocracy in the North and an equally conservative Catholic bourgeois plutocracy in the South without the need to compromise.

By the forties the Free State had become, in Yeats's words, 'a little greasy huxtering nation groping for halfpence in a greasy till ... by the light of a holy candle'.[12] As an antidote to what he termed 'the leprosy of the modern', that is, urbanization and industrialization, Yeats championed the 'wild Irishry' of the countryside. But the countryman was by no means to be spared by the all-pervading Jansenist morality of a triumphalist Church. In his long poem *The Great Hunger* Patrick Kavanagh, a former sheep-farmer from Co. Monaghan, rectifies Yeats's romanticized view of the 'spiritual peasantry' in his drastic but brilliant section XIII by contrasting the city-dweller's image of the peasantry:

> *There* is the source from which all cultures rise,
> And all religions,
> There is the pool in which the poet dips
> And the musician

with the reality as it was known to him from within:

> But the peasant in his little acres is tied
> To a mother's womb by the wind-toughened navel-cord
> Like a goat tethered to the stump of a tree —
> He circles around and around wondering why it should be.
> No crash,
> No drama.
> That was how his life happened.
> No mad hooves galloping in the sky,
> But the weak, washy way of true tragedy —
> A sick horse nosing around the meadow for a clean
>   place to die.[13]

The 'Great Hunger' depicted here is not the Famine of the late 1840's but rather a hunger caused by a very different starvation — that of enforced celibacy in the typical 'stem family' pattern of rural Ireland as described by the sociologist Anthony Coughlan:

> ... the farmer of farmer's widow passed on the holding to the eldest son, usually when the latter was middle-aged. One daughter might be dowered to enable her to marry a neighbouring smallholder and the other sons and daughters remained unmarried at home or emigrated.[14]

It was a world of ageing bachelor farmers, a flight of women from the land, and a mother-figure as the mouthpiece of a puritan, ascetic mores. Coded references in the poem to masturbation and lifelong virginity called down the forces of law and order upon Kavanagh's head — two detectives visited his house in 1943 and interrogated him on the ironic ditty in the middle of section II:

> O he loved his mother
> Above all others.
> O he loved his ploughs
> And he loved his cows
> And his happiest dream
> Was to clean his arse
> With perennial grass
> On the bank of some summer stream;
> To smoke his pipe
> In a sheltered gripe

In the middle of July —
His face in a mist
And two stones in his fist
And an impotent worm on his thigh.[15]

But although the clericalist State was quick to recognize the potential subversiveness of Kavanagh's poem, he himself abjured the role of the committed poet and adhered instead to the conventional idea of artistic detachment. In a typically truculent reaction to the public acclaim of his poem, he said in 1964:

> *The Great Hunger* is concerned with the woes of the poor. A true poet is selfish and implacable. A poet merely states the position and does not care whether his words change anything or not.[16]

By contrast, Austin Clarke did set out to change things through his poetry and, as already noted, was the object of scholarly castigation for that fact. He, too, felt the brunt of the Catholic nexus of power in the 'veritable frenzy of repression and sadistic celibacy'[17] of his early schooling, in his being sacked as English lecturer at University College Dublin for marrying in a registry office and in the banning of three of his books. He directed his poem 'Mother and Child' at perhaps the most scandalous of all Church interferences in State affairs. In 1948 an unusually progressive politician, Dr. Noel Browne, was installed as Minister for Health. At the time Ireland had an infant mortality rate five times higher than that in Britain due to rural and urban poverty, inadequate nutrition and poor hygiene. Browne devised a scheme of State-financed pre-, peri- and post-natal health care to counteract these appalling statistics. The Church immediately intervened, calling the scheme a 'ready-made instrument for future totalitarian aggression'.[18] Their real fear was that it might lead to a situation where doctors instead of priests explained sexuality to mothers in biological rather than in moral terms. The Bishops placed massive pressure on the Government, forcing it to back down from implementing the scheme even after it had been made law. As far as the Church was concerned, the infants could continue dying as long as they were baptised in time. The electorate then seemed to condone the Church's interference by voting for the opposition party Fianna Fáil, who had cunningly sat on the fence during the 'Mother and Child' debacle. Clarke did not fail to notice the irony that in the Marian Year of 1954 the new Government issued a stamp depiciting Mary and the child Jesus:

> Obedient keys rattled in locks,
> Bottles in old dispensaries
> Were shaken and the ballot boxes
> Hid politicians on their knees
> When pity showed us what we are.
> 'Why should we care', votes cried, 'for child
> Or mother? Common help is harmful
> And state-control must starve the soul'.
> One doctor spoke out. Bishops mitred.
> But now our caution has been mended,
> The side-door opened, bill amended.
> We profit from God's love and pity,
> Sampling the world with good example.
> Before you damp it with your spit,
> Respect our newest postage stamp.[19]

The poem 'Burial of an Irish President' is about the funeral of Douglas Hyde, the first President of the Irish Free State and Clarke's former lecturer. Clarke attended the funeral in the Protestant Cathedral of St. Patrick, although it had been instilled into him at school that to set foot into a Protestant Church was to risk eternal damnation. As an indication of the extent to which the Catholic parliamentarians of the Republic had internalized the sectarian values of their clergy, the then Taoiseach, John A. Costello, and his entourage remained outside the Cathedral during the ceremony. The reference to the Lord's Prayer at the end of the poem and to the minimal difference in wording between the Protestant and Catholic versions ('Our Father, which art in heaven ...' and 'Our Father, who art in heaven ...' respectively) illustrates how penetrant the taboos were that governed interdenominational relations:

> (...) At the last bench
> Two Catholics, the French
> Ambassador and I, knelt down.
> The vergers waited. Outside,
> The hush of Dublin town,
> Professors of cap and gown,
> Costello, his Cabinet,

> In Government cars, hiding
> Around the corner, ready
> Tall hat in hand, dreading
> *Our Father* in English. Better
> Not hear that 'which' for 'who'
> And risk eternal doom.[20]

In more recent times, Richard Murphy has once more pinpointed the gap between piety and charity in a petit-bourgeoisie that mixes outward sanctity and strict observance of religious duties with the mercenary spirit of gombeenism. The text 'Largesse' is based on a real incident involving a well-to-do merchant of Galway at the time of the Biafran War:

> There's a trawler at the quay landing fish.
> Could it be one of the island boats?
> Seldom we see them, but how glad we are.
> They have a generous custom
> Of giving away a box of dabs or fluke,
> For luck, of course, to the unlucky poor.
>
> And this is how it works:
> Three tramps are walking down the docks
> Casually, not hurrying, getting there
> With enough drinking time to spare,
> When a blue car fins along
> And sharks the free fish-box.
>
> Usually at this dusky hour
> That car's owner
> Is kneeling in the parlour with his wife.
> If you go into their shop you hear
> Nine decades of the rosary
> And a prayer for Biafra.[21]

The younger Paul Durcan uses the technique of surreal scurrility to combat the complacency of the Church. By describing highly improbable situations with regard to the clergy in the matter-of-fact language of newspaper reports he undermines the awe in which the priesthood is held. In the upside-down world of his fantasies a cardinal dies of a heart attack 'in the arms of his favourite prostitute',[22] or a parish priest is sentenced to two years' hard labour for 'not wearing a condom, and with intent / To cause an unwanted pregnancy'. The female judge recommends 'that while serving his sentence / Fr Mulholland should be given access to condom therapy. / Perhaps — she commented — he is lacking in condom consciousness.'[23]

Even ten years ago such poems would have been considered unpublishable. That now the clergy can be made the butt of ridicule by a very widely read author indicates that the Church's power is gradually being seen as an anachronism in accordance with Karl Marx's statement that the last stage of a historical form is its comedy, and that comedy is implemented so that mankind may part happily from his past.[24] And yet as late as 1986, as if to give the lie to the claim that their power is diminishing, the clergy and right-wing lay organizations such as SPUC (Society for the Protection of the Unborn Child) and Family Solidarity contrived to obstruct the introduction of divorce legislation to the Republic. After the defeat of the Divorce Referendum, Marian Kelly wrote her 'Ballad of the Deserted Wife' in bitterly sarcastic doggerel:

> Each night she sits there, all alone.
> 'Please ring', she begs the silent phone.
> It's hard to fill this empty space —
> A single woman has no place
> In this our land of harmony
> Where 68% agree
> The married cannot be set free,
> Despite the pain of those who wait
> Staring at the cheerless grate
> For those who left with no goodbye.
> Best be content with just a sigh
> And know that your reward is nigh
> In Paradise, where SPUC proclaim
> The meek will meet with just acclaim
> . . .
> So all of you who've blown your chance
> Your time is past for song and dance.
> For priest and people have decreed
> You'll stifle your unseemly greed.
> Failed marriages you may resent
> But with one partner be content
> Even in absentia!

And if you feel that you're not free,
Accept the pity and agree
To play the role assigned:
You'll find the world a glorious place
Of whispers and averted face
Where condescending people praise
Your fortitude, your martyred gaze.
Cold comfort in the years ahead
To contemplate an empty bed
Warmed only by the glacial glow
Of righteous strikers of the blow
For family solidarity.
So where does the solution lie?
The simplest, it would seem, to die.[25]

Parallel to the all-too-slow liberation from Church domination there is the slow and sometimes painful process of urbanization. The urban sprawl brought about by uncontrolled speculative building and ribbon development as well as the replacement of indigenous house types by hacienda-type bungalows, causing both rural and urban Ireland 'to converge on a state of placelessness',[26] has been hurtful to older poets such as Austin Clarke, Pearse Hutchinson, Thomas Kinsella and John Montague. Clarke lamenting the 'sewered city with a rump of suburbs' and 'Air-scrooging builders, men who buy and sell fast',[27] or mountain brooks 'Man-trapped in concrete',[28] while Hutchinson observes the final attack on inner-city nature:

Bright red berries, bright-dark-red,
thronged in a small tree's dullish green,
between the women's convenience
and the brand-new Luxury Apts.[29]

Their sense of outrage does not only reflect a nostalgic pastoralism but touches, if only in passing, upon the economic forces behind the mutilation: 'Our neighbourhood developer / thinking big in his soiled crombie' (Kinsella),[30] the 'grey monoglot piss' and the 'bijou brick barbarity' of 'speculation's path' (Hutchinson)[31]. In Montague's 'Hymn to the New Omagh Road' it is the motor-car lobby that triumphs over the flora, fauna and ancient earthworks of his native landscape Garvaghey:

As the bull-dozer bites into the tree-ringed hillfort
Its grapnel jaws lift the mouse, the flower,
With equal attention, and the plaited twigs
And clay of the bird's nest, shaken by the traffic,
Fall from a crevice under the bridge
Into the slow-flowing mud-choked stream
Below the quarry, where the mountain trout
Turns up its pale belly to die.[32]

The poem 'Springs' in Montague's most recent collection takes on an added poignancy by focussing on an animal that played such a central role in ancient Galeic lore — the salmon, fish of wisdom:

Dying, the salmon
heaves up its head
in the millstream.
Great sores ring
its gills, its eyes,
a burning rust
slowly corrodes
the redgold skin.
. . .
Prince of ocean, from
what shared springs
we pay you homage
we have long forgotten
but I mourn your passing
and would erase
from this cluttered earth
our foul disgrace:

Drain the poison
from the streams,
cleanse the enormous
belly of ocean, tear
those invisible miles
of mesh so that your
kin may course again
through clear waters.[33]

The poem strikes a deep chord at a time when not only massive fish kills through chemical effluent in the rivers are reported every month but the Irish Sea is the most polluted in the world due to the Sellafield plutonium reprocessing plant and our Atlantic fishing waters are teeming with both American and Russian nuclear submarines.

Most of the same poets are perturbed by the ongoing process of Ireland's absorption into the great network of multinational capitalism. The former civil servant, Kinsella, observed from close quarters the beginnings of the Irish Government's disastrous policy of luring foreign concerns to Ireland by offering tax exemptions, factory buildings and cheap labour, instead of developing an independent industrial infrastructure based on native resources:

> ... Robed in spattered iron
> At the harbour she stands, Productive Investment,
> And beckons the nations through our gold half-door:
> Lend me your wealth, your cunning and your drive,
> Your arrogant refuse;
>   let my people serve them
> Bottled fury in our new hotels,
> While native businessmen and managers
> Drift with them, chatting, over to the window
> To show them our growing city, give them a feeling
> Of what is possible; our labour pool,
> The tax concessions to foreign capital,
> How to get a nice estate through German,
> Even collect some of our better young artists.[34]

Now, twenty years on, thirty-four per cent of the country's manufacturing workforce are dependent on the whims of eight hundred firms with their headquarters outside Ireland. These firms, mainly American, British and West German, expatriate sixty-six per cent of their profits to their parent companies to the tune of IR£1.5 billion per year. American companies make their highest profits in the world in Ireland at a rate of over thirty per cent.[35] To quote from a recently published manual:

> Multinational compaines use Ireland as an operations base — importing their raw materials and exporting their products. Closures in rural towns have devastated local economies as multinational com-

panies move their capital from place to place searching for the most profitable location.[36]

The young Patrick Deeley from the country town of Athenry writes in 'The Mine' about the sudden disappearance of a Canadian firm that fully exploited the zinc deposits of Tynagh, leaving behind a devastated landscape and a displaced and stranded labour force:

> Silver lights no longer stud
> the zinc horizon. Machines
> that through two decades droned
> are empty now of purpose,
> their dull will wound down.
> I plod heart-scalded acres,
>
> a strange dust burnishing my boots,
> dip a tentative finger
> in the emulsified face of a well,
> taste bitterness where once
> there was faith. Soon, earth
> chasms, rubble rears skyward.
>
> Buildings sink into neglect.
> A few technicians dismantle things.
> Water lodges in tyre-tracks
> of lorries whose slow
> convoys of ore-rich dirt
> have all been brought to port.
> . . .
> Now the last miners have climbed
> to the redundant surface;
> the company has moved elsewhere.
> There remains only an echo
> of the boom years, hunting
> down sealed mine-shafts
>
> to honeycombed earth, a useless
> residue of rich resources
> sold to the stranger for a song.
> Awkwardly I stand, impaled
> by anger. It will buckle
> in time, like a fatigued spar.[37]

Now a new form of exploitation has been added since the property market was opened up to EEC members: one third of all land sales of last year went to foreign companies and individuals. The small farmer, due to be squeezed out of existence in the next twenty years by large-scale agribusiness, is becoming a commodity on the rapidly expanding tourist market. The last verse of Michael Gorman's poem 'Erris' chronicles the reification of a human, the reduction of a personality to an ethnic 'motif' by folklore voyeurs:

> Two busloads of German tourists
> are parked towards Glencastle.
> Practical heads with efficient cameras,
> clicking together in a semi-circle,
> close in on a lone figure
> digging turf.[38]

Hand-in-hand with this wholesale sell-out of Ireland's human and natural resources there is quite an alarming polarization of classes taking place, a slow-motion version of the Bismarckian Age of Promoterism. At one end of the social scale the gombeen man of Yeats's times is being replaced by a new national idol, the jetset executive, while at the other end a new and virulent pauperization process is going on. I quote two voices on the matter. The socialist Peadar Kirby says:

> As it prepares to enter the twenty-first century, Ireland presents many differing faces. On the one hand are the faces of the young new rich, sometimes called the 'yuppies', confidently looking forward to new wealth and opportunities in the technological Ireland they are helping to create. On the other end of the scale, however, are the new poor, those increasing numbers marginalized by unemployment and with little or no hope that the future holds any improvement in store for them.[39]

The account of the free-enterprise economist and business journalist Karl Jones is, if anything, far more drastic:

> Ireland, just 366 days away from the 1990's, is a 'two nation' society — one part made up of a million people living in poverty, some 230,000 out of work and between 25,000 and 35,000 emigrating annually; yet, at the same time, the country is going through a remarkable period of national prosperity.

In this 'second nation', jobs are well paid and usually secure; talk is mainly of return of confidence to the economy, low interest and inflation rates, the dismantling of exchange controls permitting easy offshore investment, easily available money and high hopes for the post Single Market world that dawns with New Year's Day 1993. . . .

The 'first nation' faces a bleak future, and poverty seems set to be a permanent feature of Irish life — unless, that is, the rising tide of European prosperity does, in fact, lift all boats. But increasingly sophisticated technology means that, for many purposes, people are obsolete and this situation will worsen as time passes.[40]

I have quoted these reports at some length to show that the poets who have commented on this situation are not being subjective or alarmist. It is a fact that almost a third of the population of the Republic lives below the poverty line as officially defined by the EEC, or that in 1980 the richest ten per cent of Irish society had thirty per cent of the direct income, which was more than the lowest sixty per cent had between them,[41] or that 'some twenty per cent of the labour force is unable to find any kind of work and more and more of our young people opt to leave Ireland'.[42] Kathleen O'Driscoll's 'Motherland' is her caustic comment on this situation:

> So long, my mystic land of milk and honey,
> Beefy bankers, trendy lawyer-landlords,
> Faultless pedigreed, god fearing killers exchanging
> Tory blue for tory green.
> You plump complacent sow
> Devouring your fat farrow
> While you shed the half-dead weak ones
> . . .[43]

Those remaining behind are being more and more pressed by savage cutbacks on social welfare, education and health care, so that the State can pay off the interest on its huge national debt to domestic and foreign financiers which, if calculated on a per capita basis, is by far the largest national debt in the world.[44] In some working class ghettos in Dublin, unemployment runs between sixty to eighty per cent of the so-called workforce. There are families in which three generations of men have never known what it is to have a steady job.

Gorman's 'On the Streets' catches succinctly the divide between the marginalized and the 'young upwardly mobile'. The personalities mentioned are all real-life figures, as in all of Gorman's poems:

> At Eyre Square, a man
> with a hole in his throat
> grabs at passers-by.
> He carries a card
> detailing the ailment,
> frequents pubs and cafés
> seeking financial assistance.
> An unkempt grey-haired woman
> with 'striking bone structure'
> and shakily applied red lipstick
> screams in the Franciscan Abbey.
> The body of a young man
> is fished from the river.
>
> Boom and expansion continue,
> the ground is everywhere rooted up,
> new roads are named after local dignitaries.
> The newspapers reveal all.
> Two curly-headed developers,
> resplendent in tweeds,
> have purchased a racehorse.[45]

'The growing Irish economy', says Anthony Coughlan, 'has brought about the emergence of a harsher, more competitive spirit in social life and of crude forms of conspicuous consumption and display.'[46] Paul Durcan, in his most socially conscious volume to date, *Going Home to Russia* (1989), lampoons those social climbers who try to conceal their modest beginnings in the person of a ruthless property-owner who asks her 'darling' husband what she should wear to the première of a play about the Irish Famine of 1845. His answer unwittingly recalls the rags of their forefathers and -mothers: 'Your see-through, sleeveless, backless, green evening gown'. Next day, collecting the rents from her tenement properties in an Opel Kadett hatchback, she exclaims:

> 'All these unmarried young mothers
> And their frogspawn, living on the welfare —
> You would think that it never occure to them

>   That it's their rents that pay for the outfits
>   I have to wear
>   Whenever *The Great Hunger* is playing at the Peacock.
>   No, it never occurs to them that in Ireland Today
>   It is not easy to be a landlord and a patron of
>   the arts. ...'[47]

In Dublin, where the manufacture and sales of burglar alarms is a growth industry, Durcan describes the siege mentality of the *nouveau riche* in their heavily policed avenues

>   Where each detached and fortress-visaged residence
>   Has the air of a habitat inhabited by no-one.
>   ...
>   The exclusive suburbs of Dublin city
>   Are necklaces of Crossmaglens
>   In which armies of occupation fester
>   Behind fortified walls and electronically
>   controlled gates.[48]

In the last ten years under the aegis of the EEC a new caste of hard-nosed entrepreneurs has cropped up, a caste that takes seriously the advice recently given to them by Dan Flinter, the executive director of the Industrial Development Authority: 'Go on the attack. Become a Europiranha, fast, nimble and aggressive.'[49] Pearse Hutchinson has addressed himself to this new Social Darwinism, an 'achiever' ethos that is gradually transforming Irish social life and is signalled in his poem 'Traffic Lights are Dangerous' by stylish sportscars and shrill windscreen stickers. He juxtaposes two spheres of existence in alternating stanzas — the brash world of the assertive Dublin go-getter who is not content with being upwardly mobile but has to demonstrate it by means of the motorized extension of his phallic personality, and the fragile world of a gentle old woman within her own small cocoon of human warmth that is not yet encroached upon (but, one feels, will soon be) by an increasingly abrasive environment:

>   ...
>   I make it safe home, and climb the stairs
>   to borrow sugar from an old
>   old woman, there's an apple-segment

in among the sugar:
                    to keep it dry, she says.

The lout leaps out, from his shiny black car,
and tells the man he's nearly killed:
'You take my number; right?
And I'll get you.'
The rip-off republic cherishes O.K.

I climb the stairs to borrow tea,
there's orange-peel nestling in the caddy,
'I'm all fruit', she says.

You toucha my car: I breaka your neck,
one sticker grates — and to think that we thought,
in '45, the war was fought
against that kind of bullshit.
Shift your ass, another windscreen screams —
it's a wonder they can see to drive ...

I climb the carpet, the leaking roof
has washed one step quite bright,
and hear the old old woman
singing to her windowsill ring-doves
in a high, young girl's voice.[50]

Poets like Michael Gorman, Paul Durcan and Pearse Hutchinson are all in a good position to empathize with the marginalized section of society, all of them having experienced the relative destitution of artists. But Rita Ann Higgins speaks from within that section — from inside the corporation flat, the shirt factory, the TB ward, the dole-office. She is rapidly becoming the *Sansculotte* of Irish poetry, the most prominent spokesperson of the economically redundant part of the working-class, the so-called long-term unemployed. Her some-times sardonic, sometimes angry and sometimes roguish perspec-tives prove two things: firstly, that the so-called 'poor' of Ireland are certainly not always poor in spirit but can be amazingly resilient, imaginative and self-willed. Secondly, her repartee makes nonsense of the socio-linguistic theory that the speech of the 'lower' classes is restricted in scope. Hers, which she draws from the people around her, is highly inventive, ludic and pungent, even when describing the

monotony and regimentation of factory drudgery and its throttling of
the desire for self-expression and adventure:

> Nostalgia takes me back —
> the shirt factory toilet.
>
> Where country girls met
> and sucked cigarette ends on Monday mornings.
>
> Sunday night was discussed, the Ranch House,
> his acreage, physique and the make of his car.
>
> Precisely they swayed to and fro,
> tannoy blasted sweet lyrics, their hero.
>
> Two jived to the beat, two killed the smoke
> and seven sank further into hand-basins.
>
> Boisterous laughter echoed and betrayed lost time.
> 'Back to work girls', supervisor sang.
>
> A thousand buttonholes today.
> A thousand Ranch House fantasies the weekend.
>
> Work On.[51]

Even her angriest poem to date, 'Some People' has its droll moments, as for instance in the tall tales that have to be told to the various debt-collectors that come to the door, or when the poet refers to
the absurd fact that people on the dole are sometimes forced to attend
a course on how to apply for a job and conduct telephone conversations with prospective employers, in which they have to speak into
bananas because of the lack of phones. The wit does nothing, however, to lessen the impression of the humiliation and degradation of
worklessness and pennilessness in a society that fears God but adores
Mammon:

> Some people know what it is like
> to be called a cunt in front of their children
> to be short for the rent
> to be short for the light

to be short for school books
to wait in Community Welfare waiting rooms full of smoke
to wait two years to have a tooth looked at
to wait another two years to have a tooth out (the same tooth)
to be half strangled by your varicose veins, but you're 198th on
        the list
to talk into a banana on an S.E.S. scheme
to talk into a banana in an S.E.S. dream
to be out of work
to be out of money
to be out of fashion
to be out of friends
to be in for the Vincent De Paul man
to be in space for the milk man
(sorry, mammy isn't in today she's gone to Mars for the
        weekend)
to be in Puerto Rico this week for the blanket man
to be in Puerto Rico next week for the blanket man
to be dead for the coal man
(sorry, mammy passed away in her sleep, overdose of coal in
        the tea-pot).
to be in hospital unconscious for the rent man (St. Judes ward
        4th floor)
to be second hand
to be second class
to be no class
to be looked down on
to be walked on
to be pissed on
to be shat on

and other people don't.[52]

MASK LYRICS
IN THE POETRY OF
PAUL MULDOON
AND DEREK MAHON

ISTVÁN D. RÁCZ

Dramatic monologues and mask lyrics are significant in recent Irish poetry partly because they belong to a tradition some earlier Irish poets began, and partly because some outstanding poets use this technique in order to detach experience, to see it both from the inside and from the outside.

To understand the importance of detachment in contemporary Irish verse one should view it within its historical context. In an essay 'The Contemporary Situation in Irish Poetry' published in 1975, Michael Smith expressed a low opinion of 20th-century Irish poetry: 'Regrettably, Irish poetry of this century, to go no further back, is, with a few notable exceptions, a poetry of the parish pump. And herein lies the explanation for the lack of interest in it that one finds abroad'.[1] Although the main factor in the assessment of Irish poetry is the 'few notable exceptions', Smith's statement points toward a major dilemma for Irish poets: whether to write national or cosmopolitan verse, whether to stick by the parish pump or, giving up the vernacular note, turn to general human values. Obviously, the best Irish poets have always made efforts to bridge the gap between the two extremes. When successful, they illustrate the epigraph from Jorge Luis Borges, with which Smith begins his essay:

Gibbon observes that in the Arabian book *par excellence,* in the Koran, there are no camels; I believe that this absence of camels would be sufficient to prove it is an Arabian work. It was written by Mohammed, and Mohammed, as an Arab, had no reason to know that camels were especially Arabian; for him they were part of reality, he had no reason to emphasize them; on the other hand, the first thing a falsifier, a tourist, an Arab nationalist would do is to have a surfeit of camels, caravans of camels, on every page; but Mohammed, as an Arab, was unconcerned: he could be an Arab without camels.[2]

Most Irish writers and literary scholars would agree that Irish poets should write in the way that Mohammed wrote the Koran: showing cosmopolitan values, but keeping their national identity. To reconcile these two principles, as Tom Paulin has put it, 'once full Irish identity has been established then some form of sceptical detachment — a repudiation of its possible narrowness — becomes necessary and obligatory.' This scepticism is especially important in the attitude of present-day Irish poets towards the social unrest, and Blake Morrison and Andrew Motion in their introduction to *The Penguin Book of Contemporary British Poetry* see it as a major value:

> It is interesting to speculate on the relationship between the resurgence of Northen Irish writing and the Troubles. The poets have all experienced a sense of 'living in important places', and have been under considerable pressure to 'respond'. They have been brought hard up against questions about the relationship between art and politics, between the private and the public, between conscious 'making' and intuitive 'inspiration'. But on the other hand they have avoided a poetry of directly documentary reportage.[4]

Another reason why dramatic monologues and mask lyrics are so significant in contemporary Irish verse is that W. B. Yeats and Louis MacNeice already elaborated on these genres and related lyrics forms. Apparently, no Irish poetry today can avoid their impact. (This is not to say that some poets of a different kind — Patrick Kavanagh, for example — are not influential, but perhaps less significant as the forerunners of the genres discussed here.)

The importance of Yeats for this study lies in his poetry after 1916. 'Easter 1916' is a turning-point in his career not only politically, but also aesthetically speaking. Edna Longley is right in claiming that the recurrent line 'A terrible beauty is born' suggests 'that the Rising and its consequences gave him more poetry than he had solicited'.[5] At the same time Yeats started writing dramatic lyrics, which show a unity of the personal and the impersonal peculiar to his work. He was convinced: 'all that is personal soon rots; it must be packed in the ice or salt'.[6] The most appropriate examples of poetry based upon this principle are the twenty-five poems of

Words for Music Perhaps, although the Byzantium-poems can also
be mentioned.

Louis MacNeice's impact upon the new generation of Ulster poets
has often been noted: Paul Muldoon has emphasized his role in forming Irish culture,[7] Derek Mahon and Michael Longley have praised
him.[8] MacNeice also proves to be an essential source of mask lyrics
and dramatic monologues in today's Irish poetry. He wrote:

> The word 'lyric' has always been a terrible red herring. It is taken to
> connote not only comparative brevity but a sort of emotional parthe-
> nogenesis which results in a one-track attitude labelled 'spontaneous'
> but verging on the imbecile. In fact all lyric poems, though in varying
> degrees, are *dramatic* ... there may be only one actor on the stage but
> the Opposition are on their toes in the wings — and crowding the
> auditorium; your lyric in fact is a monodrama.[8]

Yeats's and MacNeice's conviction that there must be a dramatic
element in lyric poetry paved the way towards the dramatic monologues and mask lyrics in recent Irish verse as well as similar models in the post-war English poetry of Philip Larkin, Ted Hughes, Peter Porter and so forth. Before discussing some poems of Paul Muldoon and Derek Mahon, however, I wish to clarify what I mean by
'mask lyrics'.

In a study on 'The Dramatic Monologue and Related Lyric Forms'
Ralph W. Rader distinguishes between dramatic monologues proper
(such as Browning's 'My Last Dutchess') and mask lyrics:

> Turning now to the problem of distinguishing between the dramatic
> monologue and other poems — 'Prufrock', 'Ulysses', Browning's
> 'Childe Rowland' — often so called, I remark that the most general
> difference between the two groups is that the actor-speaker in the
> second group is not a simulated natural person in contrast with the
> poet, a mask through which he speaks. This familiar concept, devel-
> oped originally by Pound and Eliot, indicates that the poems
> described by it are really a kind of indirect lyric, mask lyrics
> I will call them for convenience. In such poems, we may say, adapting
> Eliot's notion of the objective correlative, the poet creates an artificial
> outward correlative of an emotion inwardly real in him.[10]

In mask lyrics it is the reader who is addressed, not a dramatic audi-
tor. As a result, says Rader, 'we feel Prufrock's predicament not with

the superiority or inferiority of the dramatic monologue, in terms of his difference from us, but in terms of similarity, as if his predicament were ours. Similarly, we experience the old Ulysses as we experience the old man in 'Sailing to Byzantium' not in terms of contrast but of identity.[11] Therefore, what Robert Langbaum has written about the dramatic monologues also applies to mask lyrics in Rader's system:

> The difference between the dramatic monologue and other forms of dramatic literature is that the dramatic monologue does not allow moral judgement to determine the *amount* of sympathy we give to the speaker. We give him all our sympathy as a condition of reading the poem, since he is the only character there.[12]

Rader relegates even Eliot's *Waste Land* to the category of mask lyric.[13] He summerizes his differentiation between the dramatic monologue and the mask lyric as:

> In the dramatic monologue the person and objects are not symbolic but literal, natural but not actual. ... In the mask lyric, in contrast, nothing is literal and everything is symbolic and is so registered by the reader; consider the fog in 'Purfrock', the squat tower in 'Childe Rowland', the golden bird in 'Sailing to Byzantium'.[14]

The mask lyric is a 'modern' genre in the sense Stephen Spender uses this word:

> The faith of the moderns is that by allowing their sensibility to be acted upon by the modern experience as suffering, they will produce, partly through the exercise of critical consciousness, the idioms and forms of new art. The modern is the realized consciousness of suffering, sensibility and awareness of the past.[15]

Spender claims that the author of any mask lyric in most cases expresses a tension between the past and the present, as 'with his sensibility he is committed to the present; with his intellect he is committed to criticizing that present by applying to it his realization of the past'.[16]

Poets from Northern Ireland today cannot and do not want to avoid facing the troubles in their homeland. Paul Muldoon has said: 'one of my main duties as a writer is to write about what is immediately in front of me, or immediately over my shoulder'[17]. But he

does this writing with detachment which is what makes the difference between his poems and the more openly expressive poetry of
Seamus Heaney, for example. As Edna Lognley writes:

> ... technically, Muldoon has learned from his Ulster predecessors, as
> well as from international influences. An heir to alienation as well as
> roots, he can criticize from both inside and outside the catholic com-
> munity. Heaney's richly created early world (a genuinely prelapsa-
> rian vision) has a boundless self-confidence which seems no longer
> possible without running into the barbed-wire of ideology. What is
> physical in Heaney becomes metaphysically problematic in Mul-
> doon.[18]

The mask lyric has been a genre of central importance in Muldoon's poetry since the publication of his first volume, *New Weather*
(1973). As the title and the title poem of *Why Brownlee Left* (1980)
suggests, this book is about the irrational motives of various personalities and also those of his nation. The last, long poem, 'Immram',
one of Muldoon's greatest achievements, is told by an Irishman
searching for his father, or at least for the memory of him, in America.
The title itself is a Celtic word, literally meaning 'rowing around'; it
also used to refer to an Irish genre relating voyages to fantastic is-
lands.[19] The basic literary model for Muldoon was a nineth-century
Irish narrative, *Immram Maíle Dúin,* as Edna Longley suggests[20],
adding that

> 'Immram' might be termed, as Byron terms the 'wandering' *Don Juan,*
> a 'half-serious rhyme': thus toned and tuned because 'if I laugh at any
> mortal thing', 'Tis that I may not weep'. Muldoon too on close in-
> spection might be accused 'of a strange design / Against the creed and
> morals of the land'. More practically, his ten-line stanzas close in
> couplets like Byron's eight-liners.[21]

To these two literary models, the 'Immram' itself and the Byronic
narrative, I will add a third one: the 'circuitous journey' type of Romantic narrative, described by M. H. Abrams.[22] The reader witnesses three stages in the formation of a personality. In the beginning the
primal unity of an innocent young man is shown, although with a
touch of self-irony ('fairly and squarely'), foreshadowing the disintegration of the personality. This latter takes place while the narrator
tries to find his own identity by searching for his father. The disinteg-

ration seems to be complete when the elements of time and space are indistinguishable:

> I was just about getting things into perspective
> When a mile-long white Cadillac
> Came sweeping out of the distant past
> Like a wayward Bay mist,
> A transport of joy. There was that chauffer
> From the 1931 Sears Roebuck catalogue,
> Susannah, as you guessed,
> And this refugee from F. Scott Fitzgerald
> Who looked as if he might indeed own the world.
> His name was James Earl Caulfield III.
>   'Immram', 11. 241-50[23]

Finally, the regained unity of the personality, the situation of a 'sadder and a wiser' man is suggested in the last stanza. Thus 'Immram' is a peculiar combination of a traditional Celtic form, the Byronic narrative, the 'circuitous journey' type of Romantic narrative, and the mask lyric.

In *Quoof* (1983) Muldoon goes even further in the process of impersonalization: by including two translations, 'The Mirror' and 'The Hands' in the volume and treating them as integral parts of the book. In the other poems two forms of dramatization can be discerned: the dramatic monologue and the ballad-type of narrative poem. The most typical example is the final poem, 'The More a Man Has the More a Man Wants'. Here the image of the 'double' the Doppelgänger is as important as in a number of other twentieth-century poems such as Edward Thomas, 'The Other'; Ted Hughes, 'Life is Trying to be Life'; Andrew Motion, 'Coming to Visit'; nevertheless, there is something peculiarly Irish about the approach. Here is how Edna Longley summarizes it:

> Interestingly, the quest for the self — rendered as pursuit and flight —
> is currently a growthpoint in Irish literature North and South. But the
> theme involves painful physical probing, not external questions of na-
> tional identity. Indeed one question asked is whether identity *can* be
> national.[24]

The closing poem of *Meeting the British* (1987), the mask lyric '7 Middagh Street' can be interpreted as a late twentieth-century version of *The Waste Land,* an earlier mask lyric. In the other poems, too, one of the essential conflicts of their dramatic situations is that between the past and the present (see especially: 'The Earthquake' and 'The Soap-Pig'). The past is always an integral part of the present, although people often fail to see this and the ultimate aim of poetry, Muldoon seems to suggest, is to help us understand this complicated relation.

Similarly, in Derek Mahon's poetry the genre of the mask lyric is of central importance. Seamus Deane contends:

> Many Irish writers, sensitive to the threat of provincialism, have tried to compensate for it by being as cosmopolitan as possible. In consequence, they become citizens of the world by profession. Denis Devlin and Sean O'Faolain are two outstanding examples. For them, the cultivation of the intellect is not only a goal in itself but also a means of escape from besieged and rancorous origins. Others — Joyce, Beckett, Francis Stuart, Louis MacNeice — although they also seek in the world beyond an alternative to their native culture, have come to regard their exile from it as a generic feature of the artist's rootless plight rather than a specifically Irish form of alienation.
> Derek Mahon occupies a middle ground between these choices.[25]

Mahon's attitude is well defined by Gerald Dawe in a comparison with Michael Longley:

> Longley, I would suggest, has accepted his past (the protestant city, the cultural 'duality', the shaky identity), whereas Mahon rejected his. MacNeice's spiritual sons have gone their different ways: one has remained at home, the other has left.[26]

Paulin has interpreted Mahon's poetry as that of an 'intransigent aesthete who rejects life almost completely and considers only the flotsam and jetsam along its fringes'[27], while Maurice Riordan emphasizes that Mahon has accumulated a kind of 'counter-myth' by projecting his poems into the future rather than into the past.[28] The main characteristic of his poetic diction is pointed out by Eamon Grennan:

> The strangest impression made on me when I read any poem by Derek Mahon is the sense that I have been spoken to: that the poem has established its presence in the world as a kind of speech. In addition,

I am aware that its status as speech is an important value in itself, carrying and confirming those other, more explicit values which the poem endorses as part of its overt 'meaning'. What I hear in these poems is a firm commitment to the act of civil communication enlivened, in this case, by poetic craft.[29]

This attitude forms the basis of Mahon's mask lyrics. In his first volume, *Night-Crossing* (1986) the last poem is a translation of a poem by Villon. As we have seen in Muldoon's case, treating a translation as an integral part of a book containing original poems is an emphatic form of showing the poet's endeavour to render a detached view of experience. In addition, 'Legacies' is the climax of the volume in two senses: not only is this the poem where detachment is the most complete, but it also summarizes the essence of being a vagabond, an experience that most of the mask lyrics of the book are based upon. One of the most outstanding is 'As God is My Judge', the monologue of Bruce Ismay, a *Titanic* survivor. In D.E.S. Maxwell's interpretation 'it is a powerfully compassionate apologia for a life saved by a night-crossing into life-long despair. Its feelings envelop the scenes whose sole reference now is to the one calamitous event that left Ismay shamefully alive'.[30] More than that, the poem also describes the tragedy of a man who has resigned himself to a more natural way of life than he used to lead, but is unable to leave everything behind: his mind, which has been formed by civilization, and his conscience, formed by human relations, cannot be changed.

Although *Night-Crossing* is a volume of good quality, Mahon's second collection of poems, *Lives* (1972) appears even more mature and original. Its recurrent motif is the image of the world after a cataclysm; the main literary model is Cavafy's poem 'Waiting for the Barbarians', while the peak and summary of the book is 'Entropy'. In most of these poems the 'I' is replaced by a 'we' speaking, as in a number of Philip Larkin's poems. In Mahon, however, the 'we' stands for *civilized* humanity only, as opposed to nature, whereas in Larkin the 'we' of the poem usually refers to humanity without restrictions.

In Mahon's third volume, *The Snow Party* (1975) the difference between two worlds is even more marked than in *Lives:* one world is that of nature, afterlife, myths, the other is that of civilization and limitations. Mahon does not, however, give up the hope of a possible union or return to the limitless world of nature. Those poems in which he creates a persona, fall into two categories. In the first the speaker is a man such as Basho, the haiku-poet in 'The Snow Party' or the protagonist of 'A Hermit', who lives close to nature. The second group of poems focuses on objects forming or becoming a part of nature. Three outstanding examples are 'An Unborn Child', 'An Image from Beckett' and 'A Disused Shed in Co. Wexford'.

'An Unborn Child' is one of the masterpieces of *Night-Crossing*, and is, in part, a Yeatsian poem. Edna Longley writes:

> It is not outrageous to compare the opening stanza of Mahon's 'An Unborn Child' with that of Yeats's 'A Prayer for my Daughter', two poems in which birth is embryonic of troubled futured history. ... Mahon, like Yeats, plays syntax against stanza to stake out a dramatic situation. Both poets begin with their shortest sentence unit, speaking from *in medias res* ('One more', 'already') and ending in mid-line.[31]

The poem contrasts the foetus as a biological entity and the would-be man as a social being. The image of the foetus, which is ignorant of the world outside, is deepened by the recurrent motif of water, and that of the ball, that is, the shape of the foetus itself. The final sentence — 'my days are numbered' — is a witty phrase carrying a profound thought: the foetus will really cease to exist (that is, die) as a merely biological being when it is born, and, leaving the world of nature, will enter society.

The literary model of the poem is Louis MacNeice's 'Prayer Before Birth'. In that poem the basic situation is the same as in 'An Unborn Child': the foetus, which is still a purely biological being is about to enter society. But the genres are different: Mahon's poem is a mask lyric, addressed to the reader, while MacNeice's work is a proper dramatic monologue addressed — in two equally possible interpretations — either to the mother or God. The emphases, the themes of the two poems are also different. While MacNeice stresses that through the child mankind will act and perhaps commit sins and therefore, through the foetus 'the world is speaking' in the sense of the still innocent part of humanity, the good forces of our collective unconscious, Mahon forms a pointed contrast between the unborn child as a biological entity and the born child as a social being. Consequently, the fate of the future child in Mahon's poem is existential solitude.

The speaker of 'An Image from Beckett' *(Lives)* is a Beckettian persona, a dead man lying in his grave. The characteristic of the monologue is determined by this situation: the speaker does not address posterity, although, as he admits in the final stanza, that would be his real purpose:

> This, I have left my will.
> I hope they had time, and light
> Enough, to read it.
>   'An Image from Beckett'

The most probable interpretation is that he is speaking to nothingness giving a touch of irony to the hope expressed. Time ceases to exist, history and the still split second identical.[32]

As in these two poems in 'A Disused Shed in Co. Wexford' Mahon's attention, again, is attracted by a place which exists outside history.[33] The basic situation of the description is the same as in Wordsworth's 'Daffodils', where the poet glimpses the objects of the poem all of a sudden, but the pantheism is made ironic by the triviality of the mushrooms. At the same time, Edna Longley is right in remarking that the poem proves Edward Thomas's point that 'anything, however small, may make a poem; nothing, however great, is certain to'[34].

Mahon has dedicated this piece to J. G. Farrell, author of *Troubles*. This brilliant historical novel which takes place in Ireland in 1919–1921 starts and ends with the description of a devastated hotel, the Majestic, an image which re-appears in 'A Disused Shed in Co. Wexford'. Mahon's point of view resembles Farrell's in that both writers endeavour to find analogies to and relations in Irish history in the twentieth century. Farrell does so by employing a Dos Passos-like technique, and Mahon by enriching the image of the shed with visions of holocausts in various places and ages. In a way this forms a contrast with Mahon's earlier poems, as Deane has pointed out:

> Mahon has here inverted his usual procedure. The lost lives are not lived beyond history, but before it. Their fulfilment is in history. This is a conceit and a figure in which he captures the central significance of his opening poem, 'Afterlives'. In one sense, he is saying that the only life which can produce art is one that is engaged with history, even (especially?) if it is the history of the victims, the lost, the forgotten.[35]

But the two poles of the contrast are the same as in 'An Unborn Child' viz. history and the fundamental desire to live:

> They have been waiting for us in a foetor of
> Vegetable sweat since civil war days.
> 'A Disused Shed in Co. Wexford,' 11.21–3[36]

Thus, in this interpretation the image of the shed has the same function as that of the womb in 'An Unborn Child' that is, it is a place for life to begin, for creatures to be born. But the shed symbolizes the disasters both in the history of Ireland and that of mankind, too. At a philosophical level, Riordan's analysis is also correct:

> The disused shed is also a version of Plato's cave, and the loss expressed is metaphorical: 'Let the god not abandon us / Who have come so far in darkness and in pain'. Ultimately, the poem speaks perhaps for all that is supressed in consciousness, for those impulses, desires, instincts, which, denied the light of actuality for whatever historical reasons, maintain their own weird and secret life. The poem, then, would seem to suggest a confrontation between the civilized self, the 'we' of the poem ('You with your light meter and relaxed intinerary') and the repressed self, what the civilized mind has denied.[37]

The first line of the poem ('Even now there are places where a thought might grow') is highly ironic: there are no thoughts to be expressed in our civilized world, they only grow in places conquered by nature. The image of the 'burnt-out hotel' in Farrell's novel symbolizes the tragic fate of a nation. In stanza three Mahon also refers to it as a symbol of a particular historical era the 'civil war days' of 1919–1921. In the succeeding stanzas, however, the mushrooms become a symbol of life struggling for itself, and the ruins of the hotel signify the limits of freedom. In the last lines the poem turns into a dramatic monologue as the mushrooms themselves speak, thus the speaker is transformed into a listener. The significance of this shift in viewpoint is twofold. On the one hand, as Grennan contends, the poet 'confirms our sense of his imaginative engagement with the world as species of conversation.[38] On the other hand, the experience is detached from the poet, so the tone becomes more dramatic, and the message more convincing. All these features contribute to making this poem an outstanding representative of its genre.

Paul Mulddon and Derek Mahon, although in different ways, thus represent the mask lyric at its best in contemporary poetry in English. Both concentrate on experience, but at the same time detach it from themselves. This attitude has enabled them to both face the particularities of Irish history and find connections with English and European literary traditions at the same time.

YEATS'S PREOCCUPATION WITH SPIRITUALISM AND HIS BYZANTIUM POEMS

MARIUS BYRON RAIZIS

W. B. Yeats's overall poetic vision differed substantially from the panoramic vistas in the visions of his two cherished poets, Blake and Shelley. Even John Keats's vision, as described by Yeats in his spiritualist Manuscript 'The Poet and the Actress', though quite positive, indicates Yeats's emphasis on Keats's typically Romantic vision: 'Keats, for instance, who gave us the vision only ... creates the vision of luxury and of Greece and alters the history and direction of our poetry'.[1] Keats's vision, however, was entirely founded on classical literature (read in translation) and admiration of Greek art (seen in museums). Keats had had no supernatural, or paranatural, revelation of what Greece really was at her period of cultural glory.

Yeats's Byzantium poems, on the other hand, are not so much lyrical effusions praising in verse Constantinople and her Empire at the time of highest cultural and spiritual glory — specific references to relevant details are missing from both — as they are visual dramatizations of the process of attaining artistic perfection, and of the special status (secular and spiritual) of the poet who has attained excellence. Yeats's vision does not recreate historical landscapes, great monuments and places, folkloric or religious rites, cultural festivals or typical activities of Byzantium's inhabitants. Yeats does not muse on pictorial details like Keats. Unlike him in his 'Ode on a Grecian Urn', for instance, Yeats refers only to 'nightwalkers' singing and 'drunken soldiery' sleeping — two images that are hardly characteristic of Constantinople's imperial majesty and historical manifestation.[2] The sight that the poet sees and describes in rather vague terms is one seen by 'the mind's eye', as Yeats had written in *Per Amica Silentia Lunae*. It is not a photographic representation of actual reality in Justinian's time or in the poet's.

Key imagistic features in the beginning and very end of 'Byzantium' — 'great cathedral gong... dome', plus 'that gong-tormented sea' — are poetic end products of mediumistic utterances found (in seminal form) in Yeats's Leo Africanus manuscript, where we read about his 'other side' that 'the spirit world [is] a reflection of ours' (p. 268), that over there 'all was one, all was harmony a Greek cross — a city where there were many churches all one big church' (p. 269). The 'one big church' intimates the Cathedral of God's Wisdom (Santa Sophia), the 'great cathedral' in the poem 'Byzantium'.

In the same manuscript Leo speaks about himself as a spirit and specifies, 'I am of those who, feeling their imperfections, risk losing our identity by plunging into the human sea' (p. 318). Leo's 'human sea' and Yeats's 'gong-tormented sea' in 'Byzantium' are metonymies of mankind. And the last stanza includes a synecdoche of the sea, 'The smithies break the flood', which translates to: the artists tame the human multitudes to turn them into entities that can be transferred to 'the other side' — to eternity; and this is one of the main preoccupations of the artist in the Age of Modernism to which Yeats certainly belongs.

Speaking through the medium, Leo's spirit also mentioned significant details involving Yeats: Leo 'had been with the Poet since childhood'; various spirits 'wanted to use Yeats's hand and brain' (that is what characterized him as a writer) certain 'controls' (spirits) select names from the recorded or unrecorded memories of the world' (p. 241 séance of 9 May 1912). In the séance of 5 June 1912 Leo's spirit stated: 'I am lingering to teach you to write plays in a scientific way'. In the séance of 22 July 1915 Leo asked Yeats to write him a letter with 'his doubts' which Leo would answer through his 'influence' on the Poet who would then record Leo's responses — something that was actually done in the manuscript. In a séance of 27 December 1916 Leo stated that the Poet 'would write through me', something implying 'automatic writing', which is another, mediumistic phenomenon as well as a very direct admission of a creative collaboration of Leo and Yeats.

Of greater significance, however, are Leo's references to the nature and constitution of Spiritus Mundi, of Leo's part in it, and, by implication, of Yeats's relation to it. For instance, the spirits that wanted to help the Poet with his writing were part of Spiritus Mundi. Speaking of his life as a 'shade' and of his encounters with other spirits and living persons, Leo stated that the animal spirits were 'of what he [Henry More] called the "spiritus mundi"' (p. 311). And he

elaborated further: 'The Spiritus Mundi is ... the place of ... all
things that have been or yet shall be, and all things ... serpents and
animal forms (p. 312). Also, 'our images return to you and not only
in dreams' (p. 313); 'I could be overpowered by this memory of
mind — i. e., Spiritus Mundi — that gathers images about it' (p.
314) — verbal details that are ostensibly present in both Byzantium
poems. Finally, 'we are the unconscious, as you say, or as
I prefer to say, your animal spirits formed from the will, and
moulded by the images of Spiritus Mundi' (p. 319). Leo also repeated his earlier claim (p. 289). 'I am your opposite, your antithesis ... your Interlocutor,' and explained what he meant by offering
Jesus Christ as example since Christ was 'the Interlocutor of the
Pagan World ... and thereby summoned' (p. 319). The verb 'to
summon' is used in an analogous context in stanza II of 'Byzantium', whereas in stanza III of 'Sailing to Byzantium' the Poet's
summoning of the 'sages' is implied in his imperative request to
them. Since these revelatory statements by Leo cover séances of the
years 1912 through 1916, and the degree of their importance in-
creases chronologically, there is a suggestion of a process, a development of some kind.

Employing Jungian notions and terminology Spyridon Iliopoulos quite soundly makes much of this Leo–Yeats affinity or even
identification. He elaborately explains that Leo helps the Poet
transcend his ego-personality (p. 143), that he becomes his Mask,
like the Daemon in *The Player Queen* (1907) and the thought in *Per
Amica Silentia Lunae*. In the latter 'the images coming "before the
mind's eye" emerge from the Great Memory', that is, from Jung's
collective unconscious, or Leo's Spiritus Mundi. Moreover, Iliopoulos discusses the theme in 'Ego Dominus Tuus' as 'the primal
myth of the Quest for the totality of being "by the help of an image"
— the transforming symbol of the Friend' (p. 155), which in
Yeats's case is Leo, his Daemon.

Speaking of the same poem, Arnold Goldman contends that the
Interlocutor 'Ille ... summons his double, opposite, anti-self ...
walking in the moon', that is, in the unconscious.[3] Iliopoulos then
elaborates on the process of the Poet's rebirth as 'collective man'
(p. 160), and his desire to achieve permanence as expressed
symbolically by the 'stony faces' (that is, Dante) and other stone
figures featured in various poems about persons and even in 'Lapis
Lazuli'. This strange kind of rebirth is certainly echoed in the Poet's
desire to reappear as an *object d'art* in 'Sailing to Byzantium'.

Iliopoulos also suggests that the process of summoning 'the mysterious one' — in several poems by Yeats, as in Jung's theory — prepares the way for the Poet's liberation from the *enantiodromia* (εναντιοδρομια) that is, from his running forever between two opposites, like Ille–Hic, or Leo–Yeats (p. 164).

Discussing the significance of a 'loud report' that was heard during a quarrel between Freud and Jung, Iliopoulos explains it in Jungian terms as 'a catalytic exteriorisation phaenonmenon caused by a father–son conflict' (p. 146) analogous to the Leo–Yeats antithesis and, I would add, not very different from the loud sound of the gong that opens and closes the poem 'Byzantium'. In that poem 'the cocks in Hades' imply Hermes *Psychopompos* (ψυχοπομποζ), guide of souls, whose traditional symbol is the cock; and that explains, perhaps in two removes, the function of Leo's spirit as a guide to Yeats during the latter's 'translation' to the 'other side'. All of the above directly or indirectly refer to Yeats' maturation process and his final status as an individuated human and artistic entity.

Discussing the function and meaning of images in Yeats's later verse, Iliopoulos refers to Jolande Jacobi's *Complex, Archetype, Symbol in the Psychology of C. C. Jung* (1959), and concludes: 'Like myth, the process of self-transformation is best expressed in symbols and images which cannot be translated into a discursive language' (p. 166) which, I believe, is also true of Yeats's language in his Byzantium poems.

The 'otherwordly' utterances in 'Byzantium' suggest that the image does not mean photographic representation of reality, or even the Platonic *eidolon* (Ειδωλον), but is used as a means of expressing 'what cannot be translated into discursive language'. The words *image(s), shade,* and *spirit(s)* appear in all five stanzas of the poem describing Yeats's composite vision of that simultaneously real and metaphorical location, along with clusters of imagery pertaining to the other side: Hades, mummy cloth, cocks, dolphins, spirits, and so forth; while all stanzas contain successive descriptions and statements which, apart from the esotericism of their allusions and symbols, strain the comprehension of the reader because they do not sound at all like the clear speech of an articulate person in a normal state of mind. In this poem we hear the voice of a person in trance, the voice of a medium communicating to us knowledge and lore from this and from the other side, now, in the past, and at all times. To put it differently, the voice speaks of things which, according to Leo Africanus's communications to Yeats, constitute the concept of Spiritus Mundi, and imply the self-transformation of the Poet to deserve union with it.

Iliopoulos reminds us that Yeats adopted the persona of a medium in several poems in *Responsibilities* (p. 16), considered himself a dramatist and a spiritualist in his manuscript 'The Poet and the Actress' (p. 39), and that in 'The Second Coming' his method 'of trance-mediumship provides the poet with a mechanism that allows him to present a prophecy whose fulfilment is neither welcomed nor rejected by the poem' ... (p. 185). By analogy, we may say that in 'Byzantium' Yeats adopted a trance-mediumship mechanism and created a dreamy atmosphere which enabled him to describe an oneiric vision without the risk of sounding naive, or exclusively dependent on lore whose validity would be questioned by serious or skeptical intellectuals of his day and age. Also, since he wanted to emphasize his personal involvement in the context of his Byzantium pieces — this is quite apparent in 'Sailing to Byzantium', while in 'Byzantium' the same is underscored in the beginning of the second octet, 'Before me floats an image' — his use of trance-mediumship utterances and other side imagery secured both goals: Yeats's presence in the two poems, and retention of his credibility as an artist in the Age of Modernism.

The claim that Yeats's vision in both Byzantium pieces largely originated from his spiritualistic experiences of 1911–16 is further supported by a passage describing the behaviour of a female medium as recorded by Yeats in his Leo Africanus manuscript: 'Suddenly her voice changed and another personality spoke through her of my most personal affairs and changed ... more than ever the vision and dream and I would bring a closer relation between this world and the next than ever before' (p. 293).

This striking statement, I believe, explains the nature of Yeats's vision in the Byzantium poems. Another characteristic feature in 'Sailing to Byzantium' is the notion and corresponding image of the spiral movement of the widening gyre. I have already mentioned Yeats's command to the 'sages' (stanza III) to 'perne in a gyre' and 'consume my heart away', that is, to absorb him, after possessing him, into their perennially winding movement in time and space: to give him immortality as an artist. In Jungian psychology, Iliopoulos reminds us, such a symbolic rebirth must be preceded by a psychic rape; and the latter's symbolic representation is graphically shown by means of a circular, or rather spiral, movement which suggests the archetypal symbol of psychic wholeness, that is the mandala that appears in several later poems by Yeats, for instance in the opening lines of 'The Second Coming':

> Turning and turning in the widening gyre
> The falcon cannot hear the falconer;

and in the 'gyre' of 'Sailing to Byzantium', whereas in 'Byzantium' the same image is subtly transformed into the symbol-ridden image which, nonetheless, communicates Yeats's desire to be translated from this world to the other side:

> For Hades' bobbin bound in mummy cloth
> May unwind the winding path.

Psychic wholeness, however, in Yeats's Leo Africanus manuscript is suggested by Leo's repeated assertions that he has been with the poet since his birth, that he is his 'opposite', his complementary contrary mind, and that thus 'each would become more complete' (p. 289). Also, in 'The Poet and the Actress' manuscript, the poet, that is, Yeats now posing as his 'opposite', Leo, explains the necessity of violent conflicts in the artist's soul: 'Those who try to create beautiful things without this battle in the soul are mere imitators, because we can only become conscious of a thing by comparing it with its opposite. ... We need in both a violent antithesis' (p. 327). Yeats's assertion here may well justify and explain the use of the words 'fury', 'complexity', and 'gong-tormented' in three of the five octets of 'Byzantium'. Moreover, the word 'opposite' in the Leo Africanus manuscript is a Jungian term related to the process of self-transformation or individuation already discussed as Jungian psychologists and theorists of literature understand and apply it. We may say, then, that Yeats's individuation process is imagistically presented in his Byzantium and several other poems by means of the spiral-movement imagery, and that it is seminally intimated in his papers of spiritualistic experiences and related interests. In 'Sailing to Byzantium' we have some mention of elements that constitute his concept of Spiritus Mundi, whereas in 'Byzantium' we have a plethora of such elements, especially of those suggesting the figurative bridging of the gap between the world we perceive as real, and the timeless and spaceless cosmos of Spiritus Mundi (that is, spirits, images, symbols of the other world).

Spiritualist notions also explain the rather intriguing desire of the poet — as expressed in the final stanza of 'Sailing to Byzantium' to be reborn 'once out of nature' not in 'the bodily form' of a living creature of our world, but as a golden work of art that would both delight and keep wakeful an Emperor and his nobles, or would function as an oracle 'of what is past, or passing, or to come'. In other words, of what defines and constitutes Spiritus Mundi, in addition to the Jungian interpretation of such symbols of lasting existence or permanence. Certainly, readers are also amply aware of Yeats's fear of death and of the unknown that lurks beyond it (p. 231).

In the Leo Africanus manuscript shades (spirits that are part of Spiritus Mundi) speak to the living through mediums (p. 291) and can take various form (p. 309). Citing scholarly studies by Stuart Hirschberg and Brenda S. Webster and referring to Yeats's statement 'that all joyous or creative life is a re-birth as something not oneself'[4], Iliopoulos explains that 'the medium is a vehicle of what is past, or passing, or to come' — because the medium is in touch with Spiritus Mundi (p. 216). In discussing Yeats's later poem 'The Spirit Medium', he comments on those expressions and images (for example, perning in a band, those begotten or unbegotten, an old-ghost's thoughts are lightning) that bring to mind echoes from his earlier poems involving Byzantium.

Although some of the details discussed are found in the poet's volumes *Per Amica Silentia Lunae* (1918) and *A Vision* (1925, 1938), much of the new and specific information can be found only in the papers Yeats kept, or collected, during his hitherto inadequately-examined 'Spiritualist Interlude'.[5] These additional and little-known data allow us to understand how he adopted a poetic knowledge and voice which enabled him to articulate his esoteric poetic vision. The voice we hear in 'Sailing to Byzantium' and 'Byzantium' is the voice of a person in trance-mediumship utterance, and the fabric of Yeats's vision is not woven with threads of occult readings and half-digested cultural information, but is rather a poetic dramatization of telling and real-life experiences during 1911–16 which acted seminally and, in this case, catalytically on the development and increased sophistication of his mature artistic idiom.

Thus, 'Sailing to Byzantium' remains a poem about Yeats's maturation process as a poet, with the clarification, however, that this process implies psychic wholeness and transcendence of this world to approach the Spiritus Mundi. 'Byzantium' remains a poem of his having attained the completeness that enabled him to become part of Spiritus Mundi — not simply of his having gained the shores of a culturally-perfect but largely symbolic city. The substitution of a Jungian exegetical apparatus for the Platonic one of older critics,[6] evidently does justice to both Yeats the Spiritualist and Yeats the Artist, not just to one of them.

KNOWLEDGE OF THE WORLD AS THE FORBIDDEN FRUIT: CANON SHEEHAN AND JOYCE ON THE SACRIFICIUM INTELLECTUS

RUTH FLEISCHMANN

A unique combination of historical and social forces led in Ireland around the turn of the century to an extraordinary literary productivity. Many of the works which appeared during the first quarter of the century have been ranked as world literature. The value and interest of such masterpieces lies paradoxically in the fact that their authors turned their back on the world and the ruling literary fashions and dedicated themselves to the study of life on the remote, impoverished island. In so doing, and in developing new literary forms to allow of representation of the specific nature of this life, they discovered the world on the country road and in the rural Irish parish, in the city tenement and office, as well as in the big houses of the Anglo-Irish gentry.

Knowledge of the world apart from the Irish life represented was essential, for it was the contrast that opened the eyes and mind to what was, or had been, around the writer. The different life might have been that of the world of the British peerage and intelligentsia in London, Paris, or Venice, which Lady Gregory knew in addition to the life in her big house and that of her tenantry at Coole in the west of Ireland. The knowledge of the world could have been acquired through a good Irish education, such as Joyce received, and a life spent in Europe; or it could have come through migration within Ireland, as when Muiris O Súilleabháin moved from the Blaskets to become a policeman in Galway, which brought him to write of the life he had left behind him.

Irish life at all levels was becoming modernised: increasing literacy and the growing influence of newspapers, better education and cheap books meant that Irish people of the poorer classes, too, were coming into closer contact with the world around them. This was a cause of regret and unease to many: to those who hoped to see the

Irish language restored as the living language of the country, to those who treasured as the basis and justification of Ireland's potential nationhood the old pre-industrial way of life preserved in the west, and to Catholic churchmen who feared that the people might lose their religious heritage. The clerics were particularly perturbed about the vexed question of the knowledge of the world which Irish people in general and especially the young needed and might be allowed to acquire, and there was a strong tendency among conservative priests and nationalists to seek to impose strict controls.

Canon Sheehan (1852–1913), the Catholic priest who became a novelist in order to counteract the Anglo-Irish writers of the revival, began his literary career in 1881 with an article published in *The Irish Ecclesiastical Record* on Irish education. It was, as he tells us, the keynote of all his later teaching[1]. In the article, 'Religious Instruction in Intermediate Schools', he warns of the grave dangers to the young people of Ireland and to the Catholic church which the Intermediate Education Act of 1878 could entail. The Act allowed the government to give grants to secondary schools in proportion to the success of the schools' pupils at public examinations. The priest describes this as a secularisation of the educational system, as providing 'a powerful temptation to neglect religious knowledge' in favour of technical and secular learning. In 1916, observing the results of the system in operation for nearly forty years, Pádraic Pearse called it a 'mind-murder machine' which destroyed the pupils' interest in learning and their intellects. Sheehan's fears concerning the newly launched system were in 1881 of a very different nature.

He sees the young adults in secondary education as having 'matured intellects, restless, active and inquiring and far more receptive and retentive of the knowledge that is unto death, than of the wisdom that giveth life'. The young people, he says, are taught in these schools to question authority and tradition. They are introduced to scientific thinking, and are given no training to answer the 'systematized infidelity, supported by logic that is incisive enough even to well-trained minds, and presented in the finest sentences into which the English language can be moulded'. The students encounter modern literature which is filled with 'powerfully developed arguments and elaborated sarcasms against the Church and Revelation and God'. This is particularly dangerous, Sheehan says, for there is 'no country in the world in which this passion for literature has taken such firm hold of the professional and mercantile classes as in Ireland'. He telles of his astonishment at coming across 'a young commercial' on a train reading Carlyle and a periodical 'which has for contributers some of the most notorious atheists in England, and which admits every shade of opinion, no matter how advanced, provided it be representative of modern ideas'.

He considers most perilous 'the high philosophy that deifies man's intellect and humanity', so appealing to the young mind:

> How will the intellects, trained to believe in the majesty and grandeur of the human mind, suffer to have their belief shaped for them by the Divine dogmatism of the Church? How will they bend before the village curate, whose knowledge, however great, is mediaeval, and whose ideas are so reactionary, to acknowledge their weaknesses and beg pardon for their transgressions? How can they, whose ears are filled with the pet phrases of some German transcendentalist, listen to the Sunday homily according to the *Petite Methode* of St. Alphonsus, the gravity and monotony of which are unrelieved by one racy expression or one bold idea?[2]

'It takes many years and much experience', he says, to humble the human mind and force man to confess that after all he is but

> 'An infant crying in the night,
> An infant crying for the light,
> And with no language but a cry.'

The young person, however, does not see this:

> He must have knowledge even though it be forbidden. And what that forbidden knowledge is let those tell who have tasted the fruit and known the sickness of shattered faiths and dreary doubtings, and that terrible darkness that supervenes on partial or total disbelief.[3]

What is to be done? Sheehan has seen 'with pleasure the nation's pulses quicken under the new-born ambition of proving itself again a nation of scholars', and he welcomes the general interest and excitement over the educational chances now offered to the children of all classes. But human knowledge must 'be made to take its place side by side with its elder sister, the wisdom that is from above'. That is, an adequate system of comprehensive religious instruction must be made an obligatory subject in secondary schools to com-

bine a sound education with wise restraint, direction, and innocu-
lation of students against the perils of the 'forbidden knowledge'.

The fascination and danger of learning is a *leitmotif* in Canon
Sheehan's novels on clerical life. His priest-characters are all cul-
tured, scholarly men, endowed with his own passion for learning.
They are not only well-versed in the great European ecclesiastical
tradition, but often also in secular European literature, and several
are enthusiastic readers of Dante, Jean Paul, Goethe and Heine. Yet
in two of the three novels, priests renounce those scholarly pursuits
which have helped them through 'the necessary solitude' of the
priestly life. They do so with difficulty: it is a painful sacrifice to
them to give up the solace and pleasures of secular learning. The
reason why they feel obliged to abandon literature is that they
would not dream of placing their Goethe or Heine in the hands of
even 'the most enlightened' of their parishioners for fear of under-
mining their faith, and therefore consider they have no right themselves 'to indulge in secret' their taste for 'such forbidden things'[4].
So, as far as the ideal priest is concerned, the two branches of
learning, theology and secular literature, do not co-exist, the 'elder
sister' driving the younger from the presbytery, unable to tolerate
the 'blasphemous anger' with which the literary sister not infre-
quently expresses herself, although the theologian recognises it as
'the voice of bruised and wounded humanity'[5].

The two did not co-exist in the secondary schools either, contrary
to Sheehan's early hopes and expectations with regard to the education of the laity. He was later to accuse the schools of starving the
children's minds, and to deny — as Pearse did — that there was
such a thing as education in Ireland. Pearse denounced the system
for crushing the young minds with the ruthlessly efficient machinery which grinds

> ... all the raw human material in Ireland; ... and what it cannot re-
> fashion after the regulation pattern it ejects with all likeness of its
> former self crushed from it, a bruised and shapeless thing, thereafter
> accounted waste.[6]

James Joyce attended Catholic schools that came much closer to
Canon Sheehan's ideal than those the average Irish child could go
to. Clongowes and Belvedere College, the Jesuits' Dublin day
school, were far more likely than the ordinary schools to produce
students 'with large comprehensive knowledge, ready wit and fa-

cile eloquence and with all their generous impulses and enthusiasm swayed and directed by loyalty to Mother Church and to Mother Ireland'[7] — except that Sheehan's second maternal authority had no place in these schools, which were thoroughly anglicised. However, it was not loyalty and enthusiasm, but fear, which led Joyce's Stephen in the *Portrait* to submit to Mother Church. One of Stephen's first experiences in Belvedere is being accused of heresy by the lay teacher of English in front ot the class because of a phrase he used in an essay. His view of the issue in question is neither discussed nor explained, but condemned out of hand. Stephen, being 'conscious of the squalor of his own mind and home ... felt against his neck the raw edge of his turned and jagged collar'.[8] Thus painfully reminded of his status in the school as a charity boy whose father is unable to afford the fees, he makes his 'submission' and re-phrases the offending clause.

Stephen's capitulation in matters theological leads some of the most ignorant boys, who resent his academic success and sense his social stigma, to try to intimidate him into a similarly humiliating submission with regard to literature. They corner him one day after school and try to force him to denounce Lord Byron, his favourite poet, as a man of immorality and a heretic. But in this case Stephen can stand his ground, and he defies his tormentors. The characterisation of the master and apprentice bullies could have served Pearse as an illustration of the efficiency of authoritarian educational systems in producing slave mentalities.

The social descent of his family brings Stephen 'wounded pride and fallen hope and baffled desire'. (p. 56) He responds to the humiliation of poverty by plunging into desperate independence and taking up a secret sexual life, the squalor of which — being of his own doing — gives him the relief of at least a 'barren pride'. (p. 104) His rebellion is furtive; he conforms outwardly to the expectations of his masters, appearing to them to lead a life of exemplary piety and obedience. Once again, it is fear which moves him to submit to the church: the terror inculcated by the mediaeval description of hell given at the school retreat and the ensuing self-loathing which induces his own vision of the nauseating personal hell awaiting him peopled by lecherous, filthy, goatish fiends.

As he makes his way to confession in a poor quarter of the city, he broods on how it is possible that he can incur guilt through the unintended experience of sexual desire:

> It could happen in an instant. But how so quickly? By seeing or by
> thinking of seeing. The eyes see the thing, without having wished first
> to see. Then in an instant it happens. But does that part of the body
> understand or what? . . . It feels and understands and desires. What a
> horrible thing! Who made it to be like that, a bestial part of the body
> able to understand bestially and desire bestially? (pp. 139–40)

The defiant question: 'Who made it like that?' terrifies him, since
it implies that he is being unjustly punished for what is his nature:

> He cowered in the shadow of the thought, abasing himself in the awe
> of God Who made all things and all men. Madness. Who could think
> such a thought? And, cowering in darkness and abject, he prayed
> mutely to his guardian angel to drive away with his sword the demon
> that was whispering to his brain.
>   The whisper ceased and he knew then clearly that his own soul had
> sinned in thought and word and deed wilfully through his own body.
> (pp. 139–40)

Not only must he deny his physical nature as alien and threatening,
but his reason appears as an instrument of the devil. Under the impact of the volcano of shame about to erupt on him, he forces himself to accept as just the idea that he bears personal responsibility
for his unleashed sexuality. He narrows his mind, forbids himself to
think, and compels himself to a regressive simplicity of heart, reducing the question to the infantile level of naughty, wilful child
and displeased parent:

> It was easy to be good. God's yoke was sweet and light. It was better
> never to have sinned, to have remained always a child, for God loved
> little children and suffered them to come to Him. It was a terrible and
> sad thing to sin. But God was merciful to poor sinners who were truly
> sorry. How true that was! That was indeed goodness. (p. 143)

The simplicity is artificial and the repetitiveness that of self-
hypnosis: to achieve submission, Stephen must do violence to his
intellect.

During the time in which he succeeds in maintaining this frame
of mind, he does violence to his senses also, mortifying them with
the same fervour with which he previously gratified them. He remains 'meek and abased', seeking to achieve, 'virginal self-

surrender' resembling that represented in the paintings he likes to contemplate:

> The attitude of rapture in sacred art, the raised and parted hands, the parted lips and eyes as of one about to swoon, became for him an image of the soul in prayer, humiliated and faint before her Creator. (p. 150)

Stephen is rewarded for his life of deferential piety and 'quiet obedience' by being invited to join the Jesuit order. The director of studies holds out the prospect of power to him: 'secret power and secret knowledge'. Stephen has long been indulging in fantasies of himself acting the part of the self-effacing young priest, while revelling in the 'awful power' of his position and delighting in the secret knowledge of sin which studies in theology and experience as a priest would bring. He is therefore at first tempted to accept a life of intellectual submissiveness in return for power. But then, almost without noticing, as if by instinct, he decides against it. A glimpse through the open college door of the gaiety of some young people passing on the street brings back to life Stephen's sense of irony, humour and detachment, which had been driven underground by the intensities of piety, terror and lust endured. He notes the Jesuit's stony imperviousness to the scene and sees in his face 'a mirthless mask reflecting a sunken day from the threshold of the college'. Stephen is reminded of the face of another Jesuit master 'eyeless and sour-favoured and devout, shot with pink tinges of suffocated anger'; and the thought of the 'grave and ordered and passionless life' awaiting him suddenly seems repellent.

On his way home

> ... he turned his eyes coldly for an instant towards the faded blue shrine of the Blessed Virgin which stood fowl-wise on a pole in the middle of a ham-shaped encampment of poor cottages ... The faint sour stink of rotted cabbages came towards him from the kitchen gardens on the rising ground above the river. He smiled to think that it was this disorder, the misrule and confusion of his father's house and the stagnation of vegetable life, which was to win the day in his soul. Then a short laugh broke from his lips as he thought of that solitary farmhand in the kitchen gardens behind their house whom they had nicknamed the man with the hat. A second laugh, taking rise from the first after a pause, broke from him involuntarily as he thought of how

the man with the hat worked, considering in turn the four points of the sky and then regretfully plunging his spade in the earth. (pp. 162–3)

He discovers how narrow his vision had become: he now sees in the statue not only the devout intent of the poor who put it up, but at the same time the involuntarily comical result. The hard-working student is not moved to anger or contempt, but to detached amusement by the sight of the contemplative farm labourer expending as little energy on his task as is humanly possible. So the fact that Stephen does not fall for the temptation of letting his mind be tamed for the sake of power is by no means a conscious and heroic decision in favour of intellectual integrity and against corruption: it is the natural outcome of his re-discovered sense of humour.

The laughter has healed him of the morbid self-absorption of his sensual and ascetic obsessions, and restored him to sufficient generosity of spirit to make him aware of the price the younger members of his family are paying for his intellectual growth. A 'sudden instinct of remorse' overcomes him on seeing the remains of the meagre supper the children have eaten at his indigent father's table, and on hearing the 'overtone of weariness behind their frail fresh innocent voices' as they sing Tom Moore's 'Oft in the Stilly Night'[9]. He finds peace in the knowledge that there is 'in their faces no sign of rancour' towards him.

Stephen has refused the *sacrificium intellectus;* he has

.. passed beyond the challenge of the sentries who had stood as guardians of his boyhood and had sought to keep him among them that he might be subject to them and serve their ends. (p. 165)

He has resolved to 'learn his own wisdom apart from others ... wandering among the snares of the world'.

He has not allowed 'the black art of education' to combine with poverty and 'take the crown and sceptre form his spirit' — as Æ grieved to see it do to so many[10]. But, apart from the occasional period of exaltation of mind arising from the courageous decision to go his own way in life and art and from awareness as to how he would be able to do this, Stephen remains acutely conscious of the limitations of his training and of his own efforts during his studies at the Catholic university in Dublin. Every morning, as he makes his way 'amid the squalor and noise and sloth of the city', his mind wanders among works of different ages and of authors to whom he

feels drawn. The thought of Horace once brings him to dwell on his inadequacy:

> ... even for so poor a Latinist as he, the dusky verses were as fragrant as though they had lain all those years in myrtle and lavender and vervain; but yet it wounded him to think that he would never be but a shy guest at the feast of the world's culture. (p. 176)

The shy guest at the feast of the world's culture was to end up having the world as guest at the ill-provided table of his prodigal father's deprived home in the small city on the edge of Europe.

The sentries of Stephen's boyhood won their battle for the control of Irish education. They did not, on the whole, share the fears concerning the future of the Irish church of clerics like Canon Sheehan and Walter McDonald, professor of theology in Maynooth from 1881 to 1920. McDonald saw the church endangered by the sentries' inability to take cognizance of the great changes brought about in the modern *Weltanschauung* by the progress of science, and by their consequent failure to review church institutions, procedures and teaching in the light of the new knowledge. Shortly before his death in 1920, he wrote that 'Revolution' was within sight 'which the official guardians of our religion will not see coming, or will endeavour to keep out with their broomsticks'.[11]

Canon Sheehan's life was devoted to exhorting his fellow-clerics to heed the signs of the times and adapt to them in order to maintain their position in Irish society. In 1884 he wrote in *The Irish Ecclesiastical Record*:

> The Church must always be in advance of the world. The priest must lead the flock. And his spiritual instructions will carry all the more weight when it is understood that the pastor is a man of culture and refinement, and that his condemnation of new and fanciful theories comes from his belief founded on fair and exhaustive reading, that they are utterly untenable. ... Men will reverence knowledge wherever found, and the natural abilities of the scholar may lead many souls to acknowledge the supernatural mission of the priest.[12]

This response to the threat seeks a stronger and more capable church leadership of the people, who must respect the judgement of the clergy and not merely defer to it. But the laity is not to be trained to judge such issues themselves or to be allowed first-hand knowledge of them.

McDonald's view of the changes needed was radical. He not only criticised the despotic powers of the episcopate, advocated the democratic administration of the church, and urged that it publish its finances, but — convinced after bitter phases of doubt in the ultimate compatibility of science and Catholicism — he pleaded for an open-minded study of the findings of modern science with a view to correcting untenable elements of school tradition. The church's fear of acknowledging error, he says,

> ... may be good politics, but it is not the scientific spirit, which does not hesitate to admit any error that has been proved. No small part of the weakness of our theology is due to this, that we persist in maintaining positions that have been long since shown to be indefensible, with the result that the adversaries of the Church, carefully avoiding us where we are strong, defeat us easily where we are weak, and are thereby able to crow over us, with justice and to our real disgrace.

He insisted on the need for criticism within the church:

> History... proves that laws have been better made and better observed since subjects became free to criticize them ... and there would be ever so much less for history to record, with shame and tears, if there had been more criticism, reverent but fearless, of those who occupied high places, even in the Church, in the past.[13]

However, the crisis envisaged by both men did not come. The Catholic church weathered the difficult period of transition with far greater ease than either had considered possible and it emerged much strengthened in power, if not in spirit, in the Free State, in which not even broomsticks were required to defend its authority. For the poverty, stagnation, 'disorder, the misrule and confusion' which drew Joyce away from the Jesuits and back, temporally, to his father's house, prevented conditions arising in Ireland in which an intellectual life could flourish.

In one of Canon Sheehan's novels, the young priest draws the curtains of the glass doors of his bookcase, locks it, and throws the keys away.[14] But the author of the novels allows his readers many glimpses through his window of the European literature his priest feels obliged to renounce as incongruous with his calling. Frank

O'Connor tells us in his autobiography how on the way home from his dreary work as messenger boy in the Cork railway station he would talk to himself in German, quoting the poems by Goethe he had found in Canon Sheehan's books. Most of these talented young men had to escape through the opened window, though, to satisfy the appetites whetted during their schooling. But it often happened — as with that most talented of them — that they spent the rest of their lives looking back into the window on the Irish life they had been obliged to leave.

ULYSSES IN *ULYSSES:*
WHAT THE NOLAN SAID

ANDRÁS P. UNGAR

Joyce's complicated settling of accounts in *Ulysses* (1922) with Arthur Griffith's *The Resurrection of Hungary: A Parallel for Ireland* (1904) is of considerable significance. In effect, Joyce collapsed the term vital to Griffith's argument into his own work. He accomplished this with customary thoroughness in two stages. First, he ordered some aspects of his fiction in a manner analogous to Griffith's study, so that *Ulysses,* too, could be seen to have anticipated an understanding of Irish society from a distant Danubian perspective. Furthermore, to stress his right to these materials, he included allusions to his own act of authorship with the presentation. He indicated, in effect, why he would not approach the Austro–Hungarian materials as Griffith had. This self-reflexive strategy is tantamount to the foregrounding of an epistemological rupture between *The Resurrection of Hungary* and *Ulysses.* Joyce wanted to preserve Griffith's work as a variant of a subordinate structure of *Ulysses.*

Why did Joyce bother? On a first reading, nothing stands out in Arthur Griffith's study of the comparative political development of Hungary and Ireland which should have dignified the work with the status of potential rival to *Ulysses.* Still, the context of Griffith's work, and several of its salient aspects, ensured that Joyce would have felt compelled to see it in this way. He could not overlook the fact, for example, that the Irish parliamentarian, T. M. Kettle, had judged Griffith's proposal in *The Resurrection of Hungary* to be 'the largest idea contributed to Irish politics for a generation'[1]. Nor was he likely to ignore the coincidence that both *Ulysses* and *The Resurrection of Hungary* were synoptic views of the Irish situation in the same year, 1904. To be comprehensive, *Ulysses* could not avoid reviewing Griffith's evidence. Finally, by 1919–1922, a period when approaching independence and civil war in Ireland were keeping pace with Joyce's completion of *Ulysses,* a response to Griffith's ideal of Hungarian intransigeance was still more timely. Sinn Fein's misreading of history in 1904 had proven to be symptomatic of the crisis that would engulf Ireland at independence. To deal adequately with Bloomsday, *Ulysses* had to account for this misreading.

Griffith's drama in *The Resurrection of Hungary* pitted a party of far-seeing Hungarian nationalists who would not compromise their national birthright against the Habsburg despots and their lackeys. Frequently, in the course of this struggle spanning centuries, these intransigeants were pitifully few in number and their ideals seemed unrealistic in the extreme; yet, since only through self-reliance — only through the systematic boycott of all the bribes the Habsburg oppressor could offer — did the Hungarian nation have a real hope of returning to prosperity and honour, only the intransigence of these patriots mattered.

Finally, the Habsburgs, faced with defeat in Italy by Savoy and France, and in Germany by Prussia, had to pay the non-negotiable price of the intransigeants' support for the dynasty: Habsburg recognition of Hungarian constitutional autonomy. In 1867, the Austrian Emperor was crowned King of Hungary with the Crown of Saint Stephen and the Austrian Empire became the Austro–Hungarian Monarchy. Griffith proposed a similar constitutional transformation of Britain. He called for the boycott of all English political institutions and for Irish self-administration through existing local institutions. Elected Irish parliamentarians would convene a separate Irish parliament. Ireland's *de facto* constitutional autonomy under Sinn Fein's leadership would be the prelude to Britain's recognition of an independent Irish kingdom.

Ulysses' most prominent rejoinder to this scenario seems, on first view, a *non sequitor.* John Wyse Nolan, the Castle official, denies Griffith credit for the idea. 'Bloom', Nolan insists, 'gave the ideas for Sinn Fein to Griffith'.[2] Nolan gets support from Martin Cunningham for the charge. Bloom that 'perverted jew ... from a place in Hungary ... drew up all the plans according to the Hungarian system [for Sinn Fein]'. (p. 276) The apparent *non sequitor* has shifted the focus of inquiry decisively. The issue is not the adequacy of Griffith's generalization from history. We are not expected to consider Bloom in the role of historian seriously; nothing in his characterization suggests that he could have written a work like *The*

Resurrection of Hungary.[3] Nevertheless, *Ulysses* has appropriated the origins of 'the largest idea ... in Irish politics for a generation' for independent treatment.
This appropriation signals a shift in what it means to be involved with historical process. The experiential parameters of Bloom's connection with Austro–Hungarian history become the model of historical involvement which works such as *The Resurrection of Hungary* and *Ulysses* — works involved with history from a more reflective point of view — have to be able to deal with. A valuable indication of just what this criterial shift entails emerges from the use Griffith and Bloom make of the Empress Maria Theresa, a powerful symbol for both men.

For Griffith, Maria Theresa is a rhetorical counter. Her reign marked one of the lowest ebbs in the gathering force of the national feeling which would eventually win Hungary's freedom. Her appeal to Hungary had been insiduous. She struck the pose of a princess in peril and with Frederick the Great in possession of Silesia and a European coalition ready to contest her right to her remaining inheritance, her appeal was successful. In a gesture of misguided *noblesse,* Hungary accepted the embattled Habsburg as Queen, rightfully crowned with the Crown of Saint Stephen (1741). On her part, however, the reconciliation with Hungary's ancient constitution had been strategic.

> My brave brethren, ... the beautiful young queen [had said], 'my enemies assail me. I am a woman, and a woman appeals to you, chivalrous Hungarians!' And with a mighty shout Hungary went forth to battle for the beautiful young queen, and so well did it battle that it fixed the lady as securely as lady can be fixed on her throne, and placed her pretty foot as neatly as it might be placed on its own neck. And the lady did not die of laughter.[4]

Bloom's recall of Queen Maria Theresa has nothing to compare with this rhetoric. No politics are hinted at. Not even a date is supplied. In the puzzling disconnected account — a lack of concern with context which recalls the sparsity of the earliest historical annals — the name Maria Theresa is only a marker. It indicates the oldest layer of family lore transmitted to Bloom through his father. To Bloom and his father, the essential story was the odyssey of the Virags towards Ireland, the shaping of their legacy from the past. The focus on family history preempts the relevance of the drama of

Maria Theresa's fortunes, just as, for early medieval historians such
as the anonymous annalist of Saint Gall, the chronology of imminent Christian redemption deprived political and natural events of
independent significance.[5]

> What first reminiscence had [Leopold] of Rudolph Bloom (de-
> ceased)?
>
> Rudolph Bloom (deceased) narrated to his son Leopold Bloom
> (aged 6) a retrospective arrangement of migrations and settlements in
> and between Dublin, Florence, Milan, Vienna, Budapest, Szombat-
> hely with statements of satisfaction (his grandfather having seen Ma-
> ria Theresa [sic], empress of Austria, queen of Hungary), with com-
> mercial advice ... Leopold Bloom (aged 6) had accompanied these
> narrations by constant consultation of the geographical map of
> Europe (political) and by suggestions for the establishment of af-
> filiated business premises in the various centers mentioned. (*Ulysses,*
> p. 595)

At this level of involvement with the drama of state which concerns Griffith, Bloom *cum* historian of the Habsburgs can only introduce evidence through inadvertence. A case in point is the practice of naming sons in Bloom's family which commemorates
'Habsburg names ... (Leopold — Rudolph — Leopold — Rudolph)'.[6] The practice, politically meaningless to Bloom, would
have earned his forebearers the kind of treatment from Griffith's
intransigeant patriots — especially during the reigns of similarly
intransigeant centralizing Emperors such as Maria Theresa's
grandfather Leopold I or her son Joseph — which the boozy patriots
in Barney Kiernan's meted out to Bloom. The practice belongs to
the same unreflective level of historical involvement as great-
grandfather Virag's recollection of Maria Theresa. It indicates that
the Virag–Blooms had been Habsburg subjects long before they
became Hungarians. We know, for instance, that Lipoti Virag had
still spoken to his son in German. (*Ulysses*, p. 358) By the time they
decided to Hungarianize their name (Virág, the Hungarian for
'Flower'), the custom of naming sons on the Habsburg model had
become so ingrained, so 'natural', that, unlike the family name
which they readily changed, they did not even consider changing
this strictly 'family custom'.

Great-grandfather Virag's treasured recollection of Maria Theresa underscores the omnivorous pull of everyday concerns, the

power of this opaque acceptance to accomodate the most extraordinary events. The moral had worn from the anecdote in the
measure that the Virag-Blooms had become less Austrian and it
ceased to matter. On the basis of thematic coherence in *Ulysses,*
however, we can recover it. In all probability, it concerned the
Empress's exuberance at the news of her first grandson — one of
the most frequently repeated stories told of Maria Theresa,[7] and one
in accord with the theme of progenetive anxiety in *Ulysses.* The
birth guaranteed that the Habsburg sucession crisis would not be
repeated. When she got news of the birth, Maria Theresa shattered
baroque decorum. She rushed to the

> ... Imperial playhouse [where] flushed with excitement [she] leaned
> forward over the front of her box and, speaking in the broadest of
> Viennese, imparted her news ['Der Pold'l hoat a Buabn!' — 'My
> Poldy's got a boy!'] to the amazed spectators ...[8]

For Leopold Bloom, even the possibility of reflecting on the oddity
of this parallel between his anxiety and the drama of his family's
eponyms, the mighty Habsburgs, has sunk into the by-ways of
everyday habit.
    The point of view on historical process embodied in this balance
between the private and public spheres of life, between forgetting
and recollection, serves as the criterion for the relevance of the
central argument in *The Resurrection of Hungary* to Joyce's Dublin. Can the drama of Irish history be adeqately understood in the
mirror offered by the clash and reconciliation of imperial Austria
and noble Hungary? *Ulysses'* answer involves two steps. The first
takes Griffith's argument *au grand serieux* and, with the Virag-
Bloom relationship to naming as the criterion, personalizes the historical clash between Austria and Hungary as the meeting between
Leopold Bloom and Stephen Dedalus. The result is a kind of allegorical dumbshow, an historical action on stilts. The second addresses Griffith's procedure as a problem in epistemology. This
results in a prolonged meditation on the need for self-awareness in
representation and an alternative to the use of names in both the Vi-
rag-Bloom family and in Griffith.
    Ulysses plays the devil's advocate to Griffith's argument by
having the highly problematic relationship of Leopold Bloom and
Stephen Dedalus accomodate its design. Can less promising ground
be imagined for Griffith's confident parable? Exploiting the coin-

cidence between the Christian names of his characters and Saint
Leopold and Saint Stephen, the patron saints, respectively, of Austria
and Hungary, Joyce subordinates the significance of nationalist
struggles in the two multi-national empires to the meaning of Bloom
and Stephen's complicated encounter in Dublin. Like the Habsburgs
in defeat, Bloom, without a male heir, could only maintain patrilineal
continuity in his family, through the highly idiosyncratic solution of
getting Stephen to agree to live with him. Had he been able to convince Stephen to remain, he would not only have found a substitute
for the dead Rudy, but symbolically he would have recreated the cli-
mactic coronation scene in *The Resurrection of Hungary*. He would,
like the Emperor Francis Joseph, have been crowned with the Crown
of Saint Stephen (*Stephanos,* Greek for 'crown') in the interests of
dynastic continuity. The happy ending in Dublin would have dupli-
cated the profitable understanding between Germans and Hungarians
in Vienna and Budapest.[9]

Joyce rejects such a solution. On the one hand, Bloom fails (Stephen refuses to stay) because the complex reality of Dublin just
cannot be recuperated in this way. On the other, the pattern fails
because, even for its original purpose, it had been inadequate. Already in *Stephen Hero,* Joyce had rejected Griffith's highly-
abstract, highly-selective reading of history. He saw that both Irish
and Hungarian history needed a less restrictive, more open approach.

A glowing example was to be found for Ireland in the case of Hungary, an example, as these patriots imagined, of a long-suffering
minority, entitled by every right of race and justice to a separate
freedom, finally emancipating itself. In emulation of that achievement bodies of young Gaels conflicted murderously in the Phoenix
Park with whacking hurley-sticks, thrice armed in their just quarrel
since their revolution had been blessed for them by the Anointed, and
the same bodies were set aflame with indignation by the unwelcome
presence of any young skeptic who was aware of the capable aggres-
sions of the Magyars upon the Latin and Slav and Teutonic popula-
tions, greater than themselves in number, who are politically allied to
them ...[10]

Ulysses' independent approach to the issue once again has John
Wyse Nolan serving as Joyce's spokesman. This time the context is
his litany of Irish achievement and betrayal in the discussion at

Barney Kiernan's that will end with the Citizen's physical attack on Bloom. Nolan's complaint, rich in both verbal and dramatic irony, embroiders on the theme of Irish heroism in a world of uncaring strangers from the battle of the Boyne onwards. Only by proxy could Irish arms revenge their defeat by the English at home. Nolan's rhetorical high point is the expatriate Irish Brigade's performance in the French victory at Fontenoy where, to quote a contemporary account (1915): '... the Boyne [was] avenged. Never had the Irish brigade shown to such advantage. Its survivors were feted everywhere they went, its fame became universal. The Mountcassel regiment went into action several hundred strong, they came out a mere handful.'[11] Nolan's list of Irish achievements in exile passes to a mention of 'O'Donnell, the duke of Tetuan', who had threatened British Gibraltar, and concludes with the mention of Maria Theresa's most successful general, Ulysses Browne, the only Irishman with the name Ulysses in *Ulysses:*[12]

> We fought for the royal Stuarts that reneged us against the William-ites and they betrayed us. We gave our best blood to France and Spain, the wild geese. Fontenoy, eh? And Sarsfield and O'Donnell, duke of Tetuan in Spain, and Ulysses Browne of Camus that was fieldmarshall to Maria Theresa. But what did we ever get for it? (*Ulysses,* p. 271)

How was Ireland repaid for her sacrifices? The difficulty with the notion of Irish sacrifice in the service of the great Catholic powers, France and Spain, the fly in the ointment, is that Irish unity even in exile is a myth. In Nolan's litany, the one glaring exception and climax, the inclusion of Fieldmarshall Ulysses Browne undercuts the whole thrust of the rhetoric.

The one Irish Ulysses in *Ulysses* had not fought on the side of Bourbon France and Spain. At Fontenoy, Austria had been allied with England: Ulysses Browne, while not in the battle, had been allied with England. The anomaly testifies to the cross-purposes and blood-letting among the 'best blood' which Nolan so sanctimoniously invokes. What did Ireland ever get for her sacrifices in Europe? Most immediately, Nolan's blindness and the isolation of the Austrian Ulysses serve to remind the reader of Bloom, a rare immigrant to a land of emigrants, and his unlucky vulnerability among these Irish Cyclops.

How immediate is this reminder? Bloom himself, of course, has not the 'slightest inkling that he is Ulysses'.[13] His level of historical involvement excludes even the epic self-magnification to appreciate the parallel between himself and Maria Theresa's paladin. By invoking 'O'Donnell, duke of Tetuan', who, like Bloom threatened in his possession of Eccles Street and Molly, had been forced to retreat from Tetuan (1859) by British insistence that a Spanish presence there was 'inconsistent with the safety of Gibraltar',[14] the text does in a composite manner allude to Bloom's worries by way of larger European developments. Even more to the point is the apparent textual insistence on the Irishness of Ulysses Browne through the mention of 'Camus', the Irish placename associated with the family, though not with the Austrian-born Ulysses.[15] Both he and Bloom are one generation away from their ancestral homes. They represent complementary connections between the histories of the two empires.

Ulysses Browne, because he is the empirical link, also focuses Joyce's own involvement with the connection of Austro-Hungarian history and Irish life and raises the theme to a more self-reflexive compositional level.

Joyce had been familiar with the idea of the Fieldmarshall's return to Ireland long before he thought of *Ulysses* and Bloom. Conglowes Wood College, where Joyce studied from 1888–91, had originally belonged to the Brownes, the Jesuits having purchased the buildings from the family in 1813, and, after his death in Maria Theresa's service, Ulysses Browne returned to haunt the place.[16] We read, in *A Portrait,* of his ghost, 'A figure [coming] up the staircase from the hall [in] ... the white cloak of a marshall; his face ... pale and strange ... [who] had received his deathwound on the battlefield of Prague far away over the sea'. The child Stephen Dedalus had been fascinated and terrified. His imagination recoiled from everything about the Marshall which suggested the unknown and drew back into the homely and familiar, deep into the meshes of the 'nets' of family and religion which he would later strain to flee:

O how cold and strange it was to think of that! All the dark was cold and strange. There were pale strange faces there [in the dark], great eyes like carriagelamps. They were the ghosts of murderers, the figures of marshalls who had received their deathwound [sic] on battlefields far away over the sea. What did they wish to say their faces were so strange?

Visit, we beseech Thee, O Lord, this habitation and drive away from it all ...[17]

How differently 'the ghosts of murderers [and] figures of marshalls' appear in *Ulysses!* Nevertheless, the substitution of John Wyse Nolan's speech for the involuntary starts of the child Stephen has not erased the trauma of denial occasioned by the vision of the 'cold and strange'. *Ulysses* continues to code information about the Austro-Hungarian connection to Ireland in a very special way; the adequacy of its representation, whether by Griffith, Bloom, or Nolan, is in question time and again.

All the doubts about representational adequacy, however, are filtered through Nolan. The choice seems designed to focus attention directly on textuality for, apart from Dedalus, it is difficult to think of another name as charged with Joyce's authorship. His mysterious reference to 'the Nolan' when he protested the nationalist pieties of the Irish Literary Theater in the 'The Day of the Rabblement' (1901) had earned him early notoriety.

No man, said the Nolan, [Joyce wrote] can be a lover of the true and the good unless he abhors the multitude ... the artist, though he may employ the crowd, is very careful to isolate himself.[18]

The crowd was certainly puzzled by the cryptic reference.

No one knew who the Nolan was. As Joyce told Herbert Gorman later 'University College was much intrigued by this personage whom it supposed to be an ancient Irish chieftain like the MacDermott or the O'Rahilly'. Some students thought it was Joyce himself, later identified in the columns of *St. Stephen's* as 'the dreamy one of Nola'; others thought it was the porter at the Cecilia medical school, whose name was Nolan. 'Said the Nolan' became a catch phrase. Stanislaus had urged him to clarify this reference ..., but James replied, 'Laymen should be encouraged to think' ...[19]

When John Wyse Nolan inadvertently connects Bloom and Ulysses Browne, raising the issue of fact and fiction, his own fictional identity becomes as problematic as the various Griffith-Bloom-Nolan approximations of adequate historical synthesis.

The profound autobiographical resonances of this turn confront the reader as a kind of realistic imperative. The Nolan of the 'Day of the Rabblement' had been Giardano Bruno, the Renaissance martyr to Catholic orthodoxy in whose life Joyce had seen the 'vindication of the freedom of intuition' and a 'legend . . . most honourable' for those also involved in the same struggle.[20] Both the name Browne (Bruno in Italian), and the name Ulysses echo the call to fidelity. The insistence on the consciousness of textuality is massive. It is at this inordinately self-conscious textual conjuncture, with the identity of Nolan, Joyce's spokesman on the Austro-Hungarian theme, subject to the scrutiny already familiar from the meditation on Griffith's thesis, that *Ulysses* allows the threads of the synthesis joining Austria-Hungary and Britain-Ireland to unravel. *Ulysses'* fidelity to realism means that it does not need a parallel.

BANVILLE'S FAUST:
DOCTOR COPERNICUS, KEPLER,
THE NEWTON LETTER
AND *MEFISTO* AS STORIES OF
THE EUROPEAN MIND

JOSEPH SWANN

'At first it had no name. It was the thing itself, the vivid thing'. John Banville's *Doctor Copernicus* (1980) opens inside the mind of a child lying in bed amid a world of objects that are strange but at the same time related; and this strangeness and relatedness he learns before he knows their names. 'It was a part of the world', we are told, 'and yet it was his friend'. It is only then that we learn its name: 'tree'. And this remains its name although it, the thing itself, is constantly changing. For

> everything has a name, but although every name was nothing without the thing named, the thing cared nothing for its name, had no need of a name and was itself only.[1]

Name and thing are separate; the name does not touch, does not contain, but merely signifies, the essence of the thing. It was not always so, however; and that it was not always so is being said in this text too. For the speech of these lines moves in the familiar rhythms of the fourth Gospel, and the fourth Gospel states in un-equivocal terms the primacy of the creative Word:

> He was in the beginning with God; all things were made through him, and without him was not anything made that was made. (*John,* 1, 2-3)

The sound pattern is the same, but what is being said is very differ-ent, for the *Gospel According to John* is a synthesis of Judaic transcendentalism and Hellenic reason: the divine logos bears the imprint of all creation, is indeed that transcendent imprint, and by becoming flesh redeems what is created. Banville's 'prologue', however, lives in another world, the world of the late middle ages when the nominalist philosophy had begun to subvert the scholastic synthesis and Duns Scotus could lie on the lawn at Oxford contemplating the fracturing of light in a dewdrop; noticing how light was not one thing, but changed as the sun turned. It was the nominalist movement that caused such trouble to the church, separating the word from the creative plan of God, severing the intrinsic link that bound it to the thing it named, and seeing this link as something fortuitous, a pattern placed by man across the nameless force of what impinged upon him; and what impinged upon him, the essence, the 'reality' of things, was no longer rooted in the mind, but in the will, the creative power, the unfathomable love of God. This was one side of it, the side which saw the development of the 'devotio moderna' in the Low Countries and in Germany, with its anti-intellectual, or as we might now say, anti-Aristotelean, trends; and this side was strongly represented, too, in the universities of central Europe where the teachers of Martin Luther sat. But there was another side to it, for if the name no longer 'said' the thing, it was up to man himself to find out what that thing was and how it came to be; and in this passage from received knowledge to discovery lay the beginnings of modern science. It is the names of Scotus, Bacon and the Franciscan school that are generally mentioned in this connection, and this suggests that the two sides of the movement, the spiritual and the scientific, were not unconnected. Indeed, if one thinks of the popular, lay spirituality of the Franciscans and the growing importance of the towns, one might see in the shift from a patrician, gnostic wisdom to the empirical attitudes of a burgeoning mercantile class the third strand that completes the picture of Copernicus's age.

For Copernicus himself, as Banville more than once allows the older generation to observe, was the son of a tradesman, a copper merchant settled on the borders of what was then Germany and Poland. After the death of his parents, he and his brother Andreas were sent by their powerful uncle Lucas, the churchman, to a cathedral school, and it was here, we are told, that the young Nicolas Koppernigk came under the influence of Canon Wodka, teacher of arithmetic and geometry, astronomy and music theory. Their conversation is central not only to this novel but to Banville's whole tetralogy. Is the world no more than an engine, Nicolas asks, that it can be harnessed to drive a mere sundial? Canon Wodka recites the theories of Plato, Aristotle and Pythagoras. But:

'Herr Wodka — Herr Wodka, what do you believe?'
The Canon opened wide his empty arms.
'I believe that the world is *here,'* he said, 'that it exists, and that it is inexplicable. All these great men that we have spoken of, did they believe that what they proposed exists in reality? Did Ptolemy believe in the strange image of wheels within wheels that he postulated as a true picture of planetary motion? Do *we* believe in it, even though we say that it is true? For you see, when we are dealing with these matters, truth becomes an ambiguous concept . . . Well, I leave the question to you . . . I think it will give you much heartache.' And later, as they walked across the cathedral close at dusk, the Canon halted, suddenly struck, and touched the boy lightly in exitement with a trembling hand. 'Consider this, child, listen: all theories are but names, *but the world itself is a thing'.* (p. 33).

'It was', we are told, 'as if a sibyl had spoken'. But it is one that Copernicus has great difficulty in heeding. Banville's novel evolves the intricate pattern of intellectual, political and religious forces that surrounded Copernicus's redrawing of the map of the universe. It is a story that is true to its text: Banville's astronomer has one foot at least in the old world, where words tell things exactly as they are. But his Copernicus is a synoptic figure, seeing the problems of his age in a way that makes them the problems of our own, and not just the problems of science either. For the central aporia of the book is not that of theory in the narrow sense, or what we might call the status of explanation; it is the status of language itself, or the question of how we can in any way adequately name that which has no name but is simply the raw tangle of our experience.

The distinction is one that Copernicus lives out in flesh and blood. At the house of Professor Brudzewski in Cracow he first becomes aware of the need to explain, not just to save, as the professor would have it, the phenomena. Scientifically this distinction marks off the new men from the old, for if meaning and truth are in any case revealed, one account of the phenomenal world is much as good as another. That the professor can in the same breath say that 'astronomy does not describe the universe as it is, but only as we observe it' (p. 46) is, for all its nominalist enlightenment, beside the point, for the professor simply does not take observation, or astronomy, seriously. This is the real difference between them; though it is interesting to see them agreeing on one thing at least, that nominalism was a dirty word. Banville's Copernicus is never quite sure where he stands.

Nicolas's seriousness, however, sets him apart from the traditionalists; his intensity of purpose sets him above the *uomini nuovi* among whom he and his brother move. For they have gone to Italy now, and it is here, in the house of a young aristocrat on the shores of Lake Garda, in the house of Canon Nicolas's lover, that his concern for astronomy reveals its true dimensions:

> He had often before retreated into science as a refuge from the ghastliness of life ... he had made a plaything of science ... There would be no more of that, no more play. Here was no retreat, but the conscious accepting, on its own terms, of a cold, harrowing discipline. Yet even astronomy was not the real issue. He had not spent his life pursuing a vision down the corridors of pain and loneliness in order merely to become a stargazer. No: astronomy was but the knife. What he was after was the deeper, the deepest thing: the kernel, the essence, the true. (p. 90)

What holds for science, in other words, must hold for life itself, or for that language in which we would articulate it: the Copernican question, as Banville asks it, is not just about a description of the universe, but about grasping the relation between word and flesh, between a story and its underlying experience. The young Nicolas approaches this *via* its converse: he must break his life, his love, before he may understand: 'They must destroy each other, that is, that part of each that was in the other, for only by mutual destruction would he be freed'; and 'The closed system of the science must be broken, in order that it might transcend itself and its own sterile concerns' (p. 92, p. 94). The destruction is achieved and the revolutionary insight comes: the earth is moved; the theory, the explanatory proposition, is there. But that is not all:

> What mattered was not the propositions, but the combining of them: *the act of creation.* He turned the solution this way and that, admiring it, as if he were turning in his fingers a flawless ravishing jewel. It was the thing *itself, the vivid thing.* (p. 96)

Not the word, but the act of speaking, of making — this it was that contained what it signified. But what was a psychological truth was not yet an adequate metaphysic, and Copernicus was to spend the rest of his life working out that difference.

It is here that his brother Andreas, Nicolas's companion and tormenting ghost, plays, in Banville's novel, his most important role. For Andreas is the wastrel and *bon vivant,* the spirit who constantly negates all his younger sibling stands for. Poxed and doomed to death, he accuses his brother of being a living corpse (p. 113), rotting in the spirit as he has rotted in the flesh. And yet it is Andreas who has been responsible for most of Nicolas's fame, spreading everywhere the rumour of his work. Again and again the relation between them is expressed as that between two 'sundered halves' of the one being (p. 113). Andreas is 'the ineffable thing ... the ineluctable ... the world's worst' (p. 101). But when the final redemption comes, it is through him; for when Andreas Osiander, the protestant scholar and divine, visits Copernicus on his deathbed, it is in the shape of his brother that the visitor finally appears to him. It is an important scene, for Osiander utters with the supreme ease of the commonplace the hermeneutic principles which Copernicus has always feared to speak:[2] that 'hypotheses ... are not articles of faith, but bases of computation, so that even if they are false it does not matter, provided that they save the phenomena' (p. 246); that it is not the business of astronomy to discover 'true causes', but simply to 'provide a calculus which is consistent with the observations' (p. 248). For, as Copernicus himself is reported to have said, 'at the centre of all there is nothing ... the world turns upon chaos' (p. 230).

It is this that the Canon has been afraid to say openly; afraid because of the pain it will cause the common people, who need firmer doctrines to live by. And in his conscious mind he rejects Osiander's clarity as a betrayal. But nothing in this book is simple. Copernicus, aided by his personal enemies in the church, has finally, engineered the publication of his *De revolutionibus orbium mundi;* but, in order to safeguard its contents, it has to be published by protestants; anything else would be unthinkable. And yet he cannot accept the ease with which Osiander handles the implications of his thought. The old man is, of course, out of step with his age; but there is something more in the way Banville presents this scene. For what Osiander is concerned with is knowledge; what Copernicus is concerned with is life. It is only when the visiting divine abandons his mastery and takes on for the dying man the features of his brother that the final synthesis between theory and experience is reached. It is a synthesis in which each term fulfils the other by standing against the other, defining it as the relatedness of an opposite force and nothing more. Thus Osiander (or Andreas):

> We know the meaning of the singular thing only so long as we content ourselves with knowing it in the midst of other meanings; isolate it, and all meaning drains away. It is not the thing that counts, you see, only the interaction of things; and, of course, the names ...
>
> ...
>
> But you tried to discard the commonplace truths for the transcendent ideas, and so failed. (pp. 251–2)

The thing itself, the vivid thing is not there as such, because it is not nameable. It is there only in the plural, as things: the forces, some more, some less familiar, to which we are constantly giving names. And it is to these common things that Nicolas turns his hearing, 'the herdsman's call, the cries of children at play, the rumbling of the carts returning from market' (p. 254) as they finally call him away.

Banville's Copernicus is not just the renaissance scientist who has recast our understanding of the universe, nor is he just that scientist's successors — figures like Einstein, Eddington and Planck, with whose words, too, the author has him speak. More than these he is post-christian man, for whom the word and flesh are definitely separate; and most of all, perhaps, he is the post-romantic novelist, that one among us whose task it is to articulate what we call life.

In this respect *Doctor Copernicus* is an interesting book, but a surprisingly unmodern one. True, Banville deploys a wide range of narrative skills: there is the incursion, about two-thirds of the way through the story, of an omniscient narrator in the eighteenth century mode; there is the section narrated by the pompous and wrongheaded von Luachen, which yet tells us a lot about Copernicus's real mind; there is the long exchange of letters through which we glimpse, also in an earlier mode, into the politicking that surrounded Copernicus and his work. But the vessel which contains all this is the measured prose of what for us is the traditional storyteller, the maker of fictions as images of a text that is supposed, we know, to have gone before. Thus:

> In the cold and the dark at five in the mornings he rose in the mewling dormitory, aware that somewhere a part of him was turning languidly

into a deeper lovelier sleep than his hard pallet would ever allow. Throughout his days that other self crossed his path again and again, always in sunlight, always smiling, taunting him with the beauty and grace of a phantom existence. So he waited, and endured as patiently as he could the mean years, believing that someday his sundered selves must meet ... (p. 27)

or again:

Waterborne he comes, at dead of night, sliding sleek on the river's gleaming back, snout lifted, sniffing, under the drawbridge, the portcullis, past the drowsing sentry. Brief scrabble of claws on the slimed steps. (p. 101)

There is something Ptolemaic or perhaps Pythagorean about this prose: its earth is the flat place we inhabit, its music is the music of the spheres. Or, to put it another way, it is essentially metaphoric, interpretive, rather than presentational; it points, and does so in two directions, on the one hand towards the biography, the facts as they would like to be called, on the other towards the meaning, the explanation of the facts. It too is there to save the phenomena.

Banville's second novel in this series, *Kepler,* is equally biographical. Stylistically it is less poetic than *Doctor Copernicus,* its only adventure into a more highly structured language being the acrostic pattern of its chapter headings which, as Rüdiger Imhof points out, form the names of Johannes Kepler and his three great contemporaries, Tycho Brahe, Galileo Galileus and Isaac Newton.[3] This is not in any sense a value judgement on the novel, but simply a statement that from the point of view of this argument *Kepler* may be seen as a continuation and consolidation of what Banville had done in *Doctor Copernicus;* and this, broadly speaking, reflects the relationship between the two protagonists. There is one moment in particular, however, when Kepler, now the Imperial Mathematician, writes to a colleague of the older school, making clear what he sees as the distinction between astronomy and astrology:

To enquire into nature ... is to trace geometrical relationships. Since God, in his highest goodness, was not able to rest from his labours, he played with the characteristics of things, and copied himself in the world. ... And so, instinctively or thinkingly, the created imitates the Creator ... All this doing is like a child's play, without plan, without

purpose, out of an inner impulse, out of simple joy. And the contemplating spirit finds & recognizes itself again in that which it
creates. Yes, yes, Röslin: all is play.[4]

Copernicus's theory, whether saving or explaining the phenomena,
is being moved into a new dimension, for where all is play there can
be little distinction between the game of explaining and the game
that is explained.

Which brings us to *The Newton Letter* (1984). Published only a
year after *Kepler,* this novella is based not on a life, although its
narrator is an historian, but on a conjunction of literary texts, a letter
of Isaac Newton's, Hofmansthal's *Ein Brief* (the famous 'Chandos
Letter' of 1902), and, in the background, Goethe's *Die Wahlver-
wandtschaften,* the 'Elective Affinities'. It is the novella itself,
however, that is the 'Newton Letter', a single epistle written by the
narrator to Clio, confiding to her the inner and outer adventures
which accompanied his attempt to finish his book on Newton in the
seclusion of a country house at Ferns in Ireland.

It is a story of misreading; it is about the tangled maps we make of
our experience and the tangle of that experience itself; and it is
about the silence that lies at the heart of this relation. The narrator,
installed in the lodge at Fern House, soon exchanges his interest in
Newton for an interest in the inhabitants of the house. His story relates his two-fold love affair, with Ottilie and with Charlotte; and,
true to the Goethean fore-text, there is an Edward, there are the
Mittlers and there is a child, too. But this either does not matter, or it
does not follow Goethe, or it is hugely mistaken; some, but perhaps
only some, of the mistakes being revealed as the story unfolds. Thus
the decayed protestant gentility the narrator sees before him are
Catholics; the nobly fading Charlotte, mistress of his mind, is
drugged; Edward, her husband, whose illness she would be unable
otherwise to bear, is neither a villain nor a clown, but 'has it in the
gut'; and Ottilie, the mistress of his flesh, is simply there, at the end
as at the beginning, remote from all understanding. 'Shall I awake
in a few months, in a few years, broken and deceived, in the midst of
new ruins?'[5] the narrator asks as the book closes, and his answer
would probably be 'yes'; but it would equally be that only the
breaking matters.

For what he has learned from his story is the unimportance of
explanation. 'Shall I say, I've lost my faith in the primacy of text?'

(p. 9) he asks, and a little later tells how Newton was once deranged by the loss of some papers in a fire:

> The joke is, it's not the loss of the precious papers that will drive him temporarily crazy, but the simple fact that *it doesn't matter.* It might be his life's work gone, the *Principia* itself, the *Opticks,* the whole bang lot, and still it would not mean a thing ... Someone ... asks what has been lost. Newton's mouth opens and a word like a stone falls out: *Nothing.* (p. 30)

To this 'nothing' corresponds the ineffability of the common life which Newton, disguised now as Hofmansthal's Chandos, sees in the streets around him: a life that cannot be expressed in words, for these people *'are, if you will understand it, themselves the things they they might tell. They are all a form of saying.'* And the language which this composite figure seeks in order to grasp his experience is one *'in which commonplace things speak to me ...* (p. 59). The explanation, as Copernicus already knew, does not indicate what is the case, but simply denotes an intelligible pattern; and that is all, or almost all, that words can do. But events, phenomena, people and their lives — these are all pattern too; in what language, then, can that pattern be expressed? How can the flesh become word? It is the problem of the modern novelist that Banville is addressing.

His answer lies partly in the story but more in the way it is told. For the story posits a life that is there to be explained; it is the readings that are so faulty. 'Real people keep getting in the way' of understanding, 'objects, landscapes even', the 'shy back-end of things, drainpipes and broken windows' the narrator passes on his way down, and again on his way back to Dublin, a mirror-image unaffected by his passage (p. 9, p. 88). All he can do is record, and among the things he records is his attempt, and failure, to explain anything. The pattern he makes can do no more than take its place among the other patterns of experiences which intersect with his own. It does not interpret; it is part of a set, a metonymy, therefore, no longer in any way containing what it signifies. Conversely, that which was posited to be explained has no higher ontological status, no more reality, than its explanation. But the story, moving with the rhythms of a decentred, inconsequential world, can be itself a more vivid thing than the biographies which preceded it. The Copernican revolution has been enacted: at the centre is the word. Language is itself becoming experience: an experience 'based' only on the breaking and remaking of other texts.

'In the beginning', Kepler tells us, 'is the shape' (*Kepler,* p. 145); but it is with chance that the final novel of the Copernican tetralogy begins and ends, its opening words, 'Chance was in the beginning', being mirrored at the close: 'In future, I will leave things, I will try to leave things, to chance'.[6] Between these pages it is filled with what Gabriel Swan, its young narrator, calls 'the banal mathematics of gemination', for 'I too have my equations, my symmetries, and I will insist on them' (p. 3–4). Symmetry and chance, in this post-Copernican world, are no longer opposites, but rather, at all levels of language, they are complementary facets of experience.

For if *The Newton Letter* was subtitled 'An Interlude', it is in *Mefisto* (1987) that the shape of the game is finally revealed; and that shape is mathematical. The book is built on a system of symmetries; indeed it splits in two at the centre, and the halves seem to be there only in order to reflect each other. The only continuous characters are Gabriel, the boy-mathematician, and Felix, his Mephistophelian intriguer and companion. Other figures, the two Faustian men of numbers, Kasperl and Kosok, and the two girls, Sophie and Adele, are reincarnations of each other, and the episodes of the story are strung together, too, without any apparent purpose. There is, that is to say, no stable level of reality to which this story purports to be the meaning. Life and the word which codifies it have become two sides of an equation, for in this story the postulated events can have reality in no other context than that of their postulation. It is not so much the primacy of the text that has departed, but the primacy of that fictional text which we call the real.

Mefisto, in other words, is a novel of the unreal, a novel which sets out to solve the problem of the modern novelist by demonstrating the inherent nature of language. It is no longer a metaphor for an experienced world somewhere else; nor, however, is it simply a metonymy either. It is both together: full of likenesses replicating themselves almost to infinity, but full too of breaking, displacement, and the sudden sense of absence within that likeness. That is the double sense of Gabriel's twin: 'But I, I had something always beside me. It was not a presence, but a momentous absence. From it there was no escape'. (p. 17) It is the sense, too, of the relation between order and chaos, symmetry and chance: they are not, as they were for Copernicus, mutually exclusive, but inseparable and generative the one of the other. Together, indeed, they generate this book, and it is Gabriel's central insight that 'chaos is nothing but an infinite number of ordered things' (p. 183). We are close here to the conceptions of modern mathematics about the symmetries and asymmetries of numbers, but we are closer still to the post-romantic understanding of language as penetrating and playing in a world whose opposition to it is both made by it and makes it. But this, too, comes originally from Scotus, from whom a name was not a thing, and from him to Copernicus and those others — small nations have indeed made considerable contribution to our world.

In this scheme of things language is no longer either demonstration or explanation, but act, performing what it signifies. Theory is fiction, but it is one which enacts its world, and one without which that world would not, in any true sense of the word, be. For in the heuristic ontology set in train by the nominalist schools of the middle ages, the old concept of being as identity with the self has been logically shifted to make way for a more dynamic definition of being as a relation between the self and that other which is not the self. The strange is the related; being and nothingness are constitutent, the one of the other; or, as Felix puts it of Mr. Kasperl:

He's too ... negative. Me, now, I'm for positive things, rules, order, certainty. That's how we're alike, you and me. You don't believe me? Well, you'll see. The world is wide. I have plans. (p. 94)

But, of course, Felix is Mephistopheles, 'der Geist, der stets verneint' (*Faust* I, l. 338–9), the 'spirit who constantly denies'.[7] He is the interpreter (p. 176), the fixer and arranger, who never makes anything himself, but without whom nothing is or can be made. He is the Pollux to Gabriel's Castor (p. 162), as Andreas was to Copernicus, the mocking spirit who floats so easily in and on the world, the very embodiment of chance: all those things, in other words, that were present in Goethe's Mephisto when he redefined the creative relation between darkness and light, nothingness and being, that had held good since the days of Genesis:

Ich bin ein Teil des Teils, der anfangs alles war,
Ein Teil der Finsternis, die sich das Licht gebar ...
(*Faust* I, ll. 1349–50)
(I am a part of that part which in the beginning was all
A part of the darkness of which the light was born)

Mephisto, the cynical joker, the knowing fool, is in Goethean terms the twin not only of Faust, but of God himself, who admits that 'of all those spirits that deny, the joker irks me least' (*Faust* I, 11. 338–9). And here he, Mephisto, performs a radical realignment of the cosmos, assimilating spirit to darkness, light to body or matter. Goethe's Faust does not follow him in this, but Banville's Gabriel does: for him, chance alone can be salvific.[8] He is a more modern, and a more modest Faust, the last, or latest incarnation of that series which began with Copernicus.

For all of these figures are embodiments of Faust, the man who sought to know 'was die Welt / Im Innersten zusammenhält' (*Faust* I, 11. 382–3), 'what holds the world most inwardly together'; and sought to know it, not just in word, but in the very flesh of truth. Thus it is that Goethe's Faust too sets about rewriting the Prologue to the Johannine Gospel, rejecting in turn word, meaning and power ('Wort ... Sinn ... Kraft'), as his new versions of the *logos,* and finally settling for what to him was the only thoroughly this worldly formula: 'Im Anfang war die Tat' (*Faust* I, 1. 1237), 'in the beginning was the deed'.

This was the nightmare that had troubled Copernicus: the gap between thought and action, as it had not troubled the Grand Master of the Teutonic Order, his adversary, who could lay waste, without a moment's hesitation, to whole countries, and could do so in the name of the supreme fiction of his creative soul. But the German word 'Tat' is act and action as well as deed, and it is in this sense that Banville's Fausts reinterpret it. The word that was in the beginning is now the act which makes the world and is unmade by it: it does not become flesh, it always was both flesh and form, for these are no longer opposites, but complementary terms in a single equation. And it is in this sense that we might, after *Copernicus, Newton* and *Mefisto* re-read the ending to Goethe's *Faust.* For although we are told there that 'Alles Vergängliche / Ist nur ein Gleichnis' — that 'all that passes is but likeness' —, we are also told:

> Das Unzulängliche,
> Hier wird's Ereignis;
> Das Unbeschreibliche,
> Hier ist's getan;
> (*Faust* II, 11. 12104–12109)

which we might translate as 'the contingent will be here enacted, the indescribable is here performed'. It is this experience that comes to Copernicus on his deathbed, to Kepler in his moments of insight, to the narrator of *The Newton Letter* as he travels to and away from Ferns, and to Gabriel Swan all the time. The other is integral to the self: that other whose random dark beauty defies, as Andreas's did, all system. And that other is the world, the supreme fiction that we make, as we make ourselves, in the act of language.

SPEECH AND SILENCE: BEYOND THE RELIGIOUS IN BRIAN MOORE'S NOVELS

RUTH NIEL

In one of Brian Moore's early novels, *An Answer from Limbo* (1962), an old woman dies a slow and painful death in a lonely flat in New York, with the television set blaring away in the same room. She has had a stroke. She can see, but not reach, the telephone, the only means of calling for help, of telling her son about her illness. This is the ultimate cruelty of a world which the old woman — only recently emigrated from Ireland — has already found cold and hostile, a world where language and communication are reduced to 'talking', without being interested in a response or being able to reach the person talked to. It is also a world whose lack of religious faith she could not accept. She herself believed that she could find meaning in her faith, but her way of dying is so inhuman that the very possibility of such meaning is called in question.

This example of non-communication and questioning comes from one of Moore's least 'religious' novels, for in *An Answer from Limbo* religion is only one of several themes and, on the whole, is not so much a problem of faith as of social and cultural background. Brian Moore has often been called a religious novelist, and all his novels contain some religious element, even if questions of faith are not always the central theme. But Moore is also a writer who is widely praised by critics for never attempting the same thing twice. In his fifteen novels to date he has employed a wide range of formal devices, he has moved from realism to novels containing elements of the unreal, the fantastic and the miraculous, and to novels which can be interpreted as parables. A similar diversity can be found in the characters he has invented, in his settings and particularly in his plots. Despite this diversity, however, one can find recurring patterns and themes in Moore's work: his novels are all about a moment of crisis. This can be an individual, a social, a cultural, a psychological or a spiritual crisis, but Moore is always interested in the individual's reaction to this crisis; and it is here that religion plays a frequent role.

Many critics, however — and not just those who call Moore a religious writer — divide his novels into the 'religious' and the 'secular'.[1] 'Religious' novels in this categorization are usually those which centre around problems of belief — doubt, loss of faith, the meaning of religion in the modern world — and they often have priests as central characters. The most obvious examples of this are his novella *Catholics* (1972) and his two latest novels *Black Robe* (1985) and *The Colour of Blood* (1987).[2] His 'secular' novels, according to this distinction would, then, be those in which religion is only a minor issue or where the church and its social functions are criticized and satirized.[3] The problem with such divisions is that they separate aspects of Moore's oeuvre which are inseparable. Only when these elements are seen as a unity does it become clear that religion is not merely a theme which the author for some personal, autobiographical reason cannot get away from, but a focal point for depicting the crisis which is a central experience of modern man. This point has been made quite clear by Moore himself:

> Although I am not a religious writer, religion — the Catholic religion — has played a major role in many of my novels . . . I use religion as a metaphor.[4]

Terence Brown and the Jesuit critic Michael Paul Gallagher interpret Moore's use of religion in this sense, but on the whole critics concentrate on the thematic aspects of the subject, notably the two main types of religious problem presented in the novels: (1) the crisis of religious faith and (2) the question of meaning in both 'religious' and 'a-religious' worlds. If, however, one sees religious faith as a metaphor for belief as such, then the crisis of faith of an individual in a world with which he or she cannot communicate is one in which the division of the sacred from the secular is no longer valid. What is at issue is the relation between belief and language, between speech and the moment which precedes it. For communication, as the old woman in *An Answer from Limbo* found, must, if it is to be more than an empty ritual, be based on a real encounter, and at the heart of every encounter is the speechless moment called faith. In this sense Moore's novels cease to be 'religious' or 'secular' and become attempts to show various aspects of the human search for a unifying moment, a coherent pattern in life.

The opening example from *An Answer from Limbo* is a case in point: The three central characters in the novel are very different in their attitudes, desires and ambitions, but what they have in common is their search for — and lack of — a meaning and purpose in life. The old woman looks for this in religion. The fact that faith and communication — speech — are linked in this novel is symptomatic for Moore's work as a whole. For, like religion, language can also be seen as an abstraction, as a central metaphor, rather than just as a topic. As a modern writer, Moore is aware of the fact that world and meaning can rarely be grasped and understood directly; they need a medium:[5] Language is one and, for many of Moore's characters — at least as an attempt — faith is the other.

Moore does not present the reader with any value judgements about religion, he is neither for nor against belief. He often implicitly criticizes the Church as an institution — as in *Catholics* or *Judith Hearne* (1955) — or makes fun of the Church's representatives, like Monsignor Cassidy in *Cold Heaven* (1983), who is once referred to as 'God's golfer',[6] golf being, it seems, his main interest in life. He belongs to the harmless variety of Moore's priests, the sort who does no wrong to others simply because he is too lazy to do anything. Other priest-figures are less attractive: the power-ridden Father Keogh in *The Feast of Lupercal* (1957), for example, and, particularly, Father Quigley in *Judith Hearne,* whose lack of interest in Judith's problem is instrumental in finally destroying her faith. But in all these instances the novelist's attacks aim at the *institution,* the form; he never criticizes — and never praises — faith. Whether a person loses or regains his faith in a spiritual crisis is never morally judged, but is presented exclusively as that individual's struggle for meaning and salvation.

Thus there is no spiritual dominance of faith over absence of faith. This becomes evident if one looks at the different ways Moore shows of reacting to such a crisis. Moore's novels are always written in a way that the reader has to feel with the central character, and the reader's reaction will depend on whether the choice made by this character helps him or her to overcome the crisis, or whether it will lead to despair. Thus the endings of *Judith Hearne* and *Catholics* — where the protagonists both lose their faith — are catastrophic, whereas the rejection of faith in *Cold Heaven* must be seen quite differently.

The main character of *Cold Heaven,* Marie Davenport, is a young American woman who intends to leave her husband for her lover. Marie was educated at a Catholic convent but does not believe. Despite this fact she — and with her the reader — has to come to terms with miracles: her husband is killed in an accident but miraculously leaves the mortuary and returns to life (although he sometimes goes back to a death-like trance). Marie sees this as connected to something that happened to her after her first meeting with her lover a year earlier: Close to a convent at Carmel in California she had an apparition of the Virgin Mary, who told her to tell the priests about this vision and let a shrine be built on that spot. But Marie never told anyone — she rejected the religious vision and also wanted to keep her affair a secret — and now she interprets her husband's death and resurrection as a sign from the powers in which she refuses to believe. At the end of the novel, after a second vision, which was also witnessed by a young nun, and after several encounters and conversations with believers, she finally decides never to talk about her visions again, to return to her 'normal' life and to leave her husband. Marie's rejection of faith and her choice of the secular seems here to be the only possible solution.

Similarly, Moore's novel about a 'secular miracle', *The Great Victorian Collection* (1975),[7] where Anthony Maloney one night dreams a collection of Victoriana into reality, ends with a suicide which has to be accepted as the only way out. Maloney, the creator, the 'God' in this novel, has been unable to control his creation: his dream has turned into a recurring nightmare which gradually changes the marvellous collection of originals into fakes. By committing suicide Maloney admits that he has lost control, but he hopes, too, that by this total separation from it he will be able to preserve his masterpiece.

Cold Heaven and *The Great Victorian Collection* are both examples of how the secular and the religious are fused in Moore's work. Miracles need not be linked with religion, but they are, as in *The Great Victorian Collection,* linked with 'faith',[8] with belief in *something.* In the attempt to make meaning both faith and the renunciation of it can have their place, but for those characters whose life has centred on faith — like Judith Hearne or the Abbot in *Catholics* — loss of faith always means despair.

In *Cold Heaven* religion is part of a more general crisis of communication. Marie firmly believes that she has been told what to do, that she sees or receives 'signs' which give her hidden orders. Her main fault, she thinks, is not to have done what she was told; and again this is connected with talking: for the apparition had commanded her to tell the priests. After her husband's strange death and resurrection, the following of orders given by 'signs' helps him recover. But this is only one side of the dilemma: Marie never dares 'tell' anyone the whole truth. When she talks to the priests she does not tell them about her husband's death: her husband does not know about her lover or her visions, but constantly gives her orders himself, sometimes using the same words the apparition had used: and even her lover, of whom she says that he understands her and listens to her, is not informed about her strange visions. When he asks her what is wrong, Marie — who as a young girl was always 'outspoken', who 'had never kept silent when she disagreed' (p. 160) — now remains mute: 'She could not speak, could not tell him, I love you ...' (p. 157). Real communication, like belief, is impossible for her when she is faced with those unaccountable, disturbing events. Only at the end of the novel, when she has *decided* to assert her right not to believe and to keep silent about it, can she return to the ordinary world where 'normal' things can be said. She can now plan what exactly she will say when she tells her husband that she is going to leave him — and her spiritual crisis is over.

Already in Moore's first novel, *Judith Hearne,*[9] the problem of communication, or, in this case, lack of communication was one of the novel's central concerns. The lonely spinster's only links with the world around her are her faith and her dreams of friendship and love. She has some control over her life so long as she can believe that her friends, the O'Neills, love hearing her stories and talking to her, and that Mr. Madden — a man she has recently met and who believes that she has money which she might invest in a business with him — is intending to marry her. At such times going to church and talking to God in her prayers is the most stable and reassuring element in her life. She prays for a sign, a sign that her prayers have been answered in the person of James Madden. In the course of the novel Judith's dreams are gradually destroyed. Her inability to cope with this not only leads her to seek oblivion in alcohol, but is also parallelled by a gradual loss of faith. In church she prays for a sign, but suddenly

> ... it seemed as though the tabernacle were empty. ... In the tabernacle there was no God. Only round wafers of unleavened bread. She had prayed to bread. (p. 140)

She immediately asks God's forgiveness and when she leaves the church she is nearly run over by a car — for Judith this coincidence is the sign that God exists. But with the total destruction of her hopes comes the total destruction of her faith. Drunk again, she one day reveals to her friend Moira O'Neill that she never really liked her, and this will mean the end of the pretence of her belief in being part of that family. Similarly, she has to learn that all her conversations with Mr. Madden had been misunderstandings, as on both sides their words concealed more than they communicated. After the truth has finally come out, she again seeks refuge in the church:

> She began to pray . . . her mind far from the sacrifice. The Our Fathers and Hail Marys stumbled through her mind, repeating themselves until they were meaningless. . . . she slowly retraced the agony from its beginnings; . . . the things said, the cruel way he said them. They could not be washed away by repetition, those cruel words. Unlike prayers, they could not be dulled by restatement. They were the negation of prayer, the antithesis of hope. (p. 160)

Prayer has already lost its function as communication with God. At confession she has to learn that the priest, God's representative, does not listen to her either. Thus no one hears her: not her friends (cf. p. 231), nor the priest, nor even God. The sign she has asked for is never given, and in the outside world signs are just as meaningless as in church: 'A lonely tramcar clattered by, bright-lit, empty, its conductor standing alone on his platform. . . . Traffic lights flashed red, amber and green in empty futility.' (p. 212)[10] After her last attempt to talk to the priest she realizes:

> He didn't understand, he could only say the silly, ordinary things you would expect him to say. Words, all he had was words. 'Supposing he knew that there was nothing in the tabernacle — ah then, what could he say?' (p. 238)

Judith in her desperation wants to force God to reveal himself:

> 'I hate you', she said, her voice loud and shrill in the silence of the church. And she waited. Now, surely now, in His anointed, consecrated place, a thunderbolt . . . But the only sound was a banging door as a priest entered the church. No sign.
> No one.

Only bread. (p. 240)

She tries to break open the tabernacle door, to get a final proof of God's presence or absence, 'But the door rejected her. It would not open.' (p. 241) After this act of 'madness' church and outside world — the O'Neills — are united in the decision to put her into a home run by nuns, where she will probably stay for the rest of her life.

The more Judith doubts her faith, the more her prayers change from conversations with God into empty rituals. The function of prayer as ritual, or ritual as prayer, re-appears, in fact, in many of Moore's novels. Not always, however, does this imply a simple reduction to non-communication.

In *I am Mary Dunne* (1968)[11] the central character uses the language of ritual, of prayer, not as an attempt to get closer to God but as a means to overcome a crisis of identity. Mary — née Mary Dunne, now Mary Lavery — is a young woman living in New York with her third husband. She was educated at a convent school but religion plays no role in her present life. In spite of this, however, religious language and imagery permeate the novel. It is a language she learnt as a child, when life still seemed the simple following of a coherent pattern. Religion itself was such a pattern, meaningful and comforting in its rituals, and it formulated answers to all questions. Now, as an adult close to a nervous breakdown, Mary unconsciously tries to recapture some of this coherence by falling back onto the words she knew as a child. Lying in bed at night, she tries to convince herself that she is not losing her sanity and goes through the past day in her mind. She tries to remember 'her thoughts, words and deeds of today' (p. 206). This is reminiscent of the children's 'Morning Offering' — an indication that her religious development never got beyond the stage of childhood faith. The phrase also brings to mind the 'general examen', a general examination of conscience and 'traditional formalized spiritual exercise' used by Catholics to 'achieve perfection in daily life'.[12] Mary secularizes these rituals in her fight against her fears. Her identity crisis is epitomized in her constant reference to names. Names seem clear labels of identity, and the fact that she has had many names — married names, pet names, nicknames — seems to her a symptom of her problem. Whether Mary in the end succeeds in overcoming her crisis remains an open question[13], but her last words again resemble the language of ritual, and they seem to indicate insecurity rather than a sign of recovery:

... when I put my mind to it, I did manage to remember most of the
thoughts, words and deeds of today, and now I will not panic, ...
I am not losing my memory, I know who I am, ... I will not change,
... I will remember what Mama told me, I am her daughter,
I have not changed, I remember who I am, and I say it over and over
and over, I am Mary Dunne, I am Mary Dunne, I am Mary Dunne.
(p. 206)

But the most striking fusion of the religious and the secular in this
novel can be found in Mary's use of biblical language in order to
describe her feelings for her present husband, Terence. Years ago,
in a row, she had hurt her second husband by alluding to the sexual
fulfilment she had found with Terence: 'Terence is my saviour,
I shall not want, he maketh me to lie down in green pastures, he
restoreth my soul. ... He's my new religion. He's life after death.'
(p. 101) In her present crisis she is afraid of again losing faith in her
marriage, but when she realizes how Terence's presence can, at
least momentarily, restore this faith, she repeats those comforting
biblical words:

He came to me, sat on the chair with me, put his arm around me and
felt me tremble, ... saw the state I was in, but I was not afraid of him
any more, he was alive, he was life, not death, I held him and
I thought: he is my saviour, he restoreth my soul ... (p. 188)

She can find no other words to express her feelings and to reassure
herself at the same time. But more is at stake here, for in the use of
ritual, religious language to express a sexual bond there is the suggestion of a possible redemption. Both religion and sexuality are
capable of taking language to the point of silence, and the ritual repetition of word or gesture would seem to be intimately connected
with the attainment of that point. It is a moment, perhaps, at which
the sign can itself become the encountered thing. Moore repeatedly
returns to this juncture of language, hardly ever allowing the tension between a redemptive moment and the relapse into emptiness
— or garrulity — to be resolved. Thus in *I Am Mary Dunne*, language ultimately seems too limited: for Mary the mere repetition of
words is not enough to overcome the crisis.

Prayer as ritualistic language recurs as a crucial element in *Catholics*[14]. This short novel is set in the not too distant future, at a
time after 'Vatican IV', after a union of Catholicism and Protestant-

ism and at the beginning of ecumenical negotiations with Bud-
dhism. A young American priest and member of the (fictitious) Al-
banesian order, James Kinsella, is sent to a remote Irish monastery
on the island of Muck to put an end to practices still observed by the
monks there, but which have been forbidden by the new 'liberal'
church: Latin Mass, private confessions and the belief in the 'miracle' (p. 74) during Mass. Kinsella is very much at home in the new
church; he works in the Church's Ecumenical Centre and is most
interested in liberation theology. He is one of the few central characters in Moore's work who never doubts his faith. For him what
used to be miracles are merely symbolic acts. He believes in the
social function of the church, more than he believes in God. His
opponent in the novel, the other central character, is the old Abbot
Tomas O'Malley. As Abbot he *has* a social function, one which he
takes very seriously: to help the monks in his abbey to get used to
the new ideas without losing their faith in the church. O'Malley
himself had long ago begun to lose his faith, and the first moment of
doubt had occurred at Lourdes — a place usually associated with
miracles. The Abbot had been repulsed by the cheap business-side
of this 'place of worship'. When he saw this centre of organized
belief, he could not pray any more. Since his visit he has avoided
prayer in order to avoid the awareness of his loss of faith. Instead he
tries to keep the faith of others. Thus the Latin mass is kept because
'I am not a holy man, ... I felt I had no right to interfere.
I thought it was my duty, not to disturb the faith the [his monks and
the parishioners in the village] have.' (p. 56) One of the other
monks, Manus, explains why the *Latin* mass is important: it is part
of the ritual and ritual is a way of reaching God.

> It is priest and people praying to God, assisting in a miracle whereby
> Jesus Christ again comes down among us ... And the Mass was said
> in Latin because Latin was the language of the Church and the Church
> was one and universal ... And if the Mass was in Latin and people did
> not speak Latin, that was part of the mystery of it, for the Mass was
> not talking to your neighbour, it was talking to God. (p. 43)

For the 'new' Church the emphasis has of course shifted to communication in this world, and mystery is less important than intelli-
gibility. When the Abbot has to yield to the orders from Rome, he is
no longer able to avoid his own inner conflict: he wants to reassure
his monks and knows that he can do so only by leading them to

prayer: "'Prayer is the only miracle", he said. "We pray. If our words become prayer, God will come.'" (p. 91) Praying takes his monks into the world of faith; he himself enters what he most fears: '... the true hell, ... the hell of no feeling, that null, that void.' (p. 71)

Prayer has become the way to utter despair, the moment when one feels the 'silence of God'. And this phrase recurs in several of Moore's novels. Its repetition, explicitly or symbolically — for example in the figure of the tabernacle[15] — throughout Moore's work is not just accidental; it is part of a coherent pattern. Each recurrence adds new aspects of meaning to the pattern, as if trying to find answers to questions put in previous novels.

Thus for Judith Hearne God's silence had similar implications as for the Abbot. She had always seen the beauty of the silence in 'God's house', just as prayer, the silent conversation with God, had meaning. As in *Catholics* and in *Black Robe,* the tabernacle is the symbol of the absent, silent, unapproachable God. Judith tries to break through this silence, but she is doomed to fail.

In *Black Robe*[16] it is again a priest who has to come to terms with doubt. Moore's story about the Jesuit missions in Canada in the seventeenth century is yet another novel which links the secular with the religious. The novel is about a clash of cultures and with it the clash of Indian and Catholic belief. Silence is a key word in this book and refers not only to the 'silence of God'. The Jesuit Paul Laforgue is partly deaf, which is symbolic of his attitude towards Canada and the Indian 'savages': he has very concrete ideas about his mission and is reluctant to learn anything about Indian attitudes and beliefs. In the course of the novel, on his journey through Indian territory, he is forced to learn about them, but as long as his attitude remains unbroken, his hearing gets worse. Only after a severe illness — which also marks an extreme personal crisis — is he willing to accept the help of the Indians — and suddenly he can hear clearly again. Similary, sound and silence mark the differences in religious belief: for the Indians the forest is sacred, it speaks to them, warning them, for instance, of dangers. For Laforgue it is only dark, silent, threatening. He gets lost in it, a sign that the country and the Indians are still alien to him. The 'savages' have to rescue him and for the first time he is glad to be back in their habitation.

When one of the Indian leaders is dying, Laforgue has a conversation with him which will alter his attitude to his own faith. Laforgue points out that for Christians life after death is more important than life on earth. "What shit you speak", the Indian replies,

'Look around you. The sun, the forest, the animals. This is all we have. It is because you Normans are deaf and blind that you think this world is a world of darkness and the world of the dead is the world of light. We who can hear the forest and the river's warnings, we who speak with the animals and the fish and respect their bones, we know that is not the truth. If you have come here to change us, you are stupid. We know the truth. The world is a cruel place but it is the sunlight. And I grieve now, for I am leaving it.' (p. 169)

The Jesuit finds himself unable to contradict, he is impressed: 'And, at that moment, Laforgue heard a chorus of birds announce the limits of their territories.' (p. 169) He, for the first time, is capable of 'hearing', of deciphering and understanding the sounds of that strange world around him. It is after this conversation that Laforgue realizes that he is not praying any more. And a short time later, looking at the tabernacle and at a statue in the chapel of his new mission 'as though, in them, some hint might be given of that mystery which is the silence of God', he feels that

The hosts in the tabernacle were bread, dubbed the body of Christ in a ritual strange as any performed by these Savages. ... Here in this humble foolish chapel ... a wooden box and a painted statuette could not restore his faith. (p. 219)

Whether his faith is restored at the end of the novel remains unclear, but he does finally accept his new life: The Indians in his mission want to be baptized, not because they believe, but because they think that the Jesuits' God is responsible for an epidemic which has killed many villagers. Laforgue hesitates, but then realizes that the Indians' wish to obey this new God is no more true nor false than his statement of his own belief. Laforgue's God is silent, but he, Laforgue, will spend the rest of his life with the Indians — they are the new meaning in his life. And while he goes through the ritual of baptizing, while he repeats the words again and again, ... a prayer came to him, a true prayer at last. Spare them. Spare them, O Lord. (p. 224)

In his most recent book, *The Colour of Blood*[17], Moore returns to the concept of 'the silence of God'. In his previous novels this silence usually refers to God's absence or indifference. Although some characters — like the Abbot in *Catholics* or Father Laforgue — were aware of silence as the realm of infinite possibilities, of infinite faith, they could never reach that state. In *The Colour of Blood* the situation is quite different: here, 'the silence of God' never means absence, it is always a mystical place of union with God.

The central character of the novel, Cardinal Bem, never has to experience the doubt which had destroyed other characters in Moore's novels. Sometimes he can 'in prayer, in the act of prayer ... open that inner door to the silence of God, God who waited, watched and judged.' (p. 61) The absence of 'a crisis of faith' and the fact that the novel is about the role of religion and the Church in an 'atheist' world — in this case a fictitious Eastern bloc country which in many ways resembles the Poland of the mid-80s — could bring to mind the term 'religious novel'. But, as always in Moore, one cannot limit the book to this one aspect. *The Colour of Blood* is as much a social as a religious novel, it is about social worlds, about social and individual behaviour, about political beliefs, about the clash of different power groups such as a Communist government and the Catholic Church. Gallagher points out that '... it can be a study of the political underside of religion everywhere and in particular of the ambiguities of power struggles carried on in the name of religion', and he goes on to compare this book to other Moore novels: 'Where other novels took a crisis of psychological self-preservation as their focus, *The Colour of Blood* is inclined to explore the more political struggle for power within the religious structure of the church (and to a lesser extent within the State).'[18] There is no *spiritual* crisis and this, in many ways, makes *The Colour of Blood,* in spite of its religious themes and characters, a novel less interested in belief than some of Moore's so-called 'secular' novels like *I am Mary Dunne.* The secular and the religious, again, are inseparably fused.

'Speech' and 'silence' are key words in this novel where — apart from Bem's faith — nothing is certain: right to the end of the plot Bem is not sure who wants to assassinate him, he never knows whom he can trust or believe, whether what is said is what is meant and whether what he says himself will lead him into trouble, *The Colour of Blood* is a 'novel of distrust and suspicion'[19]. The importance of speech and silence — two concepts which oppose and complement each other at the same time — can be seen in the opening and the closing scenes of the novel: at the beginning Bem is sitting in the back of the car reading a book by the mystic Bernard of Clairvaux and tries to 'withdraw into that silence where God waited and judged' (p. 7). He is withdrawn from the outside world, ignorant about imminent political confrontations. He is forced into recognizing these problems when he reaches 'Proclamation Square' — and the name signifies the opposition of the noisy outside world to his spiritual silence: someone tries to kill him, an act which will finally be achieved five days later, days in which Bem increasingly grows into his role as a leader of his Church who is able to combine spiritual insight with political awareness. At the very end of the novel Bem is convinced that he has succeeded in overcoming the crisis which threatened the political stability of his country, but, typically for Moore, it remains unclear whether he has in fact preserved the peace; he is shot by religious extremists just at that moment when 'he knew peace'. Again one finds the duality of noise and silence:

> ... he saw the revolver ... and in that moment he knew: This is God's will. ... The silence of God: would it change in the moment of his death? ... He saw her finger tighten on the trigger.
> And heard that terrible noise. (p. 191)[20]

Silence is the absence of the kind of language that we are used to and seem to rely on. In Moore's work it can mean absolute despair for some characters, but for others, notably in *The Colour of Blood,* it is precisely this silence which hints at the possibility of absolute faith and absolute meaning. Here, as in other novels, Moore employs the language of religion in a secular world in order to explore the attempt of men and women at discovering, however fragmentarily, ultimate meaning.

In *Cold Heaven,* the novel where the secular and the religious are most successfully fused, we also find the most beautiful example of how meaning is rooted in belief and communication. The strongest experience of 'meeting', of that moment where the barriers of the self and the other disappear — the moment which Moore's characters try to experience in religion or love or sexuality — occurs not in the meeting with God or between lovers, but between two seemingly very different women. Marie, the nonbeliever troubled by religious visions, finds a strange and inexplicably silent form of communication with Mother St Jude, a contemplative nun, who is called a 'mystic' and a 'holy person' by the other nuns. 'She has no self', one of the sisters says (p. 88). They meet twice. At first, Marie just feels love coming from the other woman and 'There was a moment of silence while they stared into each other's eyes.' (p. 87) Marie is deeply moved, but only during their second meeting, with Marie at the most extreme point of her crisis, does the true meeting occur. Again

> ... Marie felt herself enveloped by a look of love mixed with reverence, a look she had never known from any other human being. ... The old nun came forward, holding out her arms as to embrace her and as she touched her, holding her lightly, the tension left Marie's body. In that moment, mysteriously, her fear of this place and these people was subsumed in a larger feeling, a feeling of peace. (pp. 238–9)

Together they walk to the place of Marie's vision and they have what seems to be the only authentic conversation of the book, where people listen to each other and understand each other — despite their radically different opinions. Marie says, in order to show the difference between them, 'I am your opposite' (p. 241), but the very manner of their communication shows that this is only one way of putting it. They could also be seen as complementing each other. For Mother St Jude confides in Marie and tells her that she had dreamt the vision Marie had really seen. In her dream she had been unable to understand the apparition's words and therefore thought that she had failed God. Since then, she had not felt God's presence any more. He had remained absent and silent till Marie and she first met: '"And the moment I saw you, God came back into my soul. It was true happiness, that happiness that the saints have spoken of — St John of the Cross and St Teresa."' (p. 240) This moment is not explained, not reversed, not questioned. Marie accepts it and her statement that she does not believe does not destroy their communication. Here, for once in Moore's work, the opposing forces meet: belief and non-belief, sanctity and the secular, speech and silence.

MYTH AND MOTHERLAND: EDNA O'BRIEN'S *MOTHER IRELAND*

WERNER HUBER

> Out of Ireland have we come,
> Great hatred, little room,
> Maimed us at the start,
> I carry from my mother's womb
> A fanatic heart.
> — W. B. Yeats

When Edna O'Brien's *Mother Ireland* (1978)[1] was published in 1976, critics were divided over its merits. Irish reviewers, probably because of their emotional proximity to the subject and ambivalent feelings about it, attacked its incoherence, its meandering self-indulgence and its use of stereotypes.[2] British and American critics were far more lenient in their judgements, admiring the vivid evocation and sensuous description of her memories of the Green Isle. Interestingly enough, the main objection to the book on all sides was the repetition of themes and experiences in *Mother Ireland* with which readers were already familiar from Edna O'Brien's early novels *The Country Girls* (1960), *The Lonely Girl/Girl with Green Eyes* (1962), and *A Pagan Place* (1970).[3] These concerned the early stations of her life: childhood in County Clare, convent school in County Galway, escape to Dublin, training at a pharmaceutical college.

I shall not attempt to set off fiction against truth in the works of Edna O'Brien. This distinction between *Dichtung* and *Wahrheit* becomes rather irrelevant when we are dealing with modes of experience and the images and stereotypes which serve as vehicles for narrative presentation. These concern, as the question of authenticity regarding the subject-matter is beyond reach.

This essay studies the dominant imagery pattern in *Mother Ire-*

land, starting from the assumption that *Mother Ireland* is an autobiography, that is, a statement about personal identity. The images
of Ireland and Irish history used are a functional part of this book.
They help to define personal identity via a definition of national
identity, the assumption being that in Irish autobiographies personal and national identity often go together.[4] Thus, the passages in
Mother Ireland which evoke Irish history (especially in Chapter
I 'The Land Itself') are not at all to be seen as gratuitous adjuncts or
a 'mock-heroic recreation of Irish history.'[5] They constitute a serious part of the book's impact and carry important thematic connotations, however coloured they may be by the author's idiosyncratic view of Irish history.

The opening sentences of *Mother Ireland* set the tone:

> Countries are either mothers or fathers, and engender the emo-
> tional bristle secretly reserved for either sire. Ireland has always been
> a woman, a womb, a cave, a cow, a Rosaleen, a sow, a bride, a harlot,
> and, of course, the gaunt Hag of Beare. (p. 11)

It is significant that Edna O'Brien begins her memories of Ireland
with a potted history of the country. This history is mainly the history of a series of invasions. There is first of all the mythological
story of Noah's niece, who led the first band of conquerors. Then
the stories of subsequent mythological and historic invasions are
enumerated, one wave after another: Partholans, Fomorians, the
Tuatha De Danann, Christian monks, Anglo-Normans, Elizabe-
thans, Cromwell and his soldiers and so forth. Harking back to the
first two sentences Edna O'Brien presents these various invasions
and, in a more general way, the whole of Ireland's history in sexual
terms. Most of the episodes from Irish history include what one
would normally have called a love interest but what is here better
referred to as a scene from the ever-raging battle of the sexes.

Naturally, the story of Devorgilla and her triangular relationship
with her husband Breifne O'Rourke and her lover Dermot Mac-
Murrough, who eventually seeks help from the English king, Henry
II, and brings in foreign armies, suits this purpose. Throughout the
book historical events are predominantly viewed with regard to the
sexual relations between history-making individuals and the gory
details of physical violence. In fact, the whole course of Irish history is seen as a history of forced possession. 'Rape' (p. 17) and

'violation of her [Ireland's] body and soul' (p. 11) are the actual words used.

On the level of the author's personal history, as that is what constitutes the autobiography, the story of the girl's experience of repression through indoctrination, 'warped incantation' (p. 84), is related. A series of incidents and memories are given which describe how certain physical sensations and sexual feelings are associated with guilt engendered by religion — whether this means being reprimanded for crossing one's legs for which "'Our Lady blushes whenever a woman does such an indecent thing'" (p. 38) or various attempts at seduction and carnal knowledge, 'the ultimate crime', 'a smear of the body' (p. 84).[6] One comes away with the impression that the autobiographical 'I' is simultaneously oversexed and guilt-ridden. And it is difficult to say which determines which. One instance which demonstrates this interdependence of sex, personal guilt and history very well is Queen Medb in the *Táin Bó Cuailgne,* who is the reason for the wars described in this saga. She is referred to as "'the rump of a misguiding woman'" (p. 28) and the immediate reaction of the narrator as a young girl is, 'The word rump sent shivers through you, shivers of shame' (p. 28). For Edna O'Brien looking back the tremendous influence of the Catholic Church, its teachings (especially on sexual matters in this case) and the feelings of guilt it engenders are responsible for the absence of balanced harmonious relationships between men and women. (True love must, therefore, be looked for in romances and novels.) Instead, the themes of sexual oppression and fear pervade these recollections. In her pessimistic view, courtships are referred to as 'desperate affairs', reduced to grunts behind hedges. Men seem to be lurking behind every page — or bush rather — with their flies open. From this perspective, which the adult author has not outgrown, the interdependence of, as it were, ontogenetic and phylogenetic patterns of experience in life and literature is given special emphasis. In other words, she clearly makes this connection between racial history and personal history explicit herself:

> The martyred Irish mother and the raving rollicking Irish father is not peculiar to the works of exorcized writers but common to families throughout the land. The children inherit a trinity of guilts (a Shamrock): the guilt for Christ's Passion and Crucifixion, the guilt for the plundered land, and the furtive guilt for the mother frequently defiled by the insatiable father. (p. 19)

In essence, *Mother Ireland* may be read as such 'a series of psychological projections onto Irish history and landscape.'[7] According to the double aspect of this recurrent motif or theme, which combines the realms of personal and national identity, two different sources can be isolated. Without putting too fine a point on it, one source is what one might call Edna O'Brien's sexual philosophy. In an often quoted interview with Nell Dunn, Edna O'Brien stated her idiosyncratic view of the basics of the eternal male-female difference. Of the sexual act she says,

> To some extent [a woman is] being violated or invaded because when the maidenhead is first broken it is a rupture. Each time and for evermore she must carry the memory of that first rupture no matter how she desired it. (p. 81)

The tell-tale metaphors ('violated', 'invaded') establish the basis for further metaphorical links between one Irishwoman's destiny and that of her mother country.

The other source feeding this image pattern in *Mother Ireland* must be sought in what could be termed political psychology and is far more obvious. The personification of Ireland as a woman is a traditional concept. In this concept several aspects of the female are compounded: virgin, bride, mother, old hag. In the tradition of national images and stereotypes, Hibernia is the virgin ravished or in danger of being ravished by the Sasannach, by John Bull, the masculine personification of colonial England. And in negative terms she is an old hag lifting her skirts to the invader. This tradition goes back to the Gaelic poetry of the eighteenth century and was taken up by the Anglo-Irish poets of the nineteenth century. As Richard Kearney notes, the mythical image of Ireland as a woman has also a religious, that is, Catholic, dimension from a majority point of view.[8] It was reinforced in the late nineteenth century by the emergence of a cult of the Virgin Mother. It was then given another turn around the time of the Easter Rising when Mother Eire came to be represented by Cathleen Ni Houlihan, the mother goddess who called her sons away from their brides in order to fight and eventually fulfill their blood-sacrifice for her. Yeats's eponymous play is the best-known manifestation of this image.[9]

Ernest Jones, the psychoanalyst, has claimed that 'references to Ireland as a woman, and especially as a mother, are innumerable in poems, speeches, and writings . . . .'[10] He argued that the idea of an island home fosters the central psychological concept of the womb of a virgin mother as the universal goal of unconscious desires (1:98). And Edna O'Brien seems to have adopted this archetypal sexual psychology. In the interview already mentioned she expatiates on the differences between men and women in this vein:

> [. . .] the reason I think on the whole that women are more discontent than men is [. . .] that there is, there must be, in every man and every woman the desire, the deep primeval desire to go back to the womb. Now physically and technically really, [. . .] a man partly and symbolically achieves this when he goes into a woman. He goes in and becomes sunken and lost in her. A woman never, ever, approaches that kind of security.[11]

This denial of the possibilities of the Oedipal myth is, as Edna O'Brien called it elsewhere, the 'principal crux of female despair' (Roth p. 40) and constitutes a central theme in her work. According to Peggy O'Brien, it is at the base of her most authentic writing.[12] It also gives away the clue to an understanding of the ending of *Mother Ireland,* which the reader without this background knowledge may find mystifying and pathetic:

> I live out of Ireland because something in me warns me that I [. . .] might grow placid when in fact I want yet again and for indefinable reasons to trace that same route, that trenchant childhood route, in the hope of finding some clue that will, or would, or could, make possible the leap that would restore one to one's original place and state of consciousness, to the radical innocence of the moment just before birth. (p. 89)

Apart from being a description in so many words of the autobiographical impulse, the land itself once again becomes associated with that archetypal psycho-mythical desire.

The attitude of the writer towards her country is at best ambivalent, a love-hate relationship. In *Vanishing Ireland,* a travelogue which summarizes her observations on a recent visit to Ireland and which, for the most part, is a blasting comment on Irish backwardness, she continues this theme:

> I was coming home to the country of my birth, the country I could hardly claim to have left, since it occupies so much of my

thoughts and a great deal of my fiction. The old emotions started up
— pity, exasperation, heartache, the need to flee. Growing up in Ireland is unlike growing up anywhere else. There is more emotion per
square yard than there is anywhere else. That has not changed, at least
not in the country, where the attachment to home and hearth is as deep
and as binding as the longing to escape it.[13]

There is uppermost 'the quarrel with Ireland', the resentment she
still feels for having been 'warped' and psychologically stifled. To
escape this she had of course to go into exile. On the other hand she
bears a deep affection and loyalty for the country. 'Irish? In truth
I would not want to be anything else', she confesses at the end of
Mother Ireland. (p. 88)

Having to leave one's country in order to be able to write about it
has been treated definitively in Joyce's life and work. And Edna
O'Brien like many another modern Irish writer follows his
example. Cynics will argue that Ireland has not changed much
since Joyce's time and childhood experiences must necessarily be
similar and precipitate similar results. However, beyond following
the model set by Joyce's real-life exodus from Ireland Edna O'Brien
also follows very closely in his wake as regards the transposition of
that life experience into her work and into *Mother Ireland* in particular. In the context of her psychosexual philosophizing it is not
surprising to note that Edna O'Brien takes a special interest in the
intimate details of Joyce's life, as is evident from her essay 'A
Portrait of Joyce's Marriage.'[14] She has often acknowledged
Joyce's influence on her own work.[15] Joycean echoes pervade her
oeuvre and have been pointed out[16] where they are not obvious.
There are, for example, the parallels between the beginning of
A Portrait and *A Pagan Place,* between the final chapter of *Ulysses*
and the interior monologues of *Night* and *Johnny I Hardly Knew
You. Mother Ireland* itself takes up some of the crucial scenes from
A Portrait while touching on them and presenting them in a slightly
less exalted atmosphere: the vocation to become a nun (p. 71), the
vivid descriptions of hell-fire (p. 59), and throughout, the associa-
tion of sex with guilt. Most important of all, however, is the theme
of exile. Stephen Dedalus when asked by a friend about the motives
for his intended departure from Ireland had entered into his diary:
'Told him that the shortest way to Tara was via Holyhead.' And
Edna O'Brien, as we know from her last chapter entitled 'Escape to
England,' took exactly the same route. In the very last paragraph

she tells us that she lives out of Ireland, because it is only when she is free from the manacles of fear and repression that she can explore 'that trenchant childhood route.'[17] As discussed, that route in psychological terms leads to an archetypal nostalgia for the womb or a pre-lapsarian state of grace. This may not sound like much but read in conjunction with the themes of exile and nationhood the psychological and personal acquires racial dimensions.

In the final chapter Edna O'Brien also reflects on the function of the autobiographical memory:

> It is true that a country encapsulates our childhood and those lanes, byres, fields, flowers, insects, suns, moons and stars are forever recurring and tantalizing me with a possibility of a golden key which would lead beyond birth to the roots of one's lineage. Irish? (p. 88)

Could it be that 'the roots of one's lineage' are synonymous with 'the uncreated conscience of his race' which Stephen Dedalus sailing for Europe is going 'to forge in the smithy of his soul'? Racial memory and the deepest psycho-sexual desires of the returning exile may well be the same thing for Edna O'Brien given her pan-sexual world-view. If this is so, then the models of Joyce and the artist in exile go a great way towards reinforcing an interpretation which stresses the interdependence of personal and national identity (and psychology) in Irish autobiographies.

'PROPER WORDS IN PROPER PLACES': JONATHAN SWIFT ON LANGUAGE

VERONIKA KNIEZSA

With *A Proposal for Correcting, Improving and Ascertaining the English Tongue* (Swift 1957b:1–21) Jonathan Swift joins the ranks of those English men of letters who thought necessary to found an Academy following the model of the Italian Accademia della Crusca and the French Academie. In his opinion the main tasks of such an academy would be the correction and fixing of the language. Improvements should be based on the text of the Holy Script and the fixing of the standard forms would be necessary, where again the Bible could be taken as an example. In his opinion language should change as little as possible, after all, he argued, the Bible's two hundred year old text was still understandable all over the country. He believed linguistic changes to be weaknesses which should be avoided. In *Gulliver's Travels* he described the drawbacks of such changes: 'The language of this country being always upon the Flux, the Struldbruggs of one Age do not understand those of another; neither are they able after two Hundred Years to hold any Conversation (farther than by a few general Words) with their Neighbours the Mortals, and thus they lye under the Disadvantage of living like Foreigners in their own Country' (Swift 1959:213). Swift also warns against newfangled words, '...I have since found that the Sea-Yahoos are apt, like the Land ones, to become new fangled in their Words; which the latter change every Year, insomuch, as I remember upon each Return to mine own Country, their old Dialect was so altered, that I could hardly understand the new.' In the letter published in the *Tatler* No. 230 (1711) (Swift 1957a:173–7), he gives a list of such lexical innovations which he greatly disapproved on stylistic principles: fashionable colloquialisms creeping into the written medium. He repeated his disagreement in the *Letter to a Young Gentleman Lately Entered into*

Holy Orders where he warned the addressee from using fashionable words. 'I suppose the Hearers can be little edified by the terms of Palming, Shuffling, Biting, Bamboozling and the like if they have not been sometimes conversant among Pick-pockets and Sharpers' (Swift 1963:68). In his opinion 'Proper Words in Proper Places, makes the true definition of a Style' (1963:65). Swift's aim apparently was the standardisation of written language where he praised clarity of expressions and simplicity of words. Barbara Strang in an essay on Swift's ideas and practice quotes from the introduction to the 1786 edition of *Gulliver's Travels,* on Swift's asking two menservants whether they had understood the meaning of the writing read out before them (Strang 1968:1949). The idea occurs also in the *Letter to a Young Clergyman* where he suggests avoiding hard words. He explained how Lord Falkland 'when doubted whether a word was perfectly intelligible or no ... used to consult one of his Lady's Chambermaids (not the Waiting woman, because it was possible she might be conversant in Romances)'. Harold Williams was of the opinion that the advice given to the Young Clergyman set down the rules for the standardisation of the spoken medium as well.

Swift disapproved of the coinage of new words. Strang has discovered that though the OED lists a considerable number of new coinages and nonce words which are marked by their first occurrence in Swift's works, these are much less than in the writing of any other author of similar authority in the seventeenth or eighteenth centuries. One of the major issues in Swift's writings is the so-called clipped or curtailed words, which Strang also treats at length.

Swift was immediately accepted as a prose writer and though his style seemed too barren to his contemporaries, too much lacking in adornment and graceful terms, his 'masterly conciseness' was greatly admired. Moreover, his prose continues to be admired and analysed in our times. Swift the poet, on the other hand seems to be more neglected. Linguists do not appear to be interested in the material the poet has to offer. Starting out from the remark made by the editor, Harold Williams, that Swift followed the same high stylistic aims in his poetry that he set up in his prose works, a brief description of his poems follows. There is a considerable change in Swift's poetic achievements through the decades of his activity. In the early poems written at the period when he published them in *Miscellanies,* a joint venture with Pope, he followed the require-

ments of heroic poetry both in topic and form and used elevated
expressions in carefully set stanzas with very complicated rhyme
patterns. In his late poetry topic, style, rhyme, verse form changed
into ironically phrased occasional pieces expressed in everyday
terms in couplets. Since the prose writings in which he set down his
ideals concerning language and style are contemporary to the early
poems, it should be interesting to confront them with the late
poems in order to find out how his theory compares to his later
practice.

One of the major topics in the prose essays, the Letter in the *Tatler* and the *Proposal* is Swift's stand against the so-called clipped
or curtailed words. There is a long list of them in *Tatler* 230. *Phizz,
Hipp, Mobb, Pozz, Rep,* also 'Some words are hitherto but fairly
split, and therefore only in their way to perfection; as *Incog* and
Plenipo's. But in a short Time it is to be hoped, they will be further
docked to *Inc* and *Plen*' (Swift 1975a:175–6). He remarked further on that he had tried to stop the progress of *mob* with no avail,
and complained that he had been let down by people who promised
assistance in his struggle against this form. This may be a reference
to Addison, who published a letter in the *Spectator* No. 135 a year
later, in 1711, in which he raised the same issues as Swift in the
Tatler letter. Addison raised his word against *mob, rep, poz, incog,*
wryly adding 'as all ridiculous Words take their first entry into a
Language by familiar Phrases, I dare not answer for them that they
will not in time be looked upon as a part of our Tongue' (Bolton
1966:104). In the case of *mob* Addison has been proven right! 'It is
well known that Swift returns to these issues in later life, in *Polite
Conversation* (1738)' — continues Strang, 'perhaps less well
known that similar points are made in a 1737 letter to Pope'. Herbert Davies dates — at least the beginning — of the composition of *Polite Conversation* to the 1710s, thus the clipped words
in it may be contemporary to the *Tatler* Letter and the *Proposal.* In
the letter to Pope Swift complains again about 'abominable cur-
tailing and quaint modernisms' which according to Professor
Sherburn (as quoted by Harold Williams) may be an objection
against some characteristics of Pope's text itself. (It is interesting to
note that the OED has several quotations for *mob* from Pope's
writings). It is even less known perhaps that there is a brief reference of the issue in *Gulliver's Travels,* where in the School of
Languages of Laputa three professors sat in Consultation upon
improving the language of their country. Their first project was 'to

shorten Discourse by cutting Polysyllables into one, and leaving out Verbs and Participles' (Swift 1957:185). And maybe the least expected is the appearance of these clipped words in the late poems. All the words Swift objected to, with the exception of the most hated *mob,* appear in his poems. That these forms, however, conveyed special stylistic values and represented a deliberate poetic purpose is indicated by the fact that all of them occur in rhyme-position which draws special attention to them; moreover, they usually are emphasized by different type-characters. (At the end of the quotations there is the date of the composition of the poem.) We can check each of the items of the *Tatler* list of clipped words against Samuel Johnson's Dictionary to find out their stylistic value almost half a century later, especially since the OED claims that the first appearance of these forms in written texts were found about the end of the seventeenth century: *plenipo* 1687, *phizz, mob* 1688, *incoq* 1700, *rep* 1705, *hip, poz* 1710.

> But now observe my Councel *(viz)*
> Adapt your Habit to your PHIZ
> (1720. Swift 1958. III.779:211–1)

Phiz received a separate entry in Samuel Johnson's Dictionary (1834:873): 'This word is formed by a ridiculous contraction from *physiognomy* and should therefor, if written at all, be written *phyz'*, showing Johnson's doubt about the justification of the form, but it is accompanied by a quotation by Stepney. The OED merely explains the abbreviation without stylistic remarks.

> And all Men believe he presides there *incog.*
> To give them Turns as invisible Jog.
> (1724; Swift 1958, III.805:15–6)

'INCOG adv. [corrupted by mutilation from *Incognito* Lat.]' followed by a quotation from Addison (Johnson 1834:621). 'HIP adj. a corruption of *Hypochondriack*' without any quotations in Johnson (1834:580). According to OED, *hip, hipps* (since 1710) developed a special meaning: 'Morbid depression of the spirit, the "blues"', already discernible in the Swift letter (1957b:172). *Poz, Plenipo, Rep* were not entered into Johnson's dictionary.

When you're advance'd above Dean VIZ
You'll never think of Googy GRIZ
(1724; Swift 1958, II.362:43–4).

Griz is not entered into the dictionaries; *viz* is strongly disapproved
by Johnson: 'A barbarous form of an unnecessary word'
(1834:1270), which is dated to 1540 by OED. The Johnson quotations show the stylistic status of these recent abbreviations of
which *mob* seems to be about to lose its colloquial character in the
middle of the eighteenth century; *phizz, incoq* were merely toler-
ated on a familiar level; while others apparently went out of use
quite soon.

Strang made a long list of the instances where Swift had changed
all the apostrophed past tense forms of the verbs to the more expanded *-ed* in the later editions of his writings, and doing so, he
deliberately used a more formal written form instead of the one he
used in his earlier, and especially more private writings: where, for
example, *dropt* etc. was quite common and which of course corres-
ponded also to his own pronunciation. Both in the *Tatler* letter and
the *Proposal* Swift condemned the practice of his fellow poets who,
in order to maintain the metre, would sacrifice syllables and mark
the loss of the vowel by an apostrophe: 'These Gentlemen ... to
save Time and Pains introduced that barbarous Custom of abbre-
viating Words, to fit them to the Measure of their Verse'. (Swift
1957b:11) This issue also was taken up by Addison in the Spectator
letter where Addison's text is peppered with *'d* verbs even in the
paragraphs he wrote against apostrophed forms. But what do we see
in his own poems: 'But what does our proud *Ign'rance* Learning
call' (Swift 1958. I.27:28) in an early poem written in Heroic Verse.
In the *Tatler* Letter he gives whole passages with the objectionable
forms: '...and then I'd ha' bro't 'um, but I ha'n't don't...' and so
forth, but in his poems we can find: 'Tho' the Thought be Apollo's,
'tis finally express'd' (Swift 1958, I.266:91).

There are examples of pronunciation representing more collo-
guial forms:

With Ladies what a strict Decorum:
What Devotion you adore 'um!'
(Swift 1958, III.889:51–2)

Strang was puzzled over Swift's fervour on the topic, explaining that this custom was not a new development and it had nothing whatever to do with poetic license, as Swift seems to believe it did. Or did he? An investigation of his verse reveals that all the items he condemned in his prose writing duly appeared in his own poems. It seems to be a perfect case for 'Don't do what I do, do what I say'.

Strang remarked that Swift 'was strikingly ignorant of phonology, synchronic or historical', as there is a relative absence of reference to phonology in his discussions of English (Strang 1968:1950). It is true that most of his concern was about euphony. That was the reason for his strong opposition against apostrophied words, which in his opinion unfavourably increased monosyllables in English, already abounding in consonants. In respect of pronunciation he would rather have trusted 'the Refinement of our Language, as far as it relates to Sound, to the Judgment of the Women', as they seemed to prefer vowels to consonants. He also mentioned an 'experiment' where people were asked to write letters one after the other at random, 'and upon reading this Gibberish we have found that which the Men had writ, by the frequent encountering of rough Consonants to sound like *High Dutch,* and the other by the Women, like Italian abounding in Vowels and Liquids' (Swift 1957b:13).

It would be too much to expect Swift to write on pronunciation; his age still was a transitory one where sound changes had just settled. Examining Edward Bysshe's early eighteenth-century rhyme dictionary, it becomes apparent that in poetry both old mode and new developments were used side by side, and poets especially were free to use the kind of pronunciation which fitted their verse better. There was a strong tendency in standardising grammar, usage and spelling but not in settling for a standard pronunciation. Moreover, Swift himself was a Hiberno-English speaker and could not be in an easy position to expound on the question of pronunciation. But if we scan his less theoretical writings, we find ample examples representing his ideas about pronunciation, (See, for example, 'Discourse to Prove the Antiquity of the English Language', 'A Modest Defence on Punning' and so forth with their 'shameless puns and utter nonsense' [Swift 1975:229–39; 203–10]). Besides, a poet of some standing cannot be excused on the basis of his ignorance of pronunciation, as a study of Swift's rhymes proves (Kniezsa 1986).

It is quite evident that Swift was just as aware of the diversity of the English language as authors like John of Trevisa, Chaucer, Caxton and others since the Middle English period. Swift notes that 'in London they clip their words after one Manner about the Court, another in the City, and a third in the Suburbs' (Swift 1957b:11), a remark which does not seem to carry any judgement on the variants, but from *On Barbarous Denominations in Ireland* we learn that 'the trading people have an affected Manner, and so in my time had many Ladies and Coxcombs at Court' (Swift 1957b:281).

If Swift seems to remain indifferent to the various pronunciations of England, he was far from being free from the age old prejudice against the northern way of speech, a feeling authors gave vent to since the fourteenth century. 'There is an odd provincial cant in most counties in England sometimes not very pleasing to the ear, and the Scotch cadence, as well as expression, are offensive enough' (1957b:281). But what he found most deplorable was the way people spoke in Ireland. In his opinion 'what we call the Irish Brogue is no sooner discovered, than it makes the deliverer, in the last degree, ridiculous and despised; and from such a mouth, an Englishman expects nothing but bulls, blunders and follies', he especially resents the fact that these speakers throw bad light on those who had 'the misfortune of being born in Ireland, although of English parents' (Swift 1957b:281).

From the twin burlesques: *Dialogue in Hibernian Style* and *Irish Eloquence* (Swift 1957b:277–9) we cannot learn much about the nature of this broque. The two pieces list some Hibernisms, mostly developed due to the influence of the Irish language upon the English of the planters. There are examples of sentence structure (*'Pray, how does he get his Health?'*) and vocabulary (*'stirabout'* *'porridge'*, as well as the interesting case of *'unwell'*, which apparently was unusual in standard usage in Swift's time, but since has been introduced into the standard vocabulary). In *An Examination of Certain Abuses, Corruptions and Enormities in the City of Dublin* (Swift 1955:213–33) he starts with complaints about the unintelligibility of the cries by which street vendors offered their wares. One would believe it was the curious local pronunciation, the Irish Brogue, that rendered them difficult especially for strangers, but when he gave some examples of these cries, it became apparent that it was the wording he objected to: 'Mugs, jugs, porringers, up in the garret, and down in the cellar' which announced the approach of the milkman, and 'Herrings alive, alive here!', which preceeded the fish monger (Swift 1955:213–32). There are very few indications to unusual pronunciation, only in the case of two instances may we deduct the departure from the standard spelling form can refer to the local pronunciation: 'Will you *tast* a glass of my ale?' where the short vowel could indicate a dialectal development, not necessarily Irish, but probably imported to Ireland from England. The word occurs with the standard spelling but rhyming with a word with a short vowel in: 'His way of writing now is past / The Town hath got a better Taste'. (Swift 1958, II.563:265–6) This type of rhyme was not discussed by Wyld (1965). Though Gabrielsson found hast : taste : defast and so forth rhymes used by Spenser, Pope and Byron, and in his analysis he labelled them as 'irrelevant and uncertain cases' which 'though numerous prove nothing' (Gabrielsson 1909:68, 160). He apparently did not find lists for AST : ASTE rhymes in Bysshe's rhyming dictionary (Gabrielsson 1930). Ellis quotes the rhyme past : taste from Pope with the remark that it 'would probably never have been used had they not been an heritage from the preceding century, But Pope may have had an antique pronunciation' (Ellis 1875, IV.1070ff). Dobson discusses words like taste as belonging to a Middle English quantitative variation (Dobson 1968, II.527). Thus it is difficult to decide whether the form in 'Irish Eloquence' truly represent Hiberno-English pronunciation.

There is one more instance: 'I always brew with my own Beare'. Bear 'beer' according to Bliss (1979:193) reflects a form which represented the lovering of ME (e:) > (ɛ :). He quotes another example occurring in the rhyme pair: beares : yeares, though he remarks 'it might also represent another tendency, i. e. the raising of ME (ɛ :) as in "year" to (e:) as in "beer".' The question is how much store should be set on the spelling. 'Bear' is not repeated in Irish Eloquence and in Davis's editions (Swift 1967:217) it is marked that in a deleted line it occurred with the usual spelling: <beer>.

A difficult case is 'I was at your Cozen Tom's house' (three times spelled this way, and two times with the standard spelling 'cousin' occurring in both texts (Swift 1957b:276). There is no reference anywhere to [~ u : o] correspondences exemplified by 'cozen'. (Though the same vowel appears in the abbreviated form in Shakespeare's *Henry IV:* 'coz'), neither are rhymes mentioned like Swift's

> But when her breakfast gives her courage
> Then, think of Stella's chicken porridge.
>   (Swift 1958, II.761:5—6),

which might represent parallels.

A very frequent type of rhyme in Swift's poetry may represent a west country dialect pronunciation, even if most of the rhyme pairs belonged to the contemporary poetic tradition. Such is the rhyme pair say : sea, which are homonyms in the western part of Britain and Ireland, but represent two different sounds, (e)˜(ei) : (i:) elsewhere in the country. This type of rhyme was sanctioned by tradition so much so that Wyld considered a regular merger between ME (ai) an ME (ɛ :), and described ME (ɛ :)>(i:) and its merger at this level with ME (e:) a later development (Wyld 1966). When considered in the poetry of, for example, Pope and Swift, there will be a considerable difference in the frequency of these rhymes. Though occurring quite frequently elsewhere, (ai) : (ɛ :) rhymes represent about 5.5% of all the rhymes in Swift's poetic works. (Compare with Kniezsa 1986):

> And by their never-failing ways
> Of solving all Appearance they please
>   (Swift 1958, I.19:17–8).

Rhymes between (u) and (^) also belong to the special cases of Hiberno-English pronunciation:

> A stop to Literature be put
> And the Museums's Gates be shut
>   (Swift 1958, I.19:17–18).

as in this dialect ME (u) remained a rounded high back vowel in every position. Similar rhymes were found in Byron's poems by Gabrielsson (1909) where it was the Scottish background of Byron which led him to use such rhymes, since in Scots ME (u) developed uniformly into (^) (Compare also Kniezsa 1986).

Where the written form is concerned, Swift appears to be a severe critic and condemns every deviation from the accepted norm. Therefore he rejects every attempt at spelling reform which would be phonetic: 'Which beside the obvious Inconvenience of utterly destroying our Etymology, would be a Thing we should never see

an End of ... there are different pronunciations in the country ...
All which reduced to Writing would ultimately confound Orthography'. (Swift 1957b:11) In his writings, however, if he wanted to
indicate one way of pronunciation instead of another, he himself
departed from the usual written form, as could be seen from the two
examples from 'Irish Eloquence' above. <enuff> is quite frequent
in the poems, if it appears in rhymes, especially when rhymed with
UFF words (less frequently when in connection to other OUGH
pronounced with [ˆf]:

> Carve to all but just enuff
> Let them neither starve nor stuff.
> (Swift 1958, II.633:129–30).

From Bysshe we know that in the late seventeenth through the early
eighteenth centuries *enough* could rhyme both with UFF and
OUGH words, as in Swift:

> An act for lying down the Plough,
> England will send you corn enough.
> (Swift 1958, II.422:51–2).

As enough occurs equally frequently as <enough> even when
rhyming with UFF words, it is difficult to account for the significance of the <enuff> spellings.

<agen> on the other hand is clearly intentional, as *again* usually
rhymes with other AIN words in Swift's poetry:

> Whether in time. deduction's broken chain
> Meets and salutes her sister link again.
> (Swift 1958, I.54:3–4),

as usual in the western dialects, but in the case of:

> And Vacation's over — then
> Hey for Dublin Town agen!
> (Swift 1958, II.574:55–6)

the phonetic spelling is an indication of the shortened vowel, an
East Midland feature (Dobson 1968, I.:498–9) and stresses the
ironic tone of the poem. This is proven by 'agen' appearing as the

final word in the poem, especially since this particular form appeared in the *Tatler* Letter among the abuses of the language Swift complained about: 'Tis said the *French* King will *bamboozel* us *agen*'. (Swift's italics, 1957a:174)

The context for *caveer* is a poem whose tone is also ironic:

> And for our home-bred British Chear,
> Botargo, Catsup and Caveer.
> (Swift 1958, III.895:267–8)

Samuel Johnson wrote: 'CAVI'ER: n.s. A corruption of *caviar*. See catsup' (where we can find the above Swift quotation: Johnson 1845:178). The OED gives the same quotation, but is of the opinion that '*caveer* is a recognised archaic form' (together with *caviarie* quoted from Shakespeare). But observing the context, we have to accept Johnson's explanation of the form, and that Swift intentionally used this corruption, especially if we bear in mind forms occurring elswhere:

> Ripe 'Sparagrass,
> Fit for Lad and Lass
> (Swift 1958, III. 952)

representing non-standard mispronunciation. The vowel in *caveer* seems to be a similar sound substitution for an otherwise unfamiliar sound sequence [i'a].

A quantitative and qualitative analysis of Swift's rhymes (Kniezsa 1986) allowed a glimpse into his art of versification. It revealed the fact that he was in full command of the poetic tradition and practice of his time. He preferred perfect rhymes, sometimes reflecting his own Hiberno-English pronunciation, though some features (such as, pairs like *say : sea*) were in common use among his contemporaries. He was not very fond of rhymes which, though traditional, were only eye rhymes according to contemporary pronunciation. Where he violated the rules of versification of the times, he did so in full awareness of style, and his rhymes were still acceptable for the form he had chosen, they served well the occasional, pamphlet-like character of his poems, assuring the unity of theme and form.

Swift proved to be a keen observer of the language. He noticed that pronunciation, choice of words, the whole attitude towards language greatly depends on sex, religion and social status. As every speaker of the English language, he too was aware of the great regional diversity of English and accordingly had his own likes and dislikes among the varieties.

In his writings on language: the Letter in *Tatler* No. 230, the *Proposal,* even in the *Letter to the Young Gentleman* he strived at the standardisation not only of the written language, which was the usual concept of his time, but also of the spoken medium, based on the text of the Bible which he regarded as the tool of 'use and custom' handed down by the centuries.

In the above mentioned pieces he especially warned against the danger that vulgarisms and the 'newest set of phrases' might creep into writing, where they are not only entirely improper, but run a greater risk of being imitated and thus corrupt further the language. His smaller pieces in which he collected all those linguistic sins, which form the basis of his more theoretical writings probably aim to ridicule the fashionable society who should have known better than to invent, use and what is more propagate such linguistic 'nonsense'. These various works clearly complement each other and represent Swift the stylist, whose works, prose and verse, show an admirable union of form and content.

MARIA EDGEWORTH AND THE TRADITION OF IRISH SEMIOTICS

MARTIN J. CROGHAN

Jonathan Swift had intended to publish a study of stereotyping in the form of a jeremiad against the English as revenge for their symbolic violence against the Irish; in the form of an act of homage by intellectual disciples, Maria Edgeworth, with her father, Richard Lovell Edgeworth, wrote the study of stereotyping which also manages to be a diatribe against the English. The *Essay on Irish Bulls* (1802) of the Edgeworths[1] which borrows some of its language from Swift, deals with the symbolic violence perpetrated against the Irish by the English, and in paricular it deals with the symbolic violence which was contained in what Swift called the 'Irish Brogue' and the Irish 'bulls, blunders and follies'.[2] The negative portrayal of the Irish as illustrated by the Irish bull is treated as an empirical case-study and in the best intellectual tradition the examples are used to illustrate a set of explanatory concepts which form the basis for the analysis of stereotyping.

To prove that the bull of stage-Irishism has no logical foundation, a variety of theoretical arguments are used and examples are culled from the best historical and contemporary writing, both literature and other types of writing in English, French, Latin and Greek. Because the authors also wanted to be seen to win the argument and to convince their readers absolutely, no trick is spared in the task of communication and propaganda. A variety of genres and styles are used, including stage-Irish writing, sentimental stories, and an extended Socratic type of dialogue — a form which had also been used dramatically by Swift. The language is sometimes formal, sometimes informal; standard English is used but also brogue-write. The text is peppered with sarcasm and satire, and sometimes the language of a most vicious symbolic violence is used against the English, the Scots and especially the Welsh about whom nothing good is ever said and who do not even seem to be regarded as part of the Union. Nor is the *Essay* shy about using a vast array of stage-Irish bulls and jokes, sometimes written in ridiculous brogue-write, to make sure the reader is kept amused. Ironically, the popularity of the *Essay* in the nineteenth century seems to have been due to this collection of amusing bulls, and when G. R. Neilson edited the text in 1898 he omitted those aspects of the text which he regarded as 'censorious — even ill-natured' and published only its 'stories — not its comments or moralising.' Neilson also added over fifty pages of fresh bulls 'to bring the collection made by Dr. and Miss Edgeworth up to date.'[4]

The aggressive title of the first chapter, 'Vulgar Errours', signals the authors' mood and in the first few pages a primary thesis of the *Essay* is stated. Mental conceptions may have no relationship with reality, and the proposition is supported by a quotation from Thomas Browne's *An Enquiry into Vulgar Errors,* which had been published in 1660: '... in most apprehensions the conceits of men extend the considerations of things, and dilate their notions beyond the propriety of their natures'. (p. 3) Swift had called such 'conceits' and 'notions' grossest suppositions when they generated the discourse of symbolic violence against the Irish. The Browne epistemology had been converted into a semiotic framework when Swift said in his essay 'On Barbarous Denominations in Ireland,' that it is when false conceptions are regarded as fact that the greatest damage is done; the negative portrayal of the Irish in stage-Irishism as illustrated by the brogue and the bull, becomes grossest supposition when such a portrait of the Irish is regarded as reality.[5] In the first chapter, the *Essay* also attacks the fundamental philosophy behind stage-Irishism which rests on any type of biological or mechanistic principle: 'that there exists amongst the natives of Ireland an innate and irresistible propensity to blunder'. (pp. 3–4)

The first chapter also provides plenty of examples of the type of satire and sarcasm which is found throughout the *Essay:* 'As there are no toads, or serpents, or vipers in this favoured island, it must necessarily abound with Irish bulls'. (p. 7) Sarcastic humility, a virtue also beloved of Swift, asks how could the Irish learn the English language which is so complex and difficult that it 'is only to be acquired after long labour by the brightest, and most cultivated genius, assisted by all the advantages of books and society'. (p. 8) But in the beginning of the third chapter the argument comes back to a key conceptual concern when the Edgeworths apply the Swift warning about the dangers of idle fancy being treated as reality, especially when such caprice appears in the form of international stereotypes:

> That species of monopolising pride, which inspires one nation with the belief that all the rest of the world are barbarians, and speak barbarisms, is evidently a very useful prejudice, which the English, with their usual good sense, have condescended to adopt from the Greeks and the Romans. (p. 19)

The Edgeworths provide a lenghty analysis of identity and the process involved in the formation of individual and group identity, stressing that the adoption of an identity is a mental operation. The analysis concludes with a statement about the real purpose of symbolic violence, and in particular about the danger of a group adopting the negative identity imposed on it from outside. The passage is also a good example of the Swiftean anger of the *Essay:*

> Impute a peculiar incurable mental disease to a given people, show that it incapacitates them from speaking or acting with common sense, expose their infirmities continually to public ridicule, and in time probably this people, let their constitutional boldness be ever so great, may be subjugated to that sense of inferiority, and to that acquiesence in a state of dependance, which is the necessary consequence of the conviction of imbecility. (p. 20)

The first few pages of this third chapter entitled 'Originality of Bulls Disputed', are taken up with theory and then in the rest of the chapter and in the next chapters there is an illustration of the comparative scholarship which underpins the whole *Essay,* be this a review of a French study of *bons mots* in Arabic, Farsi and Turkish or of bulls in English newspapers. Collections of jokes and bulls from English jest books from the sixteenth century onwards had also been consulted and in the middle chapters of the book, the Edgeworths pile on examples while continually reminding the reader of a theoretical perspective. The authors are also not above using an emotional historical allusion in order to fashion a mischievous analogy: 'It was formerly in law no murder to kill a *merus Hibernicus;* and it is to this day no offence against good manners to laugh at any of this species'. (p. 57)

Immediately after this extravagant comparison, the text returns to a sober argument when the furtive role of humour in symbolic violence is exposed. It is an important pointer of the standard of thinking in the *Essay on Irish Bulls,* in contrast with many present-day studies of different types of symbolic violence, that the Edgeworths never deny that Irish bulls can be funny (and they themselves provide a plentiful supply, and as stated earlier, they sometimes use Irish bulls to keep the reader's attention). In the Edgeworths there is no denial that violence can be humorous and humour can be violent. Symbolic violence is evil, but the bulls may be funny, and in countering symbolic violence the weapons of the enemy should be adopted: 'It is of a thousand times more consequence to have the laugh than the argument on our side...' (p. 58) The proposal for the defence against symbolic violence does not concern itself with morality, a philosophy which should be a warning that easy stereotypes of a country vicar and his prudish daughter might be of little use in assessing some of the writings of the Edgeworths: 'We need not in imitating them have any scruples of conscience'. (p. 58)

In a chapter called 'Little Dominick' the emphasis turns to getting sympathy for the general thesis of the *Essay.* The story is told of a young Irish orphan in Wales who is persecuted for his way of speaking English by sadistic Welsh teachers and students, and whose only friend is a young English boy. What is of interest in the chapter is how the Edgeworths use different varieties of brogue-write. A Welsh teacher who continually persecutes the young Irish boy for his defective English is portrayed as a pompous fool when he scolds the defenseless child in a dense Welsh brogue: 'Cot pless me, you plockit, and shall I never learn you enclish crammer'. (p. 60) When the boy answers the question 'Who is your father?' with 'I have no father — I am an orphan — I have only a mother', there is a reprimanding footnote to the Iliad (p. 71) — where Andromache tells Hector 'You will make your son an orphan, and your wife a widow' — as warning to the reader that it would be very stupid to regard the little Irish boy's answer as a bull. (p. 71) This reference gives notice, and this is a tactic used throughout the *Essay,* that what ignorant foreigners sometimes regard as foolish Irish bulls may also be found in the best writers and thinkers, even in the classics; bulls may be in the mind of the fool who has no understanding of the rich potential of language. We also get an example of Irish brogue-write at the end of the chapter. When 'Little Dominick' is grown up he can only remind his former English friend who he is, by reverting to his former speech: '. . . and must I spake to you again in my old irish brogue, before you ricollict your own little Dominick'. (p. 85)

The next chapter, 'The Bliss of Ignorance', returns to theory, and symbolic violence is now explained as arising from a desire to appear superior: 'Laughter always arises from a sense of real or imaginary superiority. . . (Such) laughter has its source in vanity, as the most ignorant are generally the most vain'. (p. 89)

There is nothing specifically Irish about so-called Irish bulls, the authors state, but the fallacy is facilitated by the use of some 'prefatory exclamation as — By my shoul and St. Patrick! By Jasus! Arrah Honey! My dear Joy! &c.' (p. 92) This same point is also elaborated on later in the text when the Edgeworths make the telling point that concrete imagery enhances abstract humour: 'To many people, the most stale and vulgar irish bull would appear more laughable, merely because it was Irish'. (p. 232) Similarly, the importance of the brogue as a signal of the bull is also made, a point also made first by Swift, 'Whenever we hear the tone (brogue), we expect the blunder'. (p. 192)

In Chapter 8 with its graphic title, 'Thoughts that breathe, and words that burn,' there is a change of genre again. Hyperbole is said to be at the root of many bulls and there follows a comic section written in the best stage-Irish tradition, a description of an Irish hoaxer trying to bamboozle the judge in court. Later in the same chapter, quotations are used to show that what are sometimes regarded as Irish bulls are no different from the hyperbole of great writers such as Shakespeare:

> Cowards die many times before their death
> The brave can never taste of death but once.
>   (p. 113)

In the final chapters the relationship between certain types of hyperbole and certain figures of speech found in Hiberno-English are also alluded to. In the case of catachresis, for example, 'Necessity makes it borrow and employ an expression or term, contrary to the thing it means to express' (p. 223), and this, it is stated, 'is something like the definition of an Irish bull.' A favourite Swift myth, which is still popular, especially among Dubliners, is also adapted to give another explanation for those aspects of Hiberno-English which are sometimes regarded as bulls by the English: because 'the Irish, in general, speak *better* English than is commonly spoken by the natives of England' their English may easily be misunderstood by outsiders. (p. 199) In the chapter entitled 'Irish Wit and Eloquence' this chauvinistic argument is given full vent:[6]

> The Irish nation, from the highest to the lowest, in daily conversation about the ordinary affairs of life, employ a superfluity of wit, metaphor, and ingenuity, which would be astonishing and unintelligible to a majority of the respectable body of English yeomen. Even the cutters of turf and drawers of whisky are orators; even the *cottiers* (cottagers) and gossoons (Garcons, boys) speak in trope and figure. (p. 160)

Later we are told in the same vein: '...Hibernians possess that species of quickness of intellect, which necessarily lead to blunders'. (p. 187) In the conclusion to the *Essay* the Edgeworths sum up the linguistic imaginativeness of the Irish: '...the Irish are an ingenious generous people ... the bulls and blunders, of which they are accused, are ... produced by their habits of using figurative and witty language'. (p. 308)

In the final chapters which are written in dialogue form between an Irishman, a Scotsman and an Englishman, there is one strand of the argument which does not easily fit in with the general thesis of the study. It seems strange that full agreement is given to the national characteristics model, the model which has been the basis for phenomena such as stage-Irishism, antisemitism and different kinds of racism. The authors seem to want to admit that there there are group traits, and that if there are such characteristics then there must also exist the possibility of characteristics which are negative. In the dialogue, it is the Irishman who claims that there is a peculiar Irish bull, a thesis continually disputed by the Edgeworths up to this point: 'But, alas, there are physiognomies so strongly marked with national peculiarity, that it is impossible to disguise them completely. On the face of certain things there are characteristics, which cannot be counterfeited'. (p. 238) Later in the *Essay,* Maria Edgeworth admits that her novel *Castle Rackrent* (1800), published two years before the *Essay,* had been a caricature, but she excuses herself by saying that it was a story of the Irish of a bygone age, and anyway, the Irish were amused by the novel:[7] 'The Irish were the first to laugh at the caricatura of their ancient foibles, and it was generally taken merely as good humoured raillery, not as insulting satire'. (p. 309) The Edgeworth excuse for writing stage-Irishism could also be met by the argument some pages earlier — 'An Irishman can take what's said to him, provided no affront's meant, with more good humour than any man on earth' (p. 298) — but this type of rationalization is completely at variance with the analysis of the role of humour in symbolic violence discussed above.

The *Essay on Irish Bulls* on the whole is a powerful tour de force against symbolic violence, but it is forced to admit at the end that it is not able to cope with the national characteristics model, the model which is usually used to generate inter-group symbolic violence, whether the distinction between groups is based on ethnicity, religion, nationality, or sex. But the Edgeworth acceptance of the model — and their adoption of the model could hardly be regarded as enthusiastic — is hardly surprising when it is still commonly accepted, at least implicitly, in many areas of academia, and when it is realized that this same framework is entrenched in popular cultures in Westernized societies and in many Western languages.

Perhaps the most surprising deficiency in the *Essay* is that the Edgeworths ultimately failed to come to terms with brogue-write. They seemed to want to persist in a mode of thinking which assumes that there can somehow be an absolute correlation between a graphic and a phonic medium, despite the fact that in the 'Little Dominic' episode, the Edgeworths worked with the principle that brogue-write is an index of deviancy.[8] The Edgeworth failure to come to terms with the objective purpose of the brogue is also surprising for another reason. Swift, who was the inspiration for the Edgeworth *Essay on Irish Bulls,* had explicitly stated that it is the brogue which makes the deliverer 'ridiculous and despised' and that the brogue and the bull can only be understood as expressions of stage-Irishism; it was this quotation of Swift which the Edgeworths adapted in the *Essay* (see, n. 2).

In *Castle Rackrent* there is very little brogue-write or lexical markings of the mavourneen type,[9] but this radically changes in Maria Edgeworth's three *Comic Dramas in Three Acts* (1877).[10] In one of the plays, *The Rose, Thistle and Shamrock,* a variety of brogue-write is used to portray three contrasting types of Irish. An extreme brogue including mispelling, signals an Irish comic figure or rogue; in addition, these characters may also use real Hiberno-English. The virtuous lower class Irish use real Hiberno-English or a bogus code with changes in word order which generally do not violate the syntax of standard written English; brogue-write misspellings are not usually used for this second group. The language of the Irish landlord class is not graphically marked.

The stage for the three rogues and comic figures in the *The Rose, Thistle and Shamrock,* is an inn where, we are told by the English servant of an English gentleman who is visiting the local landlord, 'the pig is in and out of the kitchen all day long ... the calf has what they call the run of the kitchen ... the poultry ... is always under one's feet, or over one's head' (p. 264). Christy Gallagher, the landlord, who admits to being a rogue and 'the laughing stock of all that's in it' (p. 378), may use an extreme brogue when he rants with his daughter or servant or when he tries to impress the gentry with his magniloquence. The fustian and the brogue are given to the English gentry: 'Oh! Please your honor, I beg your pardon for one minute; — only just give me lave to insense (Insense, — to put sense into a person) your honor's honor'. (p. 371) When he talks to his daughter the language can almost seize up with the weight of the brogue: 'Troth, Florry, 'twas not I sint you there, sorrow fut (foot) but your mother.' (p. 278) The language of Christy's daughter, Florinda, a graduate of a finishing school, 'the dancing school of Ferrinafad' (p. 278), who wants to 'have my music and my piano in the back parlor, genteel' (p. 320), is sometimes so refined she talks with her 'drunken good-fornothing' father with language such as 'La, Sir, what a coarse question' (p. 321). Maria Edgeworth plays all the notes on the linguistic piano in the character of Florinda — but it is made clear from the language used on her first entrance that an Irish girl from a humble background with linguistic pretentions above her station is destined to make a fool of herself. In one speech, Florry uses a species of rococo English, 'Hark till I hear! — Is not that a drum I hear?' (p. 273), standard written English, Hiberno-English, 'But he'll kill himself soon with the whiskey, poor man, at the rate he's going' (pp. 274–5), and a brogue-write which uses ridiculous mispellings such as 'shutable' (p. 274). Biddy, the 'Maid of the Inn', is given the misspellings of the brogue and also sometimes tortured syntax in between snatches of real Hiberno-English:

But I wouldn't value all one pin's point, if it was kind and shivil (civil) she was to me ... and when I took the innions, and took the apple-pie off her hands, and settled her behind, and all to the best of my poor ability for her, after, to go and call me Sheelah na Ghirah! though I don't rightly know who that Sheelah na Ghirah was, from Adam! —

... Oh, if it had plased Heaven to have cast my lot in the sarvice of a
raal jantleman or lady, instead of the likes of these! (p. 285)

The three Irish who are not comic figures or rogues, but who are
of a low social class, are not generally marked with the misspelling
of brogue-write except for very rare items such as 'ye' and 'edica-
tion.' The three are, the Widow Larken, 'that respectable looking
woman,' her daughter Mabel, 'that girl with the sweet countenance,'
and her son Owen, 'that boy with the quick, intelligent eyes.' The
Widow is often marked by a bogus language whose hallmark is,
firstly, a convoluted structure on the level of the phrase and sentence, and, secondly, a deviant punctuation; both stylistic devices
were also used in *Castle Rackrent.* This spurious language is used,
presumably, to give the general impression of Hiberno-English,
and, especially through the employment of abnormal punctuation,
to give the impression that this written language is a perfect repro-
duction of spoken Hiberno-English:

It's a woman sure, should know that best sure. — And it is not Mabel,
nor a daughter of mine, nor a sister of yours, Owen, should be more
forward to understand, than the man is to speak, — was the man a
prince. (p. 305)

Mabel is generally represented by standard written English or real
Hiberno-English. In the following she uses Hiberno-English:
'That's true: — and may be it was that way he took it, — and may be
it? You're talking of going?' would be the normal punctuation).
uses brogue constructions as in the following item with its deviant
punctuation: 'What is it your talking of going?' (p. 336) ('What is
it? You're talking of going?' would be the normal punctuation).
Owen is portrayed as using a standard written code, and both real
Hiberno-English and constructions which use strained syntax:

The new inn, mother ... 'Tis the very thing for you. — Neat and
compact as a nutshell, not one of them grand inns, to great for the
place, that never answers no more than the hat that's too big for the
head, and that always blows off. (pp. 301–2)

The third type of Irish character in the play, Clara O'Hara, is a reminder that a discussion of identity and symbolic violence in Ireland is complex. In the *Essay on Irish Bulls* there is bitter and vio-

lent anger against the English, but a very different picture emerges in the play, *The Rose, Thistle and Shamrock.* Clara is an 'Irish heiress' who owns the town; she inherited the property from her Irish father, but her English links are signalled by the presence of her uncle, Sir William Hamden, an 'elderly English gentleman.' Clara is given standard written English, and no Hiberno-English or bogus code purporting to be Hiberno-English is used; brogue-write and misspellings are never used. While Clara's Irishness is not marked linguistically it is commented on directly and indirectly. Indeed she is so Irish that her English uncle says that 'a cool English head will be wanting to guide that warm Irish heart' (p. 310); she acts before she thinks and is too easily seduced by poetry. In case it might be suggested that this is the usual boring picture of the weak woman, Sir William Hamden's speech about the Irish character and about Clara's father, Sir Cormac, in particular, needs to be taken into account:

> Good beginnings, it is said, make good endings; but great beginnings often make little endings, or, in this country, no endings at all. Finis — coronat opus — and that crown is wanting wherever I turn my eyes. Of the hundred magnificent things your munificent father began — ... (p. 312)

One of the strangest lines gives to Clara comes when she introduces Christy Gallagher's name to her English uncle — 'A man with a strange name — or a name that will sound strange to your English ears' (p. 317) — which seems a little Irish coming from someone by the name of Clara O'Hara.

Of the other characters in the play, Sir William uses only standard written English, and, just as Clara can throw in a French phrase, the English gentleman uses Latin. The Scots drum-major, Mr. Andrew Hope, is so burdened with the repetition of 'gude,' that Florinda mocks him with 'His gude Kate,' adding, in case her sarcasm is not understood, 'Well, I hate the Scotch accent of all languages under the sun' (p. 352). In *The Rose, Thistle, and Shamrock* and her two other plays, *Love and Law,* and *The Two Guardians,* Maria Edgeworth uses direct and indirect linguistic marking to signal class, ethnicity and nationality (and race in *The Two Guardians*). When Christy asks about the Scottish soldiers 'Is it dumb they are all? or innocents?' (p. 291), because they do not understand him, even the humble Biddy Doyle takes part in the game of linguistic marking: 'Not all innocents! nor more than myself nor your self. — Nor dumb neither, only that the Scotch tongue can't speak English as we do'.

The only other character in the play is Gilbert, the English servant to Sir William (he is never given a first name even by his intended bride). Gilbert's speech is marked by twisted syntax, presumably to give the idea of lower-class English English, though he himself professes to speak 'plain English': 'For sartain, Sir, 'tis the thing in the whole world I should like the best, and be the proudest on, and if so be it was in my power, and if so be, Sir, you could spare me'. (p. 266) The misspelling which marks three of the Irish characters and the Scots drum-major is used sparingly for Gilbert, though 'sartain, sartin, sartinty, chuse, varsal, and pa'tic'lar' are thrown in every now and then. Just as the low class Irish comment on the deviant language of the Scottish soldier, Gilbert, the English servant, comments on the language of Christy Gallagher

> CHRISTY: Oh, but I can say. — I know her egg and bird. The thing is,
>   she's mad with you, and that has set her all thro' other.
> GILBERT: Egg and bird! — mad! All through other! — Confound me,
>   if I understand one word the man is saying; but I will make
>   him understand me, if he can understand plain English.
>
> (pp. 353–4)

Maria Edgeworth uses Gilbert for the moral of the play; he is 'not fond of the Scotch' (p. 262) and has little time for the Irish, but he finishes up marrying Mabel, and both of them become the patrons of the new inn whose name symbolises the new friendship between the nations of Britain, 'The Rose, Thistle and Shamrock' (poor Wales does not seem to be looked on with favour by Edgeworth, as was seen also in the *Essay*).

In conclusion: The *Essay on Irish Bulls* was the first major study in book length of stereotyping, and the first single study of stage-Irishism. The *Essay* is still an important work because of the innovatory concepts used in the analysis of stereotyping, its uses of examples to illustrate theory, and its readiness to experiment with genre in order to communicate with the reader and to win the argument.[11] The quality of the empirical research meets the requirements of present day academic studies though the use of more than one genre of writing and the explicit display of anger would make the work unacceptable to academic publishing today.

The first noteworthy concept in the *Essay* is the complete rejection of any type of innatism which often accompanies symbolic violence; this dismissal came at the beginning of the century which was to adopt such thinking wholeheartedly, a type of thinking which, in turn, would contribute to multiple genocide in Europe in the twentieth century. The second important concept in the *Essay* is the stress on the relationship between symbolic violence and identity; a group defines itself as superior by defining the other as inferior.[12] The third critical concept is the role of humour in symbolic violence, and the Edgeworth readiness to use humour to win the argument, even when the humour is the stage-Irish humour of the bull. The second and third concept are also seen as acting together in the relationship of laughter and superiority (p. 89). It might be said in criticism, that the Edgeworths fail to provide any classification of bulls and therefore any detailed taxonomy of how the Irish are portrayed by such humour; in could be said in defense that since the *Essay* was published, there has been no study of bulls which provides any such classification or taxonomy.

The most difficult problem for the conclusion is to explain how someone who could write such a passionate critique of symbolic violence could also write stage-Irishism; the reference is to the intellectual dilemma not to any moral issue. The answer to the quandry of the 'unjustly neglected Maria Edgeworth' may be found in *Castle Rackrent,* the novel published two years before the *Essay on Irish Bulls.*[13] In *Castle Rackrent* and *The Rose, Thistle and Shamrock,* Edgeworth uses the phrase 'plain English' for, what she considers, the authentic code, and any alternative can be considered a symbol of non-authenticity.[14] So Thady, the principal character of *Castle Rackrent,* is said by the author to speak in his 'vernacular idiom,' and Edgeworth would similarly depict Irish characters in her other writings by this tactic of linguistic marking.[15]

Maria Edgeworth did not have a Somerville and Ross competence in Hiberno-English, but she was a linguist and stylist of great ability, and it would be far-fetched to claim she did not realise in some way that she was marking for deviancy when she wrote, for example, the pseudo-naturalistic language which is used by Irish characters who were not rogues or comic figures such as the Widow Larkin in *The Rose, Thistle and Shamrock,* and Thady in her novel *Castle Rackrent.* It was this novel which played an important part in the development of what is sometimes called the regional novel; from a linguistic point of view, it was this novel which inspired a whole tradition of novel writing which uses so-called dialect writing.[16] It is also reasonable to argue on the evidence of the Preface and Epilogue of *Castle Rackrent* that she knew what she doing when she used language to mark certain characters or ethnic or national groups, as other than normal. Unfortunately, many of the writers who copied Maria Edgeworth's regional writing were linguistic innocents who thought that their so-called dialect writing was an authentic expression of regional speech; many literary critics have been equally innocent, unfortunately, including many who write about Irish literature.[17]

ANGLO-IRISH AND IRISH POETRY IN HUNGARIAN: THE LITERARY OFFSHOOT OF AN HISTORICAL PARALLEL

THOMAS KABDEBO

As an historian, as well as a student of literature, I would contend that history does not create the literature that will characterise it nearly as much as literature will presage history. The ideas of the French encyclopaedists had demolished French feudalism spiritually long before the Bastille was actually razed to the ground. Through Lucretius, Petronius and, from a different angle, the writings and activities of the Stoics, the politheistic religious framework of Rome had been made ridiculous, well before the early Christians could show up its corruption. One could even go as far as to say that the spirit of a new era will come flowing steadily down the chimney and create an atmosphere in the house which, eventually, leads to an explosion. Political history will then take account of tangible events: how the windows and doors were replaced. Sometimes the roof as well. Sometimes the whole house.

Arthur Griffith, one time printer, journalist and editor, later politician and statesman, published in the 24 December 1903 issue of *The United Irishmen,* a poem by William Butler Yeats that had not been anthologised before or since. It was no literary masterpiece, and its reappearance in Griffith's journal marked a certain uneasiness in the relationship between these two great personalities of the twentieth century Irish Renaissance. Griffith had had the temerity to correct Yeats's punctuation in the poem to which the poet took exception. The poem, 'How Ferencz Renyi Kept Silent' described a Hungarian hero of the 1848–49 revolution and war of liberation, a certain Ferencz Renyi, who had withstood the most terrifying psychological pressure at the hands of his captors, the Austrians, and never betrayed his comrades. Renyi's fiancée was killed in front of his eyes yet he remained true to his friends and to the cause. Yeats wrote:

We, too, have seen our bravest and our best
To prison go, and mossy ruin rest
Where houses once whitened vale and mountain crest,
Therefore, O nation of the bleeding breast,
Libations from the Hungary of the West.[1]

Awkward as it may be and Victorian verse in style, still by virtue of its content the poem was found fit by Griffith to herald a new age. According to Griffith Ireland was to gain its independence by adopting the Hungarian method. Subsequently *The Resurrection of Hungary* — a political pamphlet — was launched in 1904 and became an instant hit.[2]

The parallel was put into practice in 1907 when *Sinn Fein* was established — a non-militant organization working for peaceful change. In 1916 an upsurge of the more violent, post-Fenian spirit resulted in the Easter Rising. After 1922 Sinn Fein became the advocate of forceful change, differing, very much, from the Sinn Fein of 1907. What is interesting, or even remarkable, is the claim by both the non-militant and militant wings of Sinn Fein, at various times in their existence, that they were equally rooted in Irish tradition and history, and that they could find parallels in Hungarian history.[3]

It was the group of Young Irelanders, John Mitchel, Thomas Davis and William Smith O'Brien who, after they had been exiled from Ireland, realized that their fate and the fate of their country, was very similar to those of Louis Kossuth's group and that of Hungary. Davis wrote in the 1840s:

And Austria on Italy — the Roman eagle chained —
Bohemia, Servia, Hungary, within her clutches grasp;
And Ireland struggles gallantly in England's loosening grasp.[4]

So it was, through the writings, correspondence and personal accounts of these *Young Irelanders* that the idea of a Hungarian parallel entered the Irish consciousness. William Smith O'Brien, for instance, visited Hungary in 1861 and observed at first hand the spirit of the so-called Hungarian passive resistance: the nonpayment of taxes, the peaceful disobedience in civic matters that eventually induced Austria to grant Hungary its constitution and restore its parliament.[5] A compromise was struck in 1867 between

Austria and Hungary and its architect was the Hungarian statesman Ferenc Deák. Hungarian resistance, similar to Ireland's, had had two different traditions. Apart from the peaceful way of Deák there was the armed resistance of Kossuth in 1849, and his conspiratorial armed struggle for independence between 1849 and 1867 directed from abroad with the help of covert international diplomacy. So when we come to a point of agreement, a Compromise, an historical watershed, it cannot be claimed unequivocally that it was the result of the peaceful resistance led by Deák solely; it was also the result of the armed resistance displayed by Kossuth in 1849 and afterwards.

In Ireland in the year of 1867 three Fenians were tried and sentenced to be executed. The affair produced a public outcry and then a protracted correspondence where two sides were polarised: those who believed that resistance by violent means was in vain, and those who claimed it was the only way to achieve independence. John Francis O'Donnell, the poet, journalist and contributor to *The Nation,* wrote a poem, 'Cui bono' in 1867 which evoked both of these Hungarian ways of resistance:

> They failed, I grant you — Klapka failed —
> But not the cause for which he bled;
> Disaster, blood and tears entailed
> Till beaten Hungary ran red
> And Europe howled and Europe railed
> Above the victors and the dead
>
> But still the mighty Magyar race
> Persisting, won the doubtful day;
> An empire charmed to sudden grace,
> Achieved its mission — forced its way:
> The nation's sons got breathing space,
> Its heart resumed its pulse and sway.
>
> Are we unworthy less renown?
> Are we unworthy less reward?
> We who, despite our master's frown,
> Cling to tradition of the sword,
> And prize the axe that strikes us down,
> More precious than the spiteful word.

I say — let history answer this —
For us, we freely risk the chance,
And, meanwhile, be it joy or bliss,
Our constant motto is: Advance.
Top ladies, whispered voice and kiss;
For freeman, rifle, sword, and lance.[6]

So there were two traditions for the parallel. Given another hundred years, or so, the configuration will have altered.

Ireland, excepting one province with two differing traditions, has achieved independence, but not the way Griffith would have conceived it: united yet free, royalist yet independent. Hungary lost many of her former territories — most notably Transylvania with over two million Hungarians living there — which changed masters and thus many former Hungarian citizens had to change their allegiance and support successor states. The remaining country of Hungary gained, lost, regained its independence much later. Meanwhile literary traditions live on and literature, particularly poetry, takes new courses, or rather, after the interlude of being filled with nationalistic fervour keeps its normal course of evoking eternal themes in novel ways.

Late twentieth century Hungarian readers are in turn attracted to Irish literature for a variety of reasons: the first was the link, the historical parallel already illustrated. Second, in the awakening of national consciousness in the early nineteenth century, Hungary took the course of hanging on to its esoteric language. One of its best poets, Ferenc Kölcsey, coined the phrase; 'a nation lives in its language'. In contrast Ireland has only kept its national language as a precious relic. English is the language of everyday communication, and most Irish poets write poetry in English, the only language they know or know well. Ireland has, however, kept its national religion through adversity. Hungarians think that the language change in Ireland may have had beneficial effects as well. Having English as a mother tongue Irish poets could immediately join the mainstream of world literature, and enjoy almost instant recognition abroad. Hungarians, locked in their own tongue, cannot communicate their poetry on a competitive world level.

So the Hungarian curiosity about Irish poetry in particular might be stated as a conundrum thus: what happens to a people who lose their language but preserve their national identity when they communicate via a world language? Furthermore: do their affinities with Celticity survive? What is it like to be sons and daughters of a small nation, economically second fiddle to a larger one, but culturally on a par with it? These are the kind of questions to which Hungarian literati are searching for answers and this is partly the reason why they would like to see a comprehensive anthology of Irish poetry available in Hungarian.

The choice of particular poets and poems for such an anthology is, to a certain extent, dictated by precedent. Thomas Moore, Oscar Wilde, James Joyce, Yeats and Samuel Beckett have already been introduced to the Hungarian public through judicious translations and/or a selection of their poetry in translation. World fame was their portent. Beyond such classical figures, selection depends upon the following: (a) Merit in contemporary literature, as already recognised by international acclaim: poets like Seamus Heaney, Thomas Kinsella, Austin Clarke, Patrick Kavanagh, Louis MacNeice. (b) Contemporary poets who have already found their way to certain Hungarian poet translators: Richard Murphy, Tom Paulin, Seamus Deane. (c) Representatives of a school of poetry, such as the earth-bound local patriots like John Hewitt of recent years, or Pierce Ferriter, the soldier poet, who seem to have near equivalents in Hungary. The same is true of the drinking songs of Carolan (though you would have to substitute wine for whiskey), folk poetry, Medieval songs written to the Virgin Mary, and love poems whose universal validity is evident. (d) Individuals who behave like Hungarian wits: such as Oliver Saint John Gogarty, hitherto unknown in Hungary.

In my anthology of Anglo-Irish poetry and poetry in Irish, *Tört álmok* ('Broken Dreams') of nearly four hundred pages there are some thirty poems offered in two different translations by two different people. Not because one is better than the other, but because both are equally convincing. For example, 'Epic' by Patrick Kavanagh was translated by Dezső Tandori and by me, separately. Both translations kept very close to the original in meaning, both attempted to approximate the original form, both texts used expressions from everyday, literary and idiomatic language, emulating the original, and both seemed to achieve a poem that could have been written in Hungarian, saving the Irish names in it.

There is a large poetry reading public in Hungary and a special demand for poetry in translation since a landlocked country, locked also into an esoteric tongue, relies to a great extent for information on translations.[7] Two thousand copies for a first volume of poetry is not rare, and the publishers of *Tört álmok* sold over five thousand copies. These numbers should convince anyone that reading poetry is not an elitist pastime but it is within the everyday experience of an educated person. It is an expectation, even though by mid-1993 there occurred a — hopefully — temporary lapse in publishing due to the withdrawal of state subsidies as publishers like all other state owned businesses became reorganised and privatised.

English is now the second language in Hungary, having overtaken German, French and the once compulsory Russian. There have been in the past bilingual volumes of poetry — *Samson Agonistes,* for instance, or *Fleur du mal.* I believe that an enterprising publisher today would recoup his investment by publishing bilingual texts, because more and more readers fancy themselves as amateur comparatists who want to see the original text and (also the compromise, which is called) the translation.

Poetry is the most instant, the most vivid, the most life-enhancing of all literary forms. Readers of poetry, at least in Hungary, want to expand their own lives through experiencing the lives of others via the medium of poetry. While in the reading experience a reader subconsciously looks for familiarity of temperament and sentiment he or she *overtly* looks for the exotic, what is to him or her exotic: the charm of a distant green island, the nearness of the sea, the spiritual dimension and the buoyancy that characterises the Irish poem — as seen from that distance.

NOTES

INTRODUCTION. A SMALL NATION'S CONTRIBUTION
TO THE WORLD. Csilla Bertha and Donald E. Morse

1 Opening Address of Welcome at the 1989 conference of the International Association for the Study of Anglo-Irish Literature held in Debrecen. All further references are to this unpublished essay.
2 András Csorba, *Magyar–ír kapcsolatok 1867-ig* (Debrecen: Tisza István Tudományegyetem Angol Szemináriuma, 1944), pp. 7–8.
3 Thomas Kabdebo, *The Hungarian-Irish 'Parallel' and Arthur Griffith's Use of his Sources* (Maynooth: St. Patrick's College, 1988), pp. 2–3.
4 Opening Address of Welcome at the 1989 conference of the International Association for the Study of Anglo-Irish Literature held in Debrecen. All further references are to this unpublished essay.
5 Kabdebo. *op. cit.,* p. 5.
6 István Pálffy, 'Hungarian Views of Ireland in the Nineteenth Century', in *Literary Interrelations, Ireland, England and the World; Reception and Translation,* ed. by Wolfgang Zach and Heinz Kosok (Tübingen: Narr Verlag, 1987), p. 33.
7 See, for instance, Duckworth Barker, 'Regionális irodalmi kísérlet Nagy-Britanniában' *Erdélyi Helikon,* 1930, 785–9.; 'Ír drámaírók', *Erdélyi Helikon,* 1931, pp. 76–9.
8 Csilla Bertha, 'Tragedies of National Fate: A Comparison between Brian Friel's *Translations* and its Hungarian Counterpart, András Sütő's *A szuzai menyegző', Irish University Review,* 17, 2 (Autumn) 1987, pp. 207–22.

STARTING FROM THE EARTH, STARTING FROM THE STARS: THE FANTASTIC IN SAMUEL BECKETT'S PLAYS AND JAMES JOYCE'S *ULYSSES.* Donald E. Morse

A portion of this essay appears within a greatly expanded context in 'More Real Than Reality': An Introduction to the Fantastic in Irish Literature and the Arts' and 'Fidelity to Failure': Time and the Fantastic in Samuel Beckett's Early Plays' in *More Real Than Reality: The Fantastic in Irish Literature and the Arts,* ed. Donald E. Morse and Csilla Bertha (Westport, CT: Greenwood Press, 1991), pp. 1–12 and 167–78. An Earlier version of much of the material on Beckett appeared as '"Moments for Nothing": Images of Time in Samuel Beckett's Plays', *Arbeiten aus Anglistik und Amerikanistik,* 15:1 (1990), pp. 27–38. I am grateful to both publishers for permission to reprint this material.

1 George P. Landow, 'And the World Became Strange: Realms of Literary Fantasy', in *The Aesthetics of Fantasy Literature and Art,* ed. Roger C. Schlobin (Notre Dame: University of Notre Dame Press, 1982), p. 107.

2 F. X. Martin, 'The Image of the Irish — Medieval and Modern Continuity and Change', in *Medieval and Modern Ireland,* ed. Richard Wall (Gerrards Cross, Bucks.: Colin Smythe, 1988), p. 2.

3 Seamus Heaney, 'Docker', in *Death of a Naturalist* (London: Faber and Faber, 1966), p. 41. The context for the remark in Heaney's poem is important:

    That fist would drop a hammer on a Catholic —
    Oh yes, that kind of thing could start again;
    The only Roman collar he tolerates
    Smiles all round his sleek pint of porter.

4 Augustine Martin, 'Fable and Fantasy' in *The Genius of Irish Prose,* ed. Augustine Martin (Dublin: The Mercier Press, 1985), pp. 110–11.

5 Dermot Mac Manus, *The Middle Kingdom: The Faerie World of Ireland* (Gerrards Cross, Bucks.: Colin Smythe, 1973), pp. 15–16.

6 For an extensive discussion of this tradition see Maureen Murphy, 'Siren or Victim: The Mermaid in Irish Legend and Poetry', and on some of the consequences of the loss of this tradition see Vernon Hyles, 'Lord Dunsany: The Geography of the Gods' in *More Real Than Reality: The Fantastic in Irish Litera-*

ture and the Arts, ed. Donald E. Morse and Csilla Bertha (Westport, CT: Greenwood Press, 1991), pp. 29–39 and 211–18.

7 F. X. Martin, *op. cit,* p. 110.

8 The 'enchanted Green Lands' at Rosses Point where Yeats 'brought his faery-obsessed friend, Æ' (Susan and Thomas Cahill, *A Literary Guide to Ireland,* [New York: Charles Scribner's Sons, 1973], p. 180) are now lined with upscale bungalows whose owners I doubt put out saucers of milk at night for the Little People; nor does the newly laid tarmac provide a congenial surface over which they can ride their fairy horses. Thus in our headlong pursuit of material pleasure and gain we continue to scrape the earth free of its magic — exactly the reverse of what Yeats and Æ believed would occur.

9 Such an attitude sharply contrasts with that of John Millington Synge who worked hard to capture the genuine folk quality of the stories and tales he retold or used on the stage, without ever condescending to either his subject or audience, as pointed out by both Toni O'Brien Johnson, 'Interrogating Boundaries: Fantasy in the Plays of J. M. Synge', and Anthony Roche, 'Ghosts in Irish Drama', in Morse and Bertha, *op. cit.,* pp. 137–50 and 41–66. For a more detailed discussion of the relation of fantasy to belief, see Donald E. Morse, 'Of Monkeys, Changelings and Asses', in *Aspects of the Fantastic,* ed. William Coyle (Westport, CT: Greenwood Press, 1986), pp. 197–202.

10 Scott Sullivan, 'The Irish Miracle', *Newsweek,* 26 June 1989, p. 21.

11 Stoppard makes his point brilliantly in *Rosencrantz and Guildenstern Are Dead:* 'The more witnesses there are [to any given fantastic event] the thinner it gets and the more reasonable it becomes until it is as thin as reality, the name we give to common experience' (New York: Grove Press, 1967), p. 21.

12 Geoffrey H. Hartman, *Criticism in the Wilderness: The Study of Literature Today,* (New Haven: Yale University Press, 1980), p. 27.

13 Samuel Beckett, *Endgame: A Play in One Act* (New York: Grove Press, 1958), p. 83; see also '"Moments for Nothing": Images of Time in Samuel Beckett's Plays,' *Arbeiten aus Anglistik und Amerikanistik,* 15:1 (1990), pp. 27–38.

14 In an interview with Tom Driver quoted in Lance Olsen, *Ellipse of Uncertainty: An Introduction to Postmodern Fantasy* (Westport, CT: Greenwood Press, 1987), p. 43.

15 'The Nayman of Noland', review of *The Beckett Country: Samuel Beckett's Ireland,* by David Davison; *Four Dubliners,* by Richard Ellmann; *On Beckett: Essays and Criticism,* ed. by S. E. Gontarski; and *Beyond Minimalism: Beckett's Late Style in the Theatre,* by Enoch Brater in *The New Republic* 6 July 1987, p. 35.
16 Samuel Beckett, *Happy Days,* (New York: Grove Press, 1958), p. 9.
17 Samuel Beckett, 'Play', *Cascando and Other Short Dramatic Pieces* (New York: Grove Press, 1968), p. 45.
18 Kathryn Hume, *Fantasy and Mimesis: Responses to Reality in Western Literature* (New York: Methuen, 1984), p. 21.
19 Rosemary Jackson, *Fantasy: The Literature of Subversion* (London: Methuen, 1981), p. 179.
20 Quoted in Ibid., p. 62.
21 Hume, *op. cit.,* p. 194.
22 'Introduction', *The Irish Mind,* ed. Richard Kearney (Dublin: The Wolfhound Press, 1985), p. 10.
23 Olsen, *op. cit.,* p. 19; compare Jackson, *op. cit.,* pp. 34–7.
24 James Joyce, *Ulysses* (New York: Random House, 1961), pp. 429–30. Because of the controversy surrounding the various texts of *Ulysses* and the non-controversial nature of the quotations in this article, I have felt free to use the Random House edition of 1961. All references to *Ulysses* are to this edition and will be given in the text in parentheses.
25 Aladár Sarbu, 'The Fantastic in *Ulysses:* Representational Strategies in "Circe" and "Penelope" in Morse and Bertha, *op. cit.,* pp. 219–29. Sarbu's and my readings of 'Circe' differ: he emphasizes 'the mind dramatized', whereas I emphasize the unconscious. I am indebted to professor Sarbu for reminding me of Iser's argument.
26 Olsen, *op. cit.,* p. 19.
27 Hartman, *op. cit.,* p. 27.
28 Surely it would be impossible to take seriously Joyce's claims for the considerable significance of Bloom, or the views of those who see him as a true hero performing extraordinary deeds in his ordinary life, or as the modern representative man, if he were a conscious participant in the truly fantastic events in 'Circe'. Richard Ellmann eloquently claims for Bloom that 'Joyce was the first to endow an urban man of no importance with heroic consequences. ... Joyce's discovery, so humanistic that he would have been embarrassed to disclose it out of context, was

that the ordinary is the extraordinary'. *James Joyce* (New York: Oxford University Press, 1959), p. 3.

29 Readers have often been misled by applying too rigidly or too generally Joyce's suggestion that the Art of 'Circe' is Magic, while the Technique is Hallucination.

30 Wolfgang Iser, *The Implied Reader: Patterns of Communication in Prose Fiction from Bunyan to Beckett* (Baltimore: The Johns Hopkins University Press, 1974), p. 216.

31 Paul Jordan Smith, *A Key to the Ulysses of James Joyce, 1927* (San Francisco: City Lights, 1970), pp. 81, 86.

32 See my forthcoming essay, "'I'm Irish! I Was Born Here!'": The Conflict Between Nationalism and Internationalism in James Joyce's *Ulysses'*.

33 'Anima' and 'animus' are Carl Jung's terms for that part of the personality rooted in characteristics of the opposite sex without which no healthy relationship is possible. For example, Jung might be accurately describing Bloom's empathy for women when he observes that 'an inherited collective image of woman exists in a man's unconscious, with the help of which he apprehends the nature of woman'. Carl G. Jung, 'Anima and Animus,' *The Relations Between the Ego and the Unconscious,* in *The Portable Jung,* ed. Violet Staub de Laszlo (New York: The Modern Library, 1971), p. 160.

34 Hume, *op. cit.,* p. 191, pp. 195–6.

35 Jackson, *op. cit.,* pp. 20–21.

36 Ibid., p. 84.

37 Quoted in Jackson, Ibid., p. 82.

38 Ibid., p. 85. For an extensive discussion of the nature of modern fantasy contrasted with traditional Victorian fantasy, see Colin Manlove, 'Victorian and Modern Fantasy: Some Contrasts', *The Celebration of the Fantastic,* ed. Donald E. Morse, Marshall B. Tymn, and Csilla Bertha (Westport, CT: Greenwood Press, 1992), pp. 9–22.

39 Ibid., p. 158.

40 Letter from G. W. Russell to William Byrne. Transcribed by Alan Denson. National Library of Ireland Ms. 9967–69.

41 Olsen. *op. cit.,* p. 49.

42 Hume, *op. cit.,* p. 98.

41 Lewis Carroll, *Through the Looking-Glass,* in *Alice's Adventures in Wonderland and Through the Looking-Glass* 1872 (New York: St. Martin's Press, 1966), p. 237.

ROMANTIC AND MODERN: VISION AND FORM IN YEATS,
SHAW AND JOYCE. Aladár Sarbu

1 F. C. McGrath, *Walter Pater and the Modernist Paradigm*
   (Tampa: U of South Florida P, 1986) p. 6.
2 Ihab Hassan, *The Postmodern Turn: Essays in Postmodern
   Theory and Culture* (Columbus: Ohio State UP, 1987), pp. 36,
   37.
3 Arthur Symons, *The Symbolist Movement in Literature* (London: Heinemann, 1899), p. 5.
4 William Butler Yeats, 'The Philosophy of Shelley's Poetry'
   (1900), *Essays and Introductions* (London: Macmillan, 1961),
   p. 87.
5 James Joyce, *A Portrait of the Artist as a Young Man* (1916;
   Harmondsworth, Middlesex: Penguin, 1960), p. 167.
6 Cf. Robert Whitman, *Shaw & the Play of Ideas* (Ithaca: Cornell
   UP, 1971), p. 129.
7 McGrath, *op. cit.,* pp. 137–8.
8 Whitman, *op. cit.,* p. 133.
9 For a lucid review of how Romanticism anticipates Modernism
   in a most direct manner, see M. H. Abrams, *Natural Supernaturalism: Tradition and Revolution in Romantic Literature* (New
   York: Norton, 1971), especially chapter eight.
10 M. H. Abrams, *The Mirror and the Lamp: Romantic Theory and
   the Critical Tradition* (New York: Oxford UP, 1953), pp. 62–4.
11 *Ibid.* p. 97.
12 Walter Pater, *The Renaissance* 1873 (New York: Random
   House, n. d.), p. 195. (The Modern Library).
13 McGrath, *op. cit.,* p. 8.
14 Thomas Carlyle, *On Heroes and Hero-Worship and the Heroic
   in History* (1841), in *Sartor Resartus, Heroes and Hero-
   Worship, Past and Present* (London: George Routledge and
   Sons, n. d.), p. 18.
15 *Ibid.,* p. 43.
16 Carlyle uses these terms in various forms in his major works,
   such as *Sartor Resartus* (1833–34), *The French Revolution*
   (1837), *Heroes and Hero-Worship* (1841), *Past and Present*
   (1843).
17 Carlyle's six incarnations of the hero are Divinity, Prophet,
   Poet, Priest, Man of Letters, King.
18 Herman Melville, *Pierre: or The Ambiguities,* Volume 9 of *The*

Writings of Herman Melville, ed. Harrison Hayford, Hershel Parker, and G. Thomas Tanselle (Evanston and Chicago: Northwestern UP and The Newberry Library, 1971), p. 285.

19 Ralph Waldo Emerson, *The Journals and Miscellaneous Notebooks of Ralph Waldo Emerson,* ed. William H. Gilman, Alfred R. Ferguson *et al.,* Volume IX, 1843–1847 (Cambridge, Mass.: The Belknap Press of Harvard UP, 1971), p. 295.

20 McGrath's phrase, in his discussion of Yeats and the Modernist vision, *op. cit.,* p. 137.

21 Robert Spiller's definition in 'The Four Faces of Emerson,' *Four Makers of the American Mind: Emerson, Thoreau, Whitman, and Melville,* ed. Thomas Edward Crawley (Durham, N. C.: Durham UP, 1976), p. 20.

22 Cf. Richard Poirier, *The Renewal of Literature: Emersonian Reflections* (New York: Random House, 1987), pp. 96–7.

'THE HARMONY OF REALITY AND FANTASY': THE FANTASTIC IN IRISH DRAMA. Csilla Bertha

This essay was first published in *Journal of the Fantastic in the Arts,* 4.3. It is reprinted here with the kind permission of the editor Carl B. Yoke.

1 Áron Tamási, *Jégtörő gondolatok.* (Budapest: Szépirodalmi, 1982), p. 224.

2 Brian Aldiss, 'Foreword', in David Pringle, *Modern Fantasy: The Hundred Best Novels,* (London, Glasgow, Toronto: Grafton Books, 1988), p. 1.

3 Kathryn Hume, *Fantasy and Mimesis. Responses to Reality in Western Literature* (New York: Methuen, 1984), p. 163.

4 Christopher Murray, 'Irish drama and the Fantastic', in *More Real Than Reality: The Fantastic in Irish Literature and the Arts,* ed. by Donald E. Morse and Csilla Bertha (Westport, CT.: Greenwood Press, 1991), p. 87.

5 David Pringle, *Modern Fantasy: The Hundred Best Novels.* London: Grafton Books, 1988), p. 10.

6 Rosemary Jackson, *Fantasy: The Literature of Subversion* (London: Methuen, 1981), p. 159.

7 Hume, *op. cit.,* p. 148.

8 Nuala Ni Dhomhnaill, Interview, in *An Nasc.* 3.1. (1990), p. 25.

9 Veronica Hollinger, 'Theater for the Fin-du-Millennium: Play-

ing (at) the End', *Journal of the Fantastic in the Arts,* 1.1 (1988), p. 30.

10 Ibid., p. 31.

11 Ibid., p. 35.

12 'What emerges as the basic trope of fantasy is the *oxymoron,* a figure of speech which holds together contradictions and sustains them in an impossible unity, without progressing towards synthesis' (Jackson, *op. cit.,* p. 21).

13 Richard Kearney, *The Irish Mind* (Dublin: Wolfhound Press, 1985), p. 9.

14 For a more detailed analysis of the difference between the mythic and the fantastic see my essay, 'Myth and the Fantastic: The Example of W. B. Yeats', in *More Real Than Reality,* pp. 17–27.

15 Colin Manlove, 'The Elusiveness of Fantasy', *Fantasy Review,* 9. 4. (1986), pp. 14, 49.

16 Richard Allen Cave, 'Johnston, Toller and Expressionism', in *Denis Johnston: A Retrospective,* ed. Joseph Ronsley (Gerrards Cross: Colin Smythe, 1981), p. 88.

17 Quoted in Harold Ferrar, *Denis Johnston's Irish Theatre* (Dublin: The Dolmen Press, 1973), p. 71.

18 Eric S. Rabkin, *The Fantastic in Literature* (Princeton: Princeton University Press, 1976), p. 8.

19 Seamus Deane, *Celtic Revivals: Essays in Modern Irish Literature* (London: Faber and Faber, 1985), p. 57.

20 Ibid., pp. 57–58.

21 Jürgen Kamm, 'The Uses of the Fantastic in the Later Plays of Sean O'Casey', in *More Real Than Reality,* p. 156.

22 Sean O'Casey, 'Cockadoodle Doo.' *Blasts and Benedictions: Articles and Stories,* ed. by Ronald Ayling (London: Macmillan; New York: St. Martin's Press, 1967), p. 144.

23 Quoted in Rosemary Jackson, *op. cit.,* p. 62.

24 See Patrick Mason, 'Directing the Gigli Concert: An Interview', *Irish University Review,* 17.1. (1987), and Fintan O'Toole, *The Politics of Magic* (Dublin: Raven Arts Press, 1987).

25 Fintan O'Toole, *op. cit.,* pp. 167ff.

26 Carl Gustav Jung, *Memories, Dreams, Reflections* (London: Fontana, 1983), p. 262.

27 For a fuller examination of the fantastic in Murphy's plays see my essay 'Thomas Murphy's Psychological Explorations', in *More Real than Reality,* pp. 179–90.

28 Christopher Murray, *op. cit.,* p. 94.
29 Thomas Mac Intyre, *The Great Hunger* in Patrick Kavanagh and Tom Mac Intyre, *The Great Hunger* (Gigginstown: The Lilliput Press, 1988), p. 3.
30 Ibid., p. 30.
31 Vincent Hurley, 'The Great Hunger: A reading', in Kavanagh and Mac Intyre, p. 31.

'BOTH HEARD AND IMAGINED': MUSIC AS STRUCTURING PRINCIPLE IN THE PLAYS OF BRIAN FRIEL. Patrick Burke

1 Brian Friel, 'Self-Portrait', *Aquarius* 5 (1972), p. 19.
2 Brian Friel, *Translations* (London and Boston: Faber and Faber, 1981), p. 49.
3 Brian Friel, *The Communication Cord* (London and Boston: Faber and Faber, 1983), p. 11.
4 Brian Friel, *Dancing at Lughnasa* (London and Boston: Faber and Faber, 1990), pp. 21–22.
5 Ibid., p. 65.
6 Brian Friel, *Philadelphia, Here I Come!* (London: Faber and Faber, 1965), p. 98.
7 In Friel's most recent play, *A Month in the Country,* that effect is reversed: in order to indicate that the elderly landowner, Bolshintsov, is less uncouth than he at first appeared, and may thereby have modest hopes of attracting the attention of the seventeen-year old Vera Aleksandrova, the play concludes with him listening, smilingly, to her playing of a John Field nocturne, and simply repeating 'Nice... nice...' to himself. See Brian Friel, *A Month in the Country* (Dublin: Gallery Books, 1992), p. 109.
8 Brian Friel, *Aristocrats* (Dublin: Gallery Books, 1980), p. 53.
9 Ibid., pp. 45–6.
10 Brian Friel, *The Loves of Cass McGuire* (Dublin: Gallery Books, 1984), p. 7.

'DEATH IS HERE AND DEATH IS THERE, DEATH IS BUSY
EVERYWHERE': TEMPORALITY AND THE DESIRE FOR
TRANSCENDENCE IN O'CASEY'S *THE SHADOW OF A
GUNMAN.* Bernice Schrank

1 See David Krause, *Sean O'Casey: The man and His Work* (New
   York: MacMillan, 1960) and Robert Hogan, *The Experiments of
   Sean O'Casey* (Carbondale: University of Illinois Press, 1960).
2 Saros Cowasjee focuses on 'the Dublin of 1920' in *O'Casey*
   (London: Macmillan, 1966), p. 21. In the same vein, Maureen
   Malone elaborates further on the background of the play in *The
   Plays of Sean O'Casey* (Carbondale: University of Illinois
   Press, 1969). Bernard Benstock in *Paycocks and Others: Sean
   O'Casey's World* (Dublin: Gill and Macmillan, 1976) and
   James Scrimgeour in *Sean O'Casey* (Boston: G. K. Hall, 1978)
   deal almost exclusively with characters. And, most recently,
   John O'Riordan provides plot summary in *A Guide to O'Casey's
   Plays* (London: Macmillan, 1984). Tragi-comic art, structure,
   background, character, plot, all of these are complementary
   approaches to the play, but they do not, either alone or when
   taken together, provide a critical reading.
3 Herbert Goldstone, *In Search of Community: The Achievement
   of Sean O'Casey* (Cork and Dublin: Mercier Press, 1972).
4 Heinz Kosok, *O'Casey, the Dramatist,* (Gerrards Cross, Bucks:
   Colin Smythe, 1985).
5 Bernice Schrank, '"You needn't say no more": Language and
   the Problems of Communication in Sean O'Casey's *The Shadow
   of a Gunman'*, *Irish University Review.* 8.1. (Spring) 1978,
   pp. 23–38.
6 Bernice Schrank, 'Poets, Poltroons and Platitudes: A Study of
   Sean O'Casey's *The Shadow of a Gunman'*, *Mosaic,* 11.1.
   (Fall), 1977, pp. 53–61.
7 Sean O'Casey, 'The Shadow of a Gunman, 1923, in *Collected
   Plays* I. London: Macmillan, 1963. All further references will
   be given in the text.

THE WAYS OF TWONESS: PAIRS, PARALLELS AND
CONTRASTS IN STEWART PARKER'S *SPOKESONG*.
Mária Kurdi

1 Ciaran Brady, Mary O'Dowd, Brian Walker (eds.), *Ulster, An Illustrated History* (London: B. T. Batsford Ltd., 1989), p. 218.
2 Christopher Murray, 'Irish Drama in Transition 1966–1978', *Études Irlandais* No. 4, 1979, p. 306.
3 Quoted by Robert Berkvist, 'A Freewheeling Play About Irish History', *The New York Times,* 11 March 1979, p. 4.
4 Quoted by Claudia W. Harris, 'The Flame That Bloomed', *The Irish Literary Supplement,* Spring 1989, p. 4.
5 Stewart Parker, 'State of Play', *The Canadian Journal of Irish Studies,* Vol. VII No. 1, June 1981, p. 9.
6 Stewart Parker, *Spokesong* (New York: Samuel French, Inc., 1980), p. 11. All further references will be given in the text.
7 Elmer Andrews, 'The Power of Play: Stewart Parker's Theatre', *Theatre Ireland* No. 18, April–June 1989, p. 24.
8 Quoted by Robert Berkvist, *op. cit.* p. 8.
9 Philomena Muinzer, 'Evacuating the Museum: the Crisis of Playwriting in Ulster', *New Theatre Quarterly* Vol. III No. 9, February 1987, p. 49.
10 Elmer Andrews, *op. cit.,* p. 24.
10 F. L. Cross, E. A. Livingstone (eds.), *The Oxford Dictionary of the Christian Church* (Oxford: University Press, 1988), p. 765.
11 Michael Etherton, *Comtemporary Irish Dramatists* (New York: St. Martin's Press, 1989), p. 23.
13 Catherine Hughes, 'Mixed Bags', *America* Vol. 140, 21 April 1979, p. 336.
14 Claudia W. Harris, 'From Pastness to Wholeness: Stewart Parker's Reinventing Theatre', *Colby Quarterly* Vol. XXVII. No. 4, Dec. 1991, p. 240.
15 Elmer Andrews, 'The Will to Freedom: Politics and Play in the Theatre of Stewart Parker', in Okifumi Komesu and Masaru Sekine (eds.), *Irish Writers and Politics* (Gerrards Cross: Colin Smythe, 1989), p. 268.

ANCIENT LIGHTS IN AUSTIN CLARKE AND THOMAS
KINSELLA. Maurice Harmon

1 All quotations from Clarke's poetry are taken from Austin
Clarke, *Collected Poems* (Dublin, 1974).
2 For a more detailed discussion of Clarke's work see Maurice
Harmon, *Austin Clarke: a Critical Introduction* (Dublin, 1989).
3 Thomas Kinsella, *Selected Poems 1956–1968* (Dublin, 1973).
4 Ibid.
5 Thomas Kinsella, *New Poems* (Dublin, 1973).
6 Thomas Kinsella, *One and Other Poems* (Dublin, 1979).
7 Ibid.
8 Thomas Kinsella, *Fifteen Dead* (Dublin, 1979).
9 Ibid.
10 Ibid.
11 For a more detailed discussion of Kinsella see Maurice Harmon,
The Poetry of Thomas Kinsella (Dublin, 1974), 'The Poetry of
Thomas Kinsella 1972–83', *Studies,* LXIV, 255 (Autumn
1975), pp. 269–281, and 'Nutrient Waters', *Poetry Ireland Review,* no. 21 (Spring 1988), pp. 20–24.

POETIC OUTRAGE: ASPECTS OF SOCIAL CRITICISM IN
MODERN IRISH POETRY. Eoin Bourke

1 Kieran Furey, *Murdering the Muse* (Dublin, 1983), p. 5.
2 J. Eglinton, W. B. Yeats et al., *Literary Ideals in Ireland* (London & Dublin, 1899), p. 36.
3 Augustine Martin, 'The Rediscovery of Austin Clarke', *Studies,*
Winter 1965, p. 418.
4 Donald Davie, Review of *Ancient Lights,* in *Irish Writing,*
XXXIV, Dublin, p. 57.
5 W. B. Yeats, *Essays and Introductions* (London, 1961), p. 185.
6 Johannes Klein, *Geschichte der deutschen Lyrik* (Wiesbaden,
1960), pp. 553ff.
7 As evidenced by the excellent anthology, *Denkzettel — poli-
tische Lyrik aus den sechziger Jahren der BRD und Westberlin*
(Leipzig, 1976, Frankfurt/Main, 1977).
8 Fintan O'Toole, *The Southern Question* (Dublin, 1987), p. 8.
9 Ibid., p. 20.

10 W. B. Yeats, 'September 1913', *W. B. Yeats: Collected Poems* (London, 1963), p. 120.
11 Patrick Kavanagh, *The Great Hunger,* in *Patrick Kavanagh: Collected Poems* (London, 1972), p. 38.
12 W. B. Yeats, *op. cit.,* p. 137. A. Norman Jeffares, *A Commentary on the Collected Poems of W. B. Yeats* (London, 1968), p. 129.
13 Patrick Kavanagh, *Collected Poems,* pp. 52ff.
14 Anthony Coughlan, 'Economic and Social Change in Ireland', *Irland — Gesellschaft und Kultur,* ed. Dorothee Siegmund-Schulze (Halle, 1982), p. 11.
15 Kavanagh, *op. cit.,* 37.
16 Ibid., p. vix.
17 Austin Clarke, *Twice Around the Black Church* (London, 1962), p. 147.
18 John Cooney, *The Crozier and the Dáil: Church and State 1922–1966* (Cork and Dublin, 1986), p. 21.
19 Austin Clarke, *Collected Poems* (London, 1974), p. 202.
20 Ibid., p. 250.
21 Richard Murphy, *High Island* (London, 1974).
22 Paul Durcan, 'Cardinal Dies of Heart Attack in Dublin Brothel', *Going Home to Russia* (Belfast and New Hampshire, 1987), p. 17.
23 Paul Durcan, 'Priest Accused of not Wearing Condom', *op. cit.,* p. 9.
24 Karl Marx, *Early Writings,* translated by Rodney Livingstone and Gregor Benton (Harmondsworth, 1975), pp. 247ff.
25 Marian Kelly, 'Ballad of the Deserted Wife', *Limerick Poetry Broadsheet,* No. 1, ed. Ciaran O'Driscoll (Limerick, 1987).
26 Fintan O'Toole, *op. cit.*
27 Austin Clarke, 'Cypress Grove', *CP,* p. 286.
28 Austin Clarke, 'The Loss of Strength', *CP,* p. 212.
29 Pearse Hutchinson, 'Bright Red Berries', *Climbing the Light* (Dublin, 1985), p. 43.
30 Thomas Kinsella, *One Fond Embrace* (Dublin, 1988), p. 8.
31 Pearse Hutchinson, 'Flowering Stump' and 'Bright Red Berries', *op. cit.,* pp. 41, 43.
32 John Montague, 'Hymn to the New Omagh Road', *The Rough Field* (Dublin, 1972), p. 53.
33 John Montague, 'Springs', *Mount Eagle* (Oldcastle, 1988), pp. 13ff.

226 *Notes to pages 98–107*

34 Thomas Kinsella, 'Nightwalker', *Nightwalker and Other Poems* (New York, 1968), p. 57.
35 Compare Peadar Kirby, *Has Ireland a Future?* (Cork and Dublin, 1988), pp. 18ff.
36 *Who Owns Ireland — Who Owns You?* ed. Carmel Jemmings et al. (Dublin, 1985), p. 138.
37 Patrick Deeley, 'The Mine', *Intimate Strangers* (Dublin, 1985), p. 138.
38 Michael Gorman, 'Erris', *Waiting for the Sky to Fall* (Galway, 1984), p. 12.
39 Peadar Kirby, *op. cit.,* p. 11.
40 Karl Jones, 'Will the Rising Tide Lift All the Boats?' *The Irish Times,* Dec. 20, 1988.
41 Compare Peadar Kirby, *op. cit.,* p. 14.
42 Ibid., p. 16.
43 Kathleen O'Driscoll, 'Motherland', in *Pillars of the House: An Anthology of Verse by Irish Women from 1690 to the Present,* ed. A. A. Kelly (Dublin, 1988), p. 133.
44 Cf. Peadar Kirby, *op. cit.,* p. 20.
45 Michael Gorman, 'On the Streets', *Waiting for the Sky to Fall,* p. 5.
46 Anthony Coughlan, *op. cit.,* p. 9.
47 Paul Durcan, 'The Great Hunger', *Going Home to Russia,* p. 23.
48 Paul Durcan, 'Anglo-Irish Agreement 1986', *Going Home to Russia,* p. 29.
49 Karl Jones, 'Market Opportunities Mean Survival of the Fittest', *The Irish Times,* Dec. 30, 1988.
50 Pearse Hutchinson, 'Traffic Lights Are Dangerous', *Climbing the Light,* pp. 47ff.
51 Rita Ann Higgins, 'Work On', *Goddess on the Mervue Bus* (Galway, 1986), p. 11.
52 Rita Ann Higgins, 'Some People', *Witch in the Bushes* (Galway, 1988), p. 59.

MASK LYRICS IN THE POETRY OF PAUL MULDOON AND DEREK MAHON. István D. Rácz

1 Michael Smith, 'The Contemporary Situation in Irish Poetry, in *Two Decades in Irish Writing,* ed. Douglas Dunn (Cheadle: Carcanet Press, 1975), p. 156.

2 Ibid., p. 154.
3 Tom Paulin, *Ireland and the English Crisis* (Newcastle, Bloodaxe Books, 1984), p. 18.
4 Blake Morrison and Andrew Motion, 'Introduction', *The Penguin Book of Contemporary British Poetry* (Harmondsworth: Penguin, 1982), p. 16.
5 Edna Longley, *Poetry in the Wars* (Newcastle: Bloodaxe Books, 1986), p. 188.
6 Quoted in Ibid., p. 17.
7 Peter McDonald. 'A Continuing Revolution', *The Times Literary Supplement* Jan. 6–12, 1989, p. 16.
8 Samuel Hynes, 'Like the Trees on Primrose Hill', *London Review of Books* 2 March 1989, pp. 6–7.
9 Quoted by E. Longley, *op. cit.,* p. 17.
10 Ralph W. Rader, 'The Dramatic Monologue and Related Lyric Forms', *Critical Inquiry* (1976), vol. 3, p. 140.
11 Ibid., p. 141.
12 Robert Langbaum, *The Poetry of Experience* (New York: Norton, 1963), p. 3.
13 Rader, *op. cit.,* pp. 141–2.
14 Ibid., 151.
15 Stephen Spender, *The Struggle of the Modern* (London: Hamish Hamilton, 1963), p. 72.
16 Ibid., p. 78.
17 Quoted by E. Longley, *op. cit.,* p. 10.
18 Ibid., p. 206.
19 Ibid., pp. 207–8.
20 Ibid., p. 211.
21 Ibid., p. 238.
22 M. H. Abrams, *Natural Supernaturalism* (New York: Norton, 1971), pp. 253–324.
23 Paul Muldoon, *Why Brownlee Left* (London: Faber and Faber, 1987), p. 46.
24 E. Longley, *op. cit.,* pp. 224–5.
25 Seamus Deane, *Celtic Revivals* (London: Faber and Faber, 1985), p. 156.
26 Gerald Dawe in *Across a Roaring Hill,* ed. Gerald Dawe and Edna Longley (Belfast: Blackstaff Press, 1985), p. 227.
27 Paulin, *op. cit.* p. 55.
28 Maurice Riordan, 'An Urbane Perspective: the Poetry of Derek

Mahon', in *The Irish Writer and the City,* ed. Maurice Harmon (Gerrards Cross, Bucks.: Colin Smythe, 1984), p. 173.

29 Eamon Grannen, "'To the Point of Speech": the Poetry of Derek Mahon' in *Contemporary Irish Writing,* ed. James D. Brophy and Raymond J. Porter (Boston: Iona College Press, 1983), p. 15.

30 D. E. S. Maxwell, 'Contemporary Poetry in the North of Ireland', in *Two Decades in Irish Writing,* p. 179.

31 Ibid., pp. 175–6.

32 Paulin, *op. cit.* p. 58. Compare to Philip Larkin's 'Days'.

33 Ibid.

34 E. Longley. *op. cit.,* pp. 205–6.

35 Deane, *op. cit.,* p. 163.

36 Derek Mahon, *The Snow Party* (London: Oxford University Press, 1975), p. 36.

37 Riordan, *op. cit.,* p. 176.

38 Grennan, *op. cit.,* p. 20.

YEATS'S PREOCCUPATION WITH SPIRITUALISM AND HIS BYZANTIUM POEMS. Marius Byron Raizis

1 Quoted in Spyridon Iliopoulos, '"Out of a Medium's Mouth": Yeats's Art in Relation to Mediumship, Spiritualism, and Psychical Research'. Unpublished Ph. D. Thesis. University of Warwick, 1985, p. 326. All further references to this work will be given by page number in the text. In addition to his scholarly interpretation Iliopoulos in several appendices gives several significant texts of Yeats from which I will quote extensively. Appendix A contains records of thirteen séances from 9 May 1912 through 27 December 1916, Iliopoulos's pages 273–288. Appendix B is the Leo Africanus Manuscript (pp. 289–321). Appendix C contains 'The Poet and the Actress' (pp. 322–329), and 'Clairvoyant Search for Will' (pp. 330–339) and Appendix D is the 'Notbook of Stainton Moses' (pp. 340–352).

2 W. B. Yeats, *The Collected Poems* (New York: The Macmillan Company, 1961), all references to the poetry of Yeats are to this edition.

3 Arnold Goldman, 'Yeats, Spiritualism, and Psychical Research', in *Yeats and the Occult,* edited George M. Harper (London: Macmillan, 1976), p. 156.

4 As quoted in Richard Ellmann, *Yeats: The Man and the Masks* (London: Faber and Faber, 1961), p. 177.
5 Arnold Goldman, *op. cit.,* p. 128.
6 For instance, in his scholarly but quite dated treatise, *W. B. Yeats and Tradition* (New York: The Macmillan Company, 1958) F. A. C. Wilson explains the Byzantium poems in the light of Platonic philosophy, in complete ignorance of the existence of Yeats's spiritualist papers (pp. 231–43).

KNOWLEDGE OF THE WORLD AS THE FORBIDDEN FRUIT: CANON SHEEHAN AND JOYCE ON THE SACRIFICIUM INTELLECTUS. Ruth Fleischmann

1 See Patrick A. Sheehan, 'Biographical Notes', unpublished manuscript, a copy of which was kindly given to me by Rev. Robert Forde of Mallow.
2 Patrick A. Sheehan, 'Religious Instruction in Intermediate Schools', *The Irish Ecclesiastical Record,* Sept, 1881, p. 528.
3 Ibid., p. 525.
4 Patrick A. Sheehan, *The Blindness of Dr. Gray: or The Final Law* (London, 1909, 2nd impr. 1918), ch. XXXI, p. 307.
5 Ibid.
6 Pádraic Pearse, 'The Murder Machine' (final form 1916), in *Collected Works of Pádraic Pearse — Political Writings and Speeches* (Dublin: Phoenix, n.d.), p. 12.
7 Patrick A. Sheehan, 'Religious Instructions' p. 531.
8 James Joyce, *A Portrait of the Artist as a Young Man* 1916 (Harmondsworth: Penguin, 1968), p. 79. All further references will be given by page number in the text.
9 Relevant lines of this nostalgic song would be:
    Fond mem'ry brings the light
    Of other days around me: ...
    The eyes that shone, now dimmed and gone,
    And cheerful hearts now broken. ...
    I feel like one who treads alone
    Some banquet hall deserted,
    Whose lights are fled, whose garlands dead,
    And all but he departed.
10 Æ (George Russell), *The National Being: Some Thouqhts on an Irish Polity,* 1916 (rpt. Dublin: Irish Academic Press, 1982), p. 68.

11 Walter McDonald, *Reminiscences of a Maynooth Professor,* ed. Denis Gwynn (London, 1925; Cork: Mercier Press, 1967), p. 269.
12 Patrick A. Sheehan, 'Free-Thought in America — The Sects — The Church', *The Irish Ecclesiastical Record,* Sept. 1884, p. 730.
13 Walter McDonald, *op. cit.,* pp. 222–3, 227.
14 Patrick A. Sheehan, *The Blindness of Dr. Gray,* p. 307.

ULYSSES IN *ULYSSES:* WHAT THE NOLAN SAID. András P. Ungar

1 Quoted in Padraic Colum, *Arthur Griffith* (Dublin: Brown and Nolan, 1959), p. 77.
2 James Joyce, *Ulysses,* The Corrected Text, ed. Hans Walter Gabler with Wolfhard Steppe and Claus Melchior (New York: Random House, 1986), p. 275. All further references are to this edition and will be given in the text.
3 Robert Martin Adams, *Surface and Symbol: The Consistency of James Joyce's Ulysses,* (New York: Oxford University Press, 1962), p. 101.
4 Arthur Griffith, *The Resurrection of Hungary: A Parallel for Ireland* (Dublin: James Duffy & Co., M. H. Gill & Son, Sealy, Bryers & Walker, 1904), p. 7.
5 Hayden White, *The Content of Form: Narrative Discourse and Historical Representation* (Baltimore and London: John Hopkins University Press, 1978), pp. 6–16.
6 Robert Tracy, 'Leopold Bloom Fourfold: A Hungarian–Hebraic–Hellenic–Hibernian Hero', *Massachusetts Review* 6, 1965, p. 227.
7 Edward Crankshaw, *Maria Theresa* (London: Longmans, 1969), p. 140.
8 Sir Horace Rumbold, *The Austrian Court in the Nineteenth Century* (London: Methuen, 1909), p. 4.
9 For a closer analysis of the role of Griffith's book as subtext in *Ulysses* see my 'Among the Hapsburgs: Arthur Griffith, Stephen Dedalus and the Dynasty of Bloom' in *Twentieth Century Literature* (forthcoming).
10 James Joyce, *Stephen Hero,* ed. Theodore Spencer (New York: New Directions, 1963), p. 62.

11 Eliot O'Donnell, *The Irish Abroad: A Record of Achievements of Wanderers from Ireland* (London: Sir Isaac Pittman & Sons, 1915), p. 104.
12 The one other non-classical occurence is Ulysses Grant (*Ulysses,* p. 623.)
13 G. J. Watson, 'The Politics of *Ulysses'*, in R. D. Newman and Weldon Thornton, *Joyce's Ulysses: The Larger Perspective* (Newark: University of Delaware Press, 1987), p. 49.
14 O'Donnell, *op. cit.,* p. 269.
15 Treating the mention of Camus as indicating a literal birthplace, Don Gifford believes Ulysses Browne to be a compound indentity for Ulysses Maxmillian, Count von Browne and Fieldmarshall (1705–57), 'and George, Count de Browne (1698–1792), [who] was born at Camus ... and became ... a field marshall in the Russian army, and was a favourite of Maria Theresia and Catherine the Great'. Don Gifford with Robert J. Seidman, *Ulysses Annotated: Notes for James Joyce's Ulysses* revised and expanded edition (Berkeley: University of California Press, 1988), p. 360. The text does not require such a conflation.
16 Richard Ellmann, *James Joyce,* New and revised edition (New York: Oxford University Press, 1982), p. 29.
17 James Joyce, *A Portrait of the Artist as a Young Man* (Harmondsworth: Penguin, 1976), p. 19.
18 James Joyce, *The Critical Writings of James Joyce,* eds. Ellsworth Mason and Richard Ellmann (New York: Viking Press, 1959), p. 69.
19 Ellmann, *op. cit.,* p. 89.
20 Joyce, *Critical Writings,* p. 134.

BANVILLE'S FAUST: *DOCTOR COPERNICUS, KEPLER, THE NEWTON LETTER* AND *MEFISTO* AS STORIES OF THE EUROPEAN OF THE EUROPEAN MIND. Joseph Swann.

1 John Banville, *Doctor Copernicus* (London: Panther Books, 1980), p. 1. All further references will be given in the text.
2 Rüdiger Imhof, in his recent study on Banville, sees Osiander rather as siding with the obscurantist forces who distinguish between hypothesis and true understanding, between knowledge of words, we might say, and knowledge of things. It is one of Banville's strengths, however, that he leaves his historical

and fictional perspectives wide open, and can allow his Osiander, like his Copernicus, to speak in voices that are authentically medieval and yet belong at the same time to a more modern physical universe where fact is just another level of interpretation. Compare Imhof, *John Banville. A Critical Introduction* (Dublin: Wolfhound Press, 1989), pp. 98–100.

3 Imhof, *Banville,* p. 132.

4 John Banville, *Kepler* (London: Panther Books, 1983), p. 142. All further references will be given in the text.

5 John Banville, *The Newton Letter* (London: Panther Books, 1984), p. 9. All further references will be given in the text.

6 Banville, John. *Mefisto* (London: Paladin Books, 1987), p. 17. All further references will be given in the text.

7 Johann Wolfgang von Goethe, *Faust* I, 1.1338. Further references will be given in the text.

8 Imhof sees Gabriel's disullusioning as mirroring and completing Copernicus's 'redemptive despair' (*Banville,* p. 169). This is a rich concept, but one based on the very parameters Banville has been so busy changing. Rarther than despair, I should like to speak of a redemptive acceptance of the unknowable, or, to put it another way, an acceptance that knowledge is not just understanding but encounter, which is something essentially random.

SPEECH AND SILENCE: BEYOND THE RELIGIOUS IN BRIAN MOORE'S NOVELS. Ruth Neil

1 Compare for example J. H., Dorenkamp, 'Finishing the Day: Nature and Grace in Two Novels by Brian Moore', *Éire-Ireland* 13 (1978), pp. 103–12.

2 It is interesting to note that whenever Moore is seen as a writer primarily concerned whit 'faith', the endings of his novels are invariably interpreted as hopeful, as a mastering of the crisis shown in the course of the novel. Other critics, in contrast to this, on the whole interpret the endings as denoting defeat or — at best — uncertainty.

3 Examples of 'secular' novels would be: *And Answer from Limbo* (Boston and Toronto: Atlantic–Little, Brown and Company, 1962), *The Feast of Lupercal* (Boston and Toronto: Atlantic–Little, Brown and Company, 1957) and *The Doctor's Wife* 1976 (London: Paladin Grafton Books, 1988), to name but a few.

4 Quoted in Michael Paul Gallagher, 'Religion as Favourite Metaphor: Moore's Recent Fiction' *Irish University Review* 18.1 (Spring 1988), pp. 50–8. Gallagher is one of the few critics who concentrate on the religious aspects of Moore's novels, but he does not read them from an orthodox Catholic point of view.

5 Moore sees himself as a traditional writer and rejects contemporary 'fashions' in fiction, but nevertheless he too is preoccupied with this particular issue of the modern dilemma. Related to the concern with 'language' is the frequent occurrence of 'signs' throughout his work. Brown's semiotic interpretation of some of Moore's novels shows the connection between these aspects. See Terrence Brown, 'Show Me a Sign: the Religious Imagination of Brian Moore' *Irish University Review* 18.1 (Spring 1988), pp. 37–49.

6 Brian Moore, *Cold Heaven* 1983 (London: Triad Panther Books, 1985). All further references will be given in the text.

7 The term 'secular miracle' can be found in the novel itself, p. 86. Religion is only one of many aspects in this complex book; for a more detailed discussion cf. Seamus Deane, 'The Real Thing: Brian Moore in Disneyland', *Irish University Review* 18.1 (Spring 1988), pp. 74–82.

8 Gallagher makes the useful distinction between 'Faith' and 'faith'. He maintains that it is a distinction which is well-established in Catholic theology. 'Faith' denotes belief in God, 'faith' 'a wider range of signifying constructs people use to find some stable anchorage for their lives', *op. cit.,* p. 51.

9 Brian Moore, *The Lonely Passion of Judith Hearne* (earlier title: *Judith Hearne*) 1955 (London: Paladin Grafton Books, 1988). All further references will be given in the text.

10 See also Brown, *op. cit.* and Brian Cosgrove, 'Brian Moore and the Price of Freedom in a Secular World', *Irish University Review* 18.1 (Spring 1988), pp. 59–73.

11 Brian Moore, *I Am Mary Dunne* 1968 (London: Triad, Panther, 1982). All further references will be given in the text.

12 Dorenkamp, *op. cit.,* pp. 108–109.

13 As often with the endings of Moore's novels, the critics' opinions diverge considerably. Hallvard Dahlie, *Brian Moore* (Boston: Twayne Publishers, 1981), Jeanne Flood, *Brian Moore* (Lewisburg: Bucknell University Press, 1974) and Dorenkamp, *op. cit.,* for example, see an optimistic ending, while David Leon Higdon is more sceptical, 'Brian Moore, *I Am Mary*

Dunne: "memento ergo sum", in *Shadows of the Past in Contemporary British Fiction,* ed. D. L. Higdon (Athens, GA: University of Georgia Press, 1984).

14 Brian Moore, *Catholics* 1972 (London: Triad Panther Books, 1983). All further references will be given in the text.

15 For a discussion of the symbol of the tabernacle see Patrick Rafroidi, 'The Temptation of Brian Moore', *Irish University Review,* Brian Moore Special Issue, 18. 1. (Spring 1988), pp. 83–87. Another such recurring symbol is that of the mirror.

16 Brian Moore, *Black Robe* 1985 (London: Paladin Grafton Books, 1987). All further references will be given in the text.

17 Brian Moore, *The Colour of Blood* 1987 (London: Paladin Grafton Books, 1988). All further references will be given in the text.

18 M. Gallagher, *op. cit.,* p. 57. Other critics stress the elements of the 'thriller' genre in this novel: Brown, for example, talks of 'a plot of Le Carré-like complexities' (*op. cit.,* p. 48); see also reviews such as Anne-Marie Conway, 'Brian Moore: *The Colour of Blood', Times Literary Supplement* October 2–8 1987: p. 1073.

19 Brown, *op. cit.,* p. 48.

20 As P. Rafroidi has poninted out (*op. cit.,* p. 87.), it is unlikely that the 'noise' of the novel's last sentence means that with death God's silence stops existing — but it is a possible reading.

MYTH AND MOTHERLAND: EDNA O'BRIEN'S *MOTHER IRELAND.* Werner Huber

1 Edna O'Brien, *Mother Ireland* (Harmondsworth: Penguin, 1978). All further references will be given in the text.

2 See, for example, Denis Donoghue, review of *Mother Ireland,* by Edna O'Brien, *New York Review of Books* 23 (14 Oct. 1976), p. 12; Roy Foster, rev. of *Mother Ireland,* by Edna O'Brien, *Times Literary Suppliment,* 4 June 1976, p. 673; and Edna O'Brien, 'The Vision of Edna O'Brien' interview with Charles E. Claffey, *Boston Globe* 27 Nov. 1988, B1.

3 Thus the late John Broderick, speaking for many, was able to write in his review of *Mother Ireland* 'One would think that Miss Edna O'Brien would be content with telling her ex-

perience in childhood and youth over and over again in her novels. But no such luck. Here she comes again with her version of Ireland, and the effect it had on her development.' Review of *Mother Ireland,* by Edna O'Brien, *The Critic* (35 (Winter 1976), pp. 72–73. For a summary assessment of her work against her Irish background see Darcy O'Brien, 'Edna O'Brien: A Kind of Irish Girlhood' in *Twentieth-Century Women Novelists,* ed. Thomas F. Staley (Totowa, NJ: Barnes and Nobel, 1982), pp. 179–90.

4 This line of thought has been developed further by Kevin P. Reilly, 'Irish Literary Autobiography: The Goddesses That Poets Dream Of', *Éire-Ireland* 16.3 (Fall 1981), pp. 57–80.

5 Richard Eder, review of *Mother Ireland,* by Edna O'Brien, *New York Times Book Review,* 19 Sept. 1976, p. 6.

6 In an interview with Philip Roth O'Brien returned to this theme as a special feature of her Irish upbringing: "In a lot of ways I feel a cripple. The body was sacred as a tabernacle and everything a potential occasion of sin. It is funny now, but not that funny — the body contains the life story just as much as the brain." Philip Roth, 'A Conversation with Edna O'Brien', *New York Times Book Review,* 18 Nov. 1984, pp. 38–40. Compare also this vitriolic comment from *Vanishing Ireland:* 'It would need more than a fleet of mobile libraries to change Ireland. It would need a hundred Sigmund Freuds to unravel the Gordian knots of guilt and anger darkness and torturous sex', Edna O'Brien, *Vanishing Ireland,* Texts by Edna O'Brien, photographs by Richard Fitzgerald (New York: Potter-Crown, 1987), p. 21.

7 Peggy O'Brien, 'The Silly and the Serious: An Assessment of Edna O'Brien', *Massachusetts Review* 28.3 (Autumn 1987), p. 486. This is a common theme throughout O'Brien's work. The short story 'A Scandalous Woman' makes the same connection between the archetypal female experience and the national character. It ends with the words of the narrator: 'I thought that ours indeed was a land of shame, a land of murder, and a land of strange, throttled, sacrificial women'. *A Fanatic Heart: Selected Stories,* (Harmondsworth: Penguin, 1987), p. 265. James M. Haule explores O'Brien's theme of the plight of Irishwomen as mothers and daughters in 'Tough Luck: The Unfortunate Birth of Edna O'Brien', *Colby Library Quarterly* 23.4 (1987), pp. 216–24.

8 Richard Kearney suggests a transition from fatherland to daughterland to motherland from the seventeenth century onwards, but the evidence for his case is all too weak. See Richard Kearney, *Myth and Motherland*. Field Day Pamphlets 5. (Derry: Field Day, 1984), pp. 20–21.

9 For a typology of imagistic models of Irish nationalism, see Klaus Lubbers, 'Literature and National Identity: The Irish Exanple', in *Nationalism in Literature — Literarischer Nationalismus: Literature, Language and National Identity,* Third International Scottish Studies Symposium — Proceedings, ed. Horst W. Drescher and Hermann Völkel (Frankfurt am Main and Berne: Peter Lang, 1989), pp. 269–79. The myth of the demanding mother goddess has been described by Patrick J. Keane, *Yeats, Joyce, Ireland, and the Myth of the Devouring Female* (Columbia, MO: University of Missouri Press, 1988).

10 Jones lists some of the names given to Ireland: 'In addition to the customary one of Erin (Ivernia), which would content most countries, Ireland is also called by, amongst other names: Cáitlin Ni Houlihan, Morrin Ni Cullinan, Roisín Dubh (little black Rose), Shan Van Vocht (old woman) ... and by the names of three queens of Tuatha Di Danann — Éire, Banba, and Fodhla'. Ernest Jones, 'The Island of Ireland: A Psychoanalytical Contribution to Political Psychology' in *Essays in Applied Psycho-analysis.* 2 vols. (London: Hogarth, 1951). 1: p. 99.

11 Ibid., p. 81.

12 Peggy O'Brien, *op. cit.,* p. 488.

13 O'Brien, *Vanishing Ireland,* p. 5.

14 There is also a biographical essay on Joyce, Edna O'Brien, 'Dear Mr. Joyce', *Audience* 1 (July–Aug. 1971), pp. 75–7, and a review of a recent biography of Nora Barnacle, 'She Was the Other Ireland', review of *Nora: The Real Life of Molly Bloom* by Brenda Maddox, *New Times Book Review* 19 June 1988, pp. 3, 33.

15 Roth, *op. cit.,* p. 39; Edna O'Brien, 'The Art of Fiction LXXXII: Edna O'Brien', Interview with Shusha Guppy, *Paris Review* 92 (1984), pp. 29, 31, 37.

16 See, for example, Grace Eckley, *Edna O'Brien* (Lewisburg, PA: Bucknell University Press, 1974), pp. 80–84 and Rita Gnutzmann, 'Die Romane Edna O'Briens', in *Einführung in die zeitgenössische irische Literatur,* ed. J. Kornelius, E. Otto, and G. Stratmann (Heidelberg: winter, 1980), pp. 157–8.

17 On this theme, which unites the heroines of Edna O'Brien's novels, see Lotus Snow, "'That Trenchant Childhood Route"?: Quest in Edna O'Brien's Novels', *Éire-Ireland* 14.1 (Spring 1979), pp. 74–83.

'PROPER WORDS IN PROPER PLACES': JONATHAN SWIFT ON LANGUAGE. Veronika Kniezsa

SOURCES

Swift, Jonathan, *The Prose Works of Jonathan Swift.* Ed. Herbert Davies (with Louis Landa). Oxford: Basil Blackwell
– – –, 1955 *Irish Tracts 1728–1733.* Vol. XII.
– – –, 1957a *Bickerstaff Papers.* Vol. II.
– – –, 1957b *A Proposal for Correcting the English Language.* Vol. IV.
– – –, 1959 *Gulliver's Travels.* Vol. XI.
– – –, 1963 *Irish Tracts 1720–1723 and Sermons.* Vol. IX.
– – –, *The Poems of Jonathan Swift.* 1958. Ed. Harold Williams. Vols. I-V. Oxford: Clarendon Press.
– – –, *The Correspondence of Jonathan Swift.* 1965. Ed. Harold Williams. Vol. I–V. Oxford: Clarendon Press.
– – –, *Swift's Polite Conversation.* 1963. With Introduction, Notes and Extensive Commentary by Eric Partridge. London: Andre Deutsch.

REFERENCES

Algeo, John 1972[2]: *Problems in the Origins and Development of the English Language.* New York: Harcourt Brace Jovanovich Inc.
Bliss, Alan J. 1977: *Spoken English in Ireland 1600–1700.* Dublin: The Dolmen Press.
Bolton, W.F. 1966: *The English Language. Essays by English and American Men of Letters 1490–1839.* Cambridge: University Press.
Dobson, E. J. 1968: *English Pronunciation 1500–1700.* Vols. I–II. Oxford: Clarendon Press.

Ekwall, Eilert 1975: *A History of Modern English Sounds and Morphology.* Translated and edited by Alan Ward. Oxford: Basil Blackwell.

Ellis, Alexander 1875: *On Early English Pronunciation.* Vol. IV. London: Trubner & Co.

Gabrielsson, Arvid 1909: *Rime as a Criterion of the Pronunciation of Spenser, Pope, Byron and Swinburn.* Uppsala: Almquist och Wiksell.

Gabrielsson, Arvid 1930: *Edward Bysshe's Dictionary of Rhymes* (1707). Uppsala: Almquist och Wiksell.

Johnson, Samuel 1834: *A Dictionary of the English Language.* London: Frederick Westley and A. H. Davis.

Kniezsa, Veronika 1986: 'Jonathan Swift's Rhymes' in *Languages in Function.* Új tendenciák az anglisztikában IV/1. Ed. by S. Rot Budapest: MTA Sokszororsítóüzem.

Luick, Karl 1964²: *Historische Drammatik der englischen Sprache.* Vols. I–II. Stuttgart: Bernhardt Tauchnitz.

Oxford English Dictionary 1933: eds. James Murray et al. Oxford: University Press.

Strang, Barbara 1968: 'Swift and the English language: a Study in Principles and Practice' in *To Honor Roman Jacobson.* Vol. III. pp. 1947–1959. The Hague: Mouton.

Wyld, Henry Cecil 1936²: *A History of Modern Colloquial English.* London.

Wyld, Henry Cecil 1965²: *Studies in English Rhymes from Surrey to Pope.* New York: Russel and Russel.

MARIA EDGEWORTH AND THE TRADITION OF IRISH SEMIOTICS. Martin J. Croghan

1 Maria Edgeworth and Richard Lovell Edgeworth, *Essay on Irish Bulls* (London: J. Johnson, 1802). Hereafter page numbers to this first edition are given in brackets in the text of the paper and in the Notes.

2 Jonathan Swift, 'On Barbarous Denominations in Ireland', ed. H. Davis, *The Prose Works of Jonathan Swift,* IV (London: Basil Blackwell, 1957), p. 281. In an advanced stage of the discussion in the *Essay* where it has been argued at length that there is nothing specifically Irish about bulls, it is stated, somewhat in despair, '. . . the Irish, if they be not blunderers, must continue to

be thought absurd and ridiculous, from the unchangeable law of the association of ideas' (p. 191), because 'whenever we hear the tone (brogue), we expect the blunder' (p. 192). Swift's words had been, 'whereas what we call the Irish Brogue is no sooner discovered, than it makes the deliverer, in the last degree, ridiculous and despised; and from such a mouth, an Englishman expects nothing but bulls, blunders and follies'.

3 G.R. Neilson, *The Book of Bulls. Being a Very Complete and Entertaining Essay on the Evolution of the Irish and other 'Bulls'. With which is Included the 'Essay on Irish Bulls', by the Edgeworths, Published Early in the Century* (London: Simkin, Marshall, Hamilton, Kent & Co., Ltd., & George Tucker, 1898), p. VI. By 1815 the *Essay* had gone into four editions, and at the end of the century Neilson was able to say: 'There are few books more often quoted from by public journals, and the copies in the British Museum and other national libraries are apparently much more in request than many more important works.' The Director of the *Academie Francaise* wrote an Appendix for a third edition of the *Essay* which contained a collection of what he called foreign bulls, to support the Edgeworth thesis that there was nothing specifically Irish about bulls.

4 Ibid., p. 147.

5 'Neither does it avail whether the censure be reasonable or not, since the fact is always so', is Swift's formulation of the semiotics of symbolic violence against the Irish: Davis, p. 281.

6 I read and re-read these pages thinking at first that the change from the more usual 'hewers of wood and drawers of water' to 'cutters of turf and drawers of whisky' was stage-Irish satire, but the wider context of the quotation indicates deadly seriousness.

7 Maria Edgeworth was obviously very conscious that her writing in *Castle Rackrent* (London: J. Johnson, 1800), could be regarded as symbolic violence against the Irish. In the Epilogue to the novel she defends herself against such a potential accusation by describing what she was doing in writing the book, as follows (Ibid., pp. 180–81):

> All the features in the foregoing sketch were taken from life and they are characteristic of that mixture of quickness, simplicity, cunning, carelessness, dissipation, disinterestedness, shrewdness and blunder, which in different forms, and with various success, has been brought upon the stage or delineated in novels.

In another part of her defense, she admits that it could be claimed that the novel is guilty of stage-Irishism, but she excuses herself by saying that the contemporary Irish had evolved and that the traits of the Irish portrayed in *Castle Rackrent* were characteristics of previous generations.

8 Such a correlation assumes that normal orthography represents elite speech and that misspelling, which may or may not masquerade as phonological transcription, can indicate other types of speech. I have dealt at some length with this transcription myth which has dogged the study of Hiberno-English and especially the study of language in Anglo-Irish literature, in *Demythologising Hiberno-English* (Boston, Mass.: Working Papers, Northeastern University, 1990), pp. 6ff. A common version of the myth is repeated by R. Wall when he claims that 'van' is 'phonetic spelling of the Irish pronunciation of one': 'Dialect in Irish Literature: The Hermetic Core', *Irish University Review*, 20 (1990), 1, p. 18: on this logic, 'one', should be replaced by 'von', and so on ad infinitum.

9 The most common change is 'e' or 'ea' to 'a' as in 'Jasus' and 'plase': cf., N. F. Blake, *Non-Standard Language in English Literature* (London: Andre Deutsch, 1981), pp. 133–37. The same phonographic rule is used in the *Essay* and in Maria Edgeworth's three plays, *Love and Law, The Two Guardians,* and *The Rose, Thistle and Shamrock.*

10 Maria Edgeworth, *The Rose, Thistle and Shamrock* (London: R. Hunter et al., 1817), pp. 255–381. Hereafter, page numbers to this edition are given in brackets, in the paper.

11 The *Essay* has been completely neglected internationally in the prolific literature produced in Western cultures in the last forty years which has dealt with the symbolic violence of antisemitism, racism and sexism. It has also been neglected in contemporary Irish studies even though it is possibly the most original intellectual work of international relevance which has appeared in Ireland over the last two centuries. My justification for the two parts of this note is that symbolic violence, including stage-Irishism, has been the main focus of my research over the last five years; this research has included bibliographical studies.

12 Croghan, *Demythologizing Hiberno-English,* p. 1ff.

13 R. Chapman, *The Treatment of Sounds in Language and Literature* (Oxford: Basil Blackwell, 1984), p. 74. See also, n. 7.

14 *Castle Rackrent,* p. VIII. &, *The Rose, Thistle and Shamrock,* p. 226.

15 *Castle Rackrent,* p. VII.
16 Blake, p. 135.
17 Croghan, *Demythologizing Hiberno-English,* passim.

ANGLO-IRISH AND IRISH POETRY IN HUNGARIAN: THE
LITERARY OFFSHOOT OF AN HISTORICAL PARALLEL.
Thomas Kabdebo

1 Warwick Gould, 'How Ferencz Renyi Spoke Up', *Yeats Annual,* vol. 3, 1985, pp. 199–205.
2 Three editions of *The Resurrection of Hungary: A Parallel for Ireland* have appeared to date: the first edition in serialised form, *United Irishmen,* January–June 1904; the second edition in book form, Dublin, 1904; and the third edition in book form, Dublin, 1918.
3 *Tracts for Irishmen,* No. 1 by 'D' argued the case for Deák in 1916.
4 *Thomas Davis,* ed. Arthur Griffith (Dublin, 1914), p. 73.
5 *Journals of William O'Brien Smith* (Vienna–Pest–Hotkocz, August–September 1861). Manuscript in the possession of Mr. Anthony O'Brien of Dublin.
6 John Francis O'Donnell (1837–1874) *a contributor to The Nation.* The Poem appeared posthumously in O'Donnell's book of verse, *Poems* (London, 1891). It was translated into Hungarian by the present author for the anthology of Irish poetry *Tört álmok* ('Broken Dreams'), szerkesztő Kabdebó Tamás (Budapest, 1988).
7 Over fifty percent of all literature published in Hungary is in translation. It is an industry with workmen at the bottom and poet-artists at the top. A volume, like *Tört álmok* attracted the top range.

NOTES ON EDITORS AND CONTRIBUTORS

CSILLA BERTHA, the first appointment in English and Irish literature in Hungary, lectures at Lajos Kossuth University, Debrecen and has held a Rockefeller fellowship with Donald E. Morse to translate contemporary Hungarian drama. Her publications include *A drámaíró Yeats* ('Yeats the Playwright'), numerous articles on Irish drama, W. B. Yeats, J. M. Synge, Brian Friel, Thomas Murphy and J. B. Keane, on Hungarian painters and on parallels between Irish and Hungarian literature.

EOIN BOURKE, Professor of German at University College Galway, has broadcast in Germany on Irish literature and history, authored articles on German authors and commentators on Ireland and with Eva Bourke published a book of translations of modern Irish poetry, *Hundsrose — neue irischer Gedichte.*

PATRICK BURKE, a well-known actor, director and drama adjudicator, lectures in English at St. Patrick's College of Education, Dublin. A specialist in Irish theatre his publications include essays on Brian Friel, Tom Murphy, Frank McGuinness and earlier dramatists such as J. M. Synge and T. C. Murray.

MARTIN J. CROGHAN teaches at Dublin City University and serves as Secretary of the International Association for the Study of Anglo-Irish Literature. He is an expert on the history of Irish Semiotics.

RUTH FLEISCHMANN, born in Cork, studied at University College Cork and in Tübingen, Germany, lectures in English at the University of Bielefeld, Germany and has published work on Daniel Corkery, Patrick Kavanagh, Brinsley McNammara, J. M. Synge and turn-of-the century Ireland.

MAURICE HARMON, Emeritus Professor of Anglo-Irish Literature at University College-Dublin, Burns Library Scholar in Irish Studies at Boston College 1993–94, former editor of the *Irish University Review,* is the official biographer of Sean O'Faolain. He has written books on Sean O'Faolain, Thomas Kinsella and Austin Clarke as well as the standard bibliography for the study of Anglo-Irish literature.

WERNER HUBER, lecturer in English literature at the University of Paterborn, Germany, received his PhD. for a study of the early novels of James Stephens. His main research interests and publications are in the fields of Irish literature, English Romanticism, Samuel Beckett and modern drama.

THOMAS KABDEBO, Librarian of Maynooth, College, is a translator, novelist, travel writer, literary critic and historian with numerous publications in English and Hungarian. He selected and edited an anthology of Irish poetry in Hungarian *Tört álmok* ('Broken Dreams').

MÁRIA KURDI teaches Anglo–Irish and American literature at Janus Pannonius University, Pécs, Hungary. Her publications include essays on Beckett, Joyce, Yeats, Arthur Miller and contemporary Irish dramatists. She reviews for *The Irish Literary Supplement* and *Filológiai Közlöny.*

DONALD E. MORSE, Professor of English and Rhetoric at Oakland University in Michigan, twice Fulbright Professor at Lajos Kossuth University, author of *Kurt Vonnequt* and over fifty essays, including those on Samuel Beckett, J. P. Donleavy and Joyce, is the editor of six books, three with Csilla Bertha including *More Real Than Reality: The Fantastic in Irish Literature and the Arts.*

RUTH NEIL is a post-graduate student at the University of Wuppertal, doing research on Brian Friel. She has published articles on Friel, Seamus Heaney and Brian Moore. Apart from Irish literature she has a particular interest in contemporary drama and Commonwealth literature.

ISTVÁN PÁLFFY, Professor of English, University of Miskolc, Hungary and long-time head of the English department at Kossuth

University, is an authority on G. B. Shaw. A frequent contributor to international journals and conferences, his books include *Az új angol dráma — mint a 'valóság drámája'* ('The New English Drama — As the Drama of Reality') and *George Bernard Shaw Magyarországon* ('The Reception of Shaw in Hungary').

M. BYRON RAIZIS chaired the Athens University English Department for ten years and has authored or edited thirteen books and several dozen articles mostly on English Romanticism and Byronism but also on Yeats and Joyce.

ISTVÁN D. RÁCZ has been a lecturer in English at Lajos Kossuth University, Hungary since 1983. His main interests are in Romanticism and post-1945 English and Irish poetry and he has published studies on Shelley, Blake, Philip Larkin, Ted Hughes and Carol Ann Duffy.

ALADÁR SARBU, Professor of English and American Literature at Loránd Eötvös University, Budapest, has published books on Joseph Conrad, Henry James, the English literary Left, and most recently on Emerson, Hawthorne and Melville. He has held research fellowships at the Universities of London, Liverpool, Harvard and Minnesota.

BERNICE SCHRANK, Professor of English at Memorial University of Newfoundland in Canada, has published extensively on Irish drama. She is currently working on a production and performance history of O'Casey's plays.

JOSEPH SWANN, lecturer in English, University of Wuppertal, has a particular interest in poetry and in literary theory. Among his numerous publications are essays on W. B. Yeats, Seamus Heaney, Richard Murphy and Tom Murphy and on various writers from Nigeria, India, Australia and New Zealand.

ANDRÁS P. UNGAR emigrated from Hungary to Canada in 1986. He received his PhD. in 1992 from McGill University, lectures at Concordia University in Montréal and has published *The Epic of the Irish Free State: Genre and History in Joyce's Ulysses.*

INDEX

The publication of this book was made possible through the
generous financial assistance of the Hungarian National
Scholarly and Scientific Research Fund (OTKA) Grant · T4682